LESSONS FOR
EXTENDING
MULTIPLICATION

GRADES 4-5

PUBLISHED TEACHING ARITHMETIC TITLES

Lessons for First Grade
Lessons for Addition and Subtraction, Grades 2–3
Lessons for Introducing Multiplication, Grade 3
Lessons for Extending Multiplication, Grades 4–5
Lessons for Introducing Fractions, Grades 4–5

FORTHCOMING TEACHING ARITHMETIC TITLES

Lessons for Place Value, Grades 1–2
Lessons for Extending Division, Grade 3
Lessons for Extending Division, Grades 4–5
Lessons for Extending Fractions, Grades 5–6
Lessons for Decimals and Percents, Grades 5–6

Teaching
ARITHMETIC

LESSONS FOR
EXTENDING
MULTIPLICATION

▲▲▲▲▲

GRADES 4–5

MARYANN WICKETT
MARILYN BURNS

MATH SOLUTIONS PUBLICATIONS
SAUSALITO, CA

Math Solutions Publications
A division of
Marilyn Burns Education Associates
150 Gate 5 Road, Suite 101
Sausalito, CA 94965
www.mathsolutions.com

Library of Congress Cataloging-in-Publication Data
Wickett, Maryann
   Lessons for extending multiplication : grades 4–5 / Maryann Wickett,
Marilyn Burns.
      p. cm. — (Teaching arithmetic)
Includes index.
    ISBN 0-941355-31-4 (alk. paper)
  1. Multiplication—Study and teaching (Primary) I. Burns, Marilyn,
1941– II. Title. III. Series.
   QA115.W64 2001
    372.7'2—dc21

                                                      2001002173

Editor: Toby Gordon
Production: Melissa L. Inglis
Cover & interior design: Leslie Bauman
Composition: Argosy Publishing

Printed in the United States of America on acid-free paper
05 04 03 02 01   ML   1 2 3 4 5

A Message from Marilyn Burns

We at Marilyn Burns Education Associates believe that teaching mathematics well calls for continually reflecting on and improving one's instructional practice. Our Math Solutions Publications include a wide range of choices, from books in our new Teaching Arithmetic series—which address beginning number concepts, place value, addition, subtraction, multiplication, division, fractions, decimals, and percents—to resources that help link math with writing and literature; from books that help teachers more deeply understand the mathematics behind the math they teach to children's books that help students develop an appreciation for math while learning basic concepts.

Along with our large collection of teacher resource books, we have a more general collection of books, videotapes, and audiotapes that can help teachers and parents bridge the gap between home and school. All of our materials are available at education stores, from distributors, and through major teacher catalogs.

In addition, Math Solutions Inservice offers five-day courses and one-day workshops throughout the country. We also work in partnership with school districts to help implement and sustain long-term improvement in mathematics instruction in all classrooms.

To find a complete listing of our publications and workshops, please visit our Web site at *www.mathsolutions.com*. Or contact us by calling (800) 868-9092 or sending an e-mail to *info@mathsolutions.com*.

We're eager for your feedback and interested in learning about your particular needs. We look forward to hearing from you.

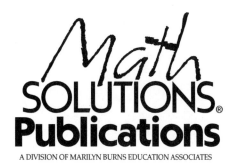

A DIVISION OF MARILYN BURNS EDUCATION ASSOCIATES

CONTENTS

ACKNOWLEDGMENTS

A special thanks to the following teachers and their students for allowing us to try out ideas in their classrooms: Carol Scurlock (Discovery Elementary School, San Marcos Unified Schools, San Marcos, California); Katie Zimmer (Carmel Creek Elementary School, Solana Beach Schools, Solana Beach, California); Annie Gordon (Marin Horizon School, Mill Valley, California); Katherine Orrell (Carmel Creek Elementary School, Solana Beach Schools, Solana Beach, California); Karen Krantz (Paloma Elementary School, San Marcos Unified Schools, San Marcos, California).

A special thanks to the following teachers for using these lessons with their students and providing valuable feedback and insights: Eunice Hendrix (Martin-Carrillo Elementary School, San Marcos Unified School District, San Marcos, California); Richard Kharas (Seymour School, Syracuse City Schools, Syracuse, New York); Suzanne McGrath (East Lake Elementary School, Chula Vista Elementary Schools, Chula Vista, California); Don Hurlbert (Carrillo Elementary School, San Marcos Unified Schools, San Marcos, California).

Thanks to these students for contributing their ideas and feedback: Jenny Wickett, who created the idea for Matilda's Mental Math; Suzanne Johnson, whose curiosity sparked the idea for Investigating Elevens; the students of room 18, 1998–1999, Paloma Elementary School, San Marcos, California; the students of room 19, 1999–2001, Carrillo Elementary School, Carlsbad, California.

Thanks to the following colleagues for reading the lessons carefully and offering feedback, insights, and encouragement: Rusty Bresser, Katharine Kharas, and Leigh Childs.

INTRODUCTION

Every morning they come. We greet each other with a hug or a high five along with a few softly spoken words. Some are well fed, some hungry, some native speakers of English, some just learning, some filled with wonder, and some full of uncertainty, each one unique: my students, all complex human beings, all capable of learning and achieving great things. It is an awesome responsibility and an honor to guide them for a year, or even two, if I am especially lucky.

Making choices about what to teach and how to teach it is one of my greatest responsibilities. There is no single, one-size-fits-all answer. That complexity is what makes teaching an art and demands that I constantly evaluate what I am doing and how it affects the children in my charge. In addition to this, I must consider what my students must take with them as a foundation for future education and their adult lives.

This book presents a collection of lessons designed to provide teachers with instructional strategies for multidigit multiplication that help children make sense of the mathematics they're learning. The lessons extend multiplication beyond concept development and attention to the multiplication table characteristic of the third-grade curriculum and build on the lessons offered in the Teaching Arithmetic series book *Lessons for Introducing Multiplication, Grade 3*. For this book, Marilyn Burns and I taught the lessons to a variety of classrooms over several years. During this time, we discussed what we had done, how the students responded, and what changes to the lessons we might make. We examined student work and analyzed the learning that occurred.

Common to all of the lessons we've included is that students share their thinking and strategies, which strengthens and expands their understanding. Through discussion, students consider a variety of approaches to solving problems, which promotes the learning of efficient, accurate computation strategies grounded in understanding. Also, the lessons encourage students to make connections among ideas as they apply previous learning to new problem-solving situations.

About half the lessons in this book use concrete materials to support student understanding and sense making. Even students who have had only, or mostly, abstract experiences benefit from using manipulative materials to explore and develop understanding about why what they have previously learned works. My belief about the benefit and usefulness of manipulative materials stems from my own experience learning mathematics. From my schooling, I gained abstract knowledge, little of which made sense. The focus was on learning *to do,* not on why what I did made sense. Some who were taught this way achieved success, especially if they were compliant, organized, and had an appreciation of the predictability of the procedures being taught. However, success was elusive for many others needing to make sense of their learning. Consequently, learning to do without making sense of what was being done created a dislike of mathematics that carried into adulthood, affecting career choices and the ability to use mathematics competently and confidently. I was astounded when, as a beginning teacher, experiences with concrete materials helped me make sense of what I had memorized; this was thrilling to me and had a profound impact on my classroom teaching methods.

I taught these lessons in a variety of classrooms, but there was one classroom in particular in which the students had learned a well-developed traditional set of abstract rules, or algorithms, for multiplication. I still chose to offer students the concrete approaches provided in the lessons along with many opportunities to discuss and justify their thinking to enhance their understanding. Concrete experiences offered students a fresh way to look at what they already knew and could do with multiplication. If they hadn't had previous abstract instruction, my choice would have been to begin with the concrete, because I think this minimizes the risk of students learning how to do procedures or learning facts without understanding why they make sense.

Goals for Multiplication Instruction

Students coming into fourth grade should be able to

▲ explain how multiplication relates to repeated addition (a numerical interpretation);

▲ explain how multiplication relates to rectangular arrays (a geometric interpretation);

▲ figure products up to 12 × 12; and

▲ solve real-world problems that involve multiplication.

While the lessons in this book build from and extend this foundation, a few focus on strengthening these prior understandings. For example, *Checking for Understanding: 8 × 7* provides a look at students' prior learning, and *Related Rectangles* and *One Hundred Hungry Ants* help students strengthen their understanding of multiplication as arrays.

The goals of the lessons in this book are to give all students the chance to learn how to

▲ mentally multiply by 10, powers of 10, and multiples of 10;

▲ use the distributive property to calculate products;

▲ use paper and pencil to record thinking when solving problems involving multi-digit multiplication;

▲ identify factors, multiples, products, primes, and composites; and

▲ explain how multiplication relates to addition and division.

As students are confronted with learning to multiply larger numbers, they need to move beyond strategies that were useful in third grade such as repeated addition, building arrays, and skip-counting. Students need to become comfortable with using the distributive property and the structure of our base ten number system to solve multidigit multiplication problems. While it is appropriate for a third grader to solve a problem like 5 × 12 by skip-counting by 5s 12 times, or by adding 5 12s, or by counting the cubes in a 5-by-12 rectangular array, older students need to approach the problem in other, more efficient ways. For example, a student might think, "Two twelves is twenty-four, and double that to get forty-eight, and then I add one more twelve to get sixty." Or a student might think of 12 as 10 plus 2 and think, "Five tens is fifty plus five twos makes sixty." Both of these ways of thinking make use of the distributive property by spreading multiplication over two or more additions. The second method also calls for understanding that multiplying by 10 results in adding a zero to a number, an idea that is based in our base ten system and is central for children to understand. With larger numbers, such as when multiplying 28×6, fourth- and fifth-grade students should be able to think of the problem as $(20 \times 6) + (8 \times 6)$, and they should be able to multiply 6 by 20 mentally, thinking perhaps that 10×6 is 60 and 60 doubled is 120, or that 2×6 is 12, so 20×6 is 120. This combination of using the distributive property and understanding how to multiply by multiples of 10, 100, or 1,000 is key to the instruction in this unit.

A Closer Look at the Mathematics

Asking students to make sense of the mathematics involved in multidigit computation is a key component of this unit. In order for teachers to support student exploration and justification of ideas and mathematical understandings, it is critical they understand the mathematics they are teaching. The "Background" section of each chapter explains the mathematics involved in the particular lesson. For easy reference, following are explanations that relate to the important underlying ideas about multidigit multiplication:

THE DISTRIBUTIVE PROPERTY SYMBOLIZED AS $a(b + c) = ab + ac$

The distributive property is a powerful tool for effectively and efficiently multiplying unwieldy numbers. The distributive property is a way to solve a multiplication problem with large and complicated numbers by breaking it into two or more easier problems, doing these calculations, and then combining the partial products for a final answer. The property is often referred to as the distributive property of multiplication over addition and can be represented algebraically as $a(b + c) = ab + ac$. As in the example discussed previously, 28×6 was broken into two easier problems by changing 28 to $20 + 8$ and multiplying 20×6 and 8×6. Adding the partial products of these two problems—120 and 48—produces the answer to 28×6: 168. So $a(b + c) = ab + ac$ becomes $6(20 + 8) = (6 \times 20) + (6 \times 8)$. $6 \times 20 = 120$ and $6 \times 8 = 48$. Add these two partial products together to get a total of 168. In this book, the lessons do not focus on learning the distributive property or its algebraic representation, but rather on using the distributive property to understand multidigit multiplication and learn to compute efficiently.

MULTIPLYING BY 10, POWERS OF 10, AND MULTIPLES OF 10

It is important for children to understand the patterns inherent in our base ten number system, which occur when multiplying by 10 and multiples of 10. For example, if students understand problems such as $10 \times 3 = 30$ and $10 \times 5 = 50$ then they can make the connection that $10 \times 15 = 150$ or $1,297 \times 10 = 12,970$. Later they can extend this understanding to $10 \times 50 = 500$ or $100 \times 23 = 2,300$. It is also useful for students to understand that problems such as $3 \times 120 = 360$ can also be thought of as $3 \times 12 \times 10 = 360$. Understanding this calls for applying the associative property of multiplication, that $(a \times b) \times c = a \times (b \times c)$, so that $3 \times (12 \times 10) = (3 \times 12) \times 10$. Again, the goal of these lessons is not to focus on the associative property, but to help students develop flexibility.

EFFICIENT COMPUTATION TECHNIQUES

When doing calculations with unwieldy numbers, it makes sense for students to use paper and pencil to keep track of their thinking. Using paper and pencil to keep track of thinking in these lessons is very different from the way using paper and pencil has been traditionally viewed. The focus of traditional instruction has been on arriving at correct answers using one consistent and standard method. Learning the algorithm too often is more important than seeking meaning and understanding. Such instruction supports the mistaken notion that the standard algorithm is the only way, or at least the best way, to calculate accurately and efficiently in all instances. The risk of making proficiency with the standard algorithm the goal of instruction is that students too often become dependent on a procedure they've memorized and not necessarily understood.

In contrast, as a result of these lessons, students will have available to them several options for doing multiplication calculations accurately and efficiently and will be able to choose an option that's appropriate based on the particular numbers involved. In addition to computation accuracy and efficiency, a broad view of proficiency with multiplication is taken and includes students learning to

▲ use multiplication to solve problems;

▲ see relationships among factors, multiples, and products;

▲ understand primes and composites; and

▲ explain how multiplication relates to addition and division.

A final thought about computation: Knowing the multiplication table is essential for students' success. A student who does not have quick, accurate access to the basic multiplication facts will have difficulties doing computation, whether with paper and pencil or mentally, and trouble with considering the reasonableness of answers. Some of the earlier lessons in the book such as *Learning the Multiplication Chart*, *Related Rectangles*, and *One Hundred Hungry Ants* can be especially helpful in providing students additional experience to support this essential learning.

The Structure of the Lessons

The lessons in the book vary in several ways. Some span one class period, others take longer, and some are suitable to repeat over and over throughout the year, giving students a chance to revisit ideas and extend their learning. Some use manipulative materials, others ask students to draw pictures, and others ask students to rely on mental reasoning. While some lessons might seem more suited for beginning experiences, at times it's beneficial for more experienced students to engage in them as well. An activity that seems simple can reinforce students' understanding or give them a fresh way to look at a familiar concept. Also, a lesson that initially seems too difficult or advanced can be ideal for introducing students to thinking in a new way.

For ease in using the lessons in this book, each is organized into the following sections:

Overview   To help you decide if the lesson is appropriate for your students, this is a nutshell description of the mathematical goals of the lesson and what the students will be doing.

Materials   This section lists the special materials needed along with quantities. Not included in the list are regular classroom supplies such as paper and pencils. Worksheets that need to be duplicated are included in the Blackline Masters section at the back of the book.

Time   The number of class periods needed is provided here. A class period is considered to be forty-five minutes to an hour. As indicated, some lessons are intended to be repeated from time to time.

Teaching Directions   To help with planning, the directions for the lesson are given in a step-by-step format.

Teaching Notes   This section addresses the mathematics underlying the lesson and at times provides information about the prior experiences or knowledge students need.

The Lesson   This is a vignette that describes what actually occurred when the lesson was taught to one or more classes. While the vignette mirrors the plan described in the teaching directions, it elaborates with details that are valuable for preparing and teaching the lesson. Samples of student work are included.

Extensions   This section is included for some of the lessons and offers follow-up suggestions.

Questions and Discussion   Presented in a question-and-answer format, this section addresses issues that came up during the lesson and/or have been posed by other teachers.

How to Use This Book

To teach the lessons as described in the thirteen chapters requires at least twenty-three days of instruction, not including time for repeat experiences, as recommended for some lessons, or for the ideas for assessment and additional ideas suggested at the end of the book. While it is possible to spend a continuous stretch of five or six weeks on these lessons, I don't think that is the best decision. In my experience, time is required for children to absorb concepts, and I would rather spend a three-week period of time and then wait two months or so before returning for another three-week period, or arrange for three chunks of time, each two weeks or so, spaced throughout the year. When students return to ideas after a break, they bring not only the learning they've done in other areas but also a fresh look that some distance can provide.

I ordered the lessons in a way that made sense to me, but the sequence is not essential. The lessons that come early in the book, such as *Checking for Understanding: 8 × 7*, *Learning the Multiplication Chart*, and *One Hundred Hungry Ants*, act as a sort of bridge. They help students revisit and strengthen their previous learning in preparation for some of the more complex ideas presented in later lessons. As the lessons progress, students are presented with opportunities to develop more efficient strategies to solve increasingly complex problems involving multidigit numbers. *Silent Multiplication* helps students explore new strategies to solve multidigit multiplication problems. *Related Rectangles* helps students by using concrete materials to understand why some of the strategies in *Silent Multiplication* work. *The Game of Target 300* is a game that helps reinforce other strategies presented using silent multiplication. In some cases I ordered lessons depending on the complexity of the numbers involved. Lessons such as *Calculating Squares, Covering Boxes,* and *Beans and Scoops* involve concrete materials, allowing students to more easily verify their thinking and their results. Lessons such as *Matilda's Mental Multiplication, French Fries,* and *Collecting Pennies* are less concrete and come later in the book. Also, *French Fries* involves a connection with division. Lessons such as *One Hundred Hungry Ants* and *Two Ways to Count to Ten* explore prime, composite, and square numbers.

Throughout the lessons in this book, students are expected to share their thinking. Students share in whole class discussions, by writing, and by talking in small groups, often preceded with a form of pair sharing called dyads. My use of dyads is based on the work of Julian Weissglass, a mathematics professor at the University of California–Santa Barbara. A dyad gives all children an opportunity to be listened to by another and to listen to another. The following are the basic guidelines for using dyads:

1. Each person is given equal time to share and listen.
2. The listener does not interrupt the person who is talking. The listener also does not give advice, analyze, or break in with personal comments.
3. The listener does not share what the talker has said with anyone else. This confidentiality allows children to more fully explore their ideas without fear of being ridiculed or having their mistakes shared publicly.

It has been my experience that using these rules has given shy, less verbal children more opportunity to voice their ideas. In many cases, as these students gain confidence by sharing in a safe environment, they share more in class discussions, which often results in deeper thinking and understanding of the mathematics along with increased confidence. Using dyads frequently also helps keep more students engaged in the learning process.

Some children are willing to share ideas more than others. It's important, however, that all students learn to participate fully in my math class. To facilitate this, I do the following:

▲ I make it a part of the classroom culture and my expectations that all students are capable and can think. They are expected to think and always do their best. Anything less is not acceptable.

▲ I support students by using my behavior as a model. I am constantly thinking and exploring ideas with them. I do not allow them to believe that I know everything—I don't! We explore ideas together constantly.

▲ To support students' thinking and development of strategies, I pose a question and then give students think time. Think time is a few moments of quiet when all students are expected to focus their attention on an idea or question.

▲ After students have a few moments to form their own thoughts, I often use a form of pair sharing called dyads, which I described earlier.

▲ Class discussions play a big role in my teaching. Before beginning a class discussion students have had the opportunity to think about the topic at hand. This opportunity to think might have been in the form of think time, a written assignment, or a dyad. Coming to a class discussion prepared creates a more lively, interesting discussion with more opportunity for both the students and me to learn.

▲ Class discussions usually include sharing of strategies that students use. These strategies are recorded on the chalkboard or some other highly visible place in the classroom. This gives students a reference list of ideas that will help keep them from getting stuck because of a lack of strategies.

As effective as this last practice is, occasionally a student will still get stuck. In this instance, it often helps to ask a question such as the following:

How might you begin?

What do you think the problem is asking you to do?

What would happen if . . . ?

Can you draw a picture that represents the problem or find a pattern?

Can you think of a smaller, similar problem?

It is likely you will choose to use these lessons along with other instructional materials or learning activities. It is important, however, to be consistent so that in all lessons you encourage students to make sense of ideas, communicate about their reasoning both orally and in writing, and apply their learning to problem-solving situations.

CHAPTER ONE
CHECKING FOR UNDERSTANDING
8×7

Overview

This lesson sets the stage and gives all students a common reference point for thinking together as a class about multiplication. Also, the lesson can serve as an assessment, allowing me to check out students' conceptual understanding of multiplication. This information can be used to guide my instructional decisions about what is appropriate for students. Students are asked to demonstrate as many ways as possible to think about and solve 8×7, first on paper, then through class discussion.

Materials

▲ none

Time

▲ one class period

Teaching Directions

1. Explain to students that you are interested in the different ways they can solve 8×7 or prove that $8 \times 7 = 56$ if they already know the fact.

2. Write the following on the board: *Using words, pictures, and numbers, show as many ways as you can to solve 8×7.*

3. Give students as much time as they need to respond to the question.

4. Ask students to share their different ways of solving this problem in a class discussion. Record their methods for finding solutions on the chalkboard to model how to represent their ideas symbolically and also as a reference for ways to multiply.

5. Collect their papers to look at later to assess individual progress.

6. Repeat from time to time with other problems.

Teaching Notes

While many students already know the product of 8×7, it should not be assumed that all do. Also, while an accurate answer is important, the strategies students use to find the product or prove that 56 is the correct answer are also important. By considering the strategies the students use, you can gain insight into their understanding of the concept of multiplication. Often as students are pushed to memorize the multiplication table, they begin to forget what multiplication is really all about. This can limit them as they go on to study division, fractions, and algebra.

Strategies indicative of good conceptual understanding include but are not limited to the following:

▲ showing multiplication as repeated addition;

▲ showing multiplication geometrically as a rectangular array;

▲ indicating an understanding of the commutative nature of multiplication;

▲ reasoning flexibly by choosing strategies particular to the numbers given (e.g., $7 \times 6 = 7 \times 5$ plus 7 more);

▲ and making a real-world connection.

The Lesson

▲▲▲

I began the lesson by writing 8×7 on the chalkboard. "Raise your hand if you know the answer to this multiplication fact," I said. Many hands went up immediately. "In a whisper voice, tell me the product of eight times seven," I continued.

"Fifty-six!" came the whispered response.

"How many of you already had this answer memorized?" I asked. Again many hands went up quickly. "Think in your head of a way you could figure this out if you hadn't already memorized it or a way that you could use to prove your answer. When you have thought of at least one way, put your thumb up so I know you are ready," I said. Some of the students had a tendency to blurt out answers and I found it useful to preface statements that might get a blurt with "Think in your head . . ." When most students were showing me with their thumbs up that they were ready, I continued. "I would like each of you to write down as

many ways as you can think of that would help you solve this problem or prove your answer. I would like you to work on this by yourself, as I am very interested in knowing how you each are thinking about this at the moment. Are there any questions?"

"Can you draw pictures?" Juan asked.

"Yes, if that would help you figure out or prove the answer," I responded.

"Can you use dots?" Dana asked.

"If drawing dots helps you think about this problem, then yes," I answered.

"Could you do fifty-four plus two equals fifty-six or fifty-five plus one equals fifty-six?" Jeremy asked.

"Your examples lead me to believe that you already know the answer is fifty-six and you are finding other ways to make fifty-six. Remember, you are supposed to figure out ways to show that eight times seven equals fifty-six. What if you don't know that the product is fifty-six? What could you do to figure out that eight times seven equals fifty-six or prove that eight times seven equals fifty-six?"

"It helps to think of it as eight groups of seven," Mia interjected.

"Mia's suggestion is a good one. It might help you to remember that another way of saying this problem besides eight times seven is eight groups of seven. Does fifty-four plus two relate to eight groups of seven?" I asked.

Jeremy shook his head no, indicating that 54 + 2 did not relate to eight groups of seven. I could see he was uncertain. The other students seemed ready to get started so I had them begin and then turned my attention back to Jeremy.

"Could I put eight plus eight plus eight plus eight plus eight plus eight plus eight equals fifty-six?" Jeremy wondered.

"Can you tell me how it relates to eight times seven, and would it help you solve the problem?" I responded.

"Well it would be adding eight seven times like the problem says to do. I could keep adding eights until I did it seven times or I think I could also count by eight seven times and both ways would give me the answer," he explained. "Boy, am I glad I memorized that one! What a pain it would be to have to do that all the time," Jeremy said, smiling.

I encouraged Jeremy to show me other ways he could solve the problem.

OBSERVING THE STUDENTS

I moved about the classroom, observing students as they worked and stopping to ask questions of the children. Children's responses to my questions helped me more clearly understand their thinking. Since the students were not yet comfortable writing about math, I also used this work period as an opportunity to encourage and guide them in learning to explain their thinking clearly by suggesting they use words, pic-

tures, and numbers in their explanations. One question I frequently ask children is why they chose to use the numbers they have written on their papers. After a student has had the chance to explain, I follow his explanation with a reminder that labels and short explanations help me understand more clearly when the students are not present to explain.

A problem that students encounter as they learn to write about their thinking in math is "getting stuck." Sometimes giving them ideas for ways to show their thinking helps. From past experience I knew that children sometimes did not include a picture or a rectangular array as possible strategies to solve 8×7.

Beckie raised her hand and stated that she was stuck. She had written $8 \times 7 = 56$ on her paper. She had used repeated addition, $7 + 7 + 7 + 7 + 7 + 7 + 7 + 7 = 56$, as one way of showing her solution.

"Besides eight times seven, what is another way this problem could be read?" I asked.

"Eight groups of seven?" Beckie offered tentatively.

"Yes, eight groups of seven is another way to read the problem. What would eight groups of seven look like if you drew a picture?" I asked, hoping to guide Beckie's thinking toward the idea of representing the problem pictorially.

"Oh, I see, I could draw eight groups of seven bugs to show that eight times seven equals fifty-six," Beckie responded.

Had Beckie not recognized that the multiplication sign could be thought of as "groups of," I would have reminded her.

Strategies I was looking for included the use of repeated addition, skip-counting, arrays, rectangles, pictures showing eight groups of seven or seven groups of eight, some indication of the commutative nature of multiplication ($7 \times 8 = 8 \times 7$), and flexibility with reasoning numerically and choosing strategies particular to the numbers given. For example, would students use strategies such as finding a friendly fact like $6 \times 8 = 48$ and add an additional group of 8 to 48 to get 56? As I moved about the classroom observing the students, I noticed that most had included the strategy of using repeated addition as a way to find the product of 8×7. What concerned me is that for some children, this was their only method for finding the product. While relying on repeated addition is appropriate for third graders just learning about multiplication, my goal for older students is to broaden their repertoire and help them develop more efficient strategies.

A CLASS DISCUSSION

I asked for the students' attention and began a class discussion to give the students the opportunity to share their strategies and consider their classmates' ideas. This discussion would also set the stage and give all students a common reference point for thinking together as a class about multiplication.

"As I watched you work, I noticed that all of you had at least one way of finding the product of eight times seven. Would someone like to share one of your strategies?" I began. I planned to record the children's ideas on the chalkboard as they shared their strategies. Often children find it difficult to put their thoughts and ideas about mathematics in writing. Recording students' thinking on the chalkboard models for students how their ideas can be represented. Recording student thinking on the chalkboard also helps children realize that their ideas are important and valued. I make sure to remind the children often that they may revise their thinking at any time.

I paused until about half the students had raised their hands. I called on Tina. "I knew that I could keep adding eight until I did it seven times."

"How did you know to add eight seven times?" I asked.

"Well the eight says that there are eight in a group and the seven tells me there are seven groups. So it is eight plus eight plus eight plus eight plus eight plus eight plus eight," Tina explained.

I wrote $8 + 8 + 8 + 8 + 8 + 8 + 8 = 56$ (Tina) on the chalkboard and asked Tina if that was what she meant. She nodded yes. "Does anyone have a question for Tina about her idea?" I asked. No one did.

"Mine is sort of like Tina's; in fact, I think it is almost the same thing," Juan said. "The thing that I think might be a little different, but it could be the same, is that you could count by eight for seven times, like eight, sixteen, twenty-four . . . But then I can't really count much higher just by eights so then I have to add."

I wrote Juan's idea as 8, 16, 24, ? ? ? (Juan).

"Juan says you can count by eights to fifty-six. Let's do it together in a whisper voice," I suggested to the rest of the students as a way to verify Juan's thinking. I replaced the question marks I had written on the board as part of Juan's thinking with the multiples of eight as the students counted by eights in whisper voices, stopping when the students got to fifty-six: 8, 16, 24, 32, 40, 48, 56.

"Oh, another way that is sort of like both of those but backwards is you could add seven eight times, seven plus seven plus seven like that. It adds up to fifty-six," Dana said. I recorded Dana's strategy: $7 + 7 + 7 + 7 + 7 + 7 + 7 + 7 = 56$ (Dana).

There was a pause for a moment as the students studied what I had been writing. "How many of you have used this way on your paper?" I asked, pointing to the first strategy, which had been suggested by Tina. Most students raised their hands. I followed this process with the other two suggestions. I did this for a couple of reasons: I wanted to survey the class at a glance for my own information to help guide me in making decisions about my questions for the next part of the discussion. I also wanted to encourage students to examine the thinking of others and compare it with their own.

"Does someone have another strategy that is different from the three we have discussed so far?" I continued. I called on Rick.

"I made a rectangle," Rick explained. "It had seven rows of boxes and each row had eight boxes." I recorded his idea of drawing a rectangle on the board.

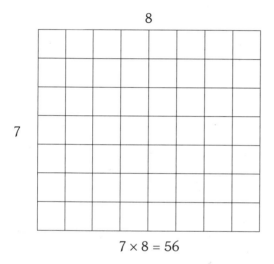

$$7 \times 8 = 56$$

"Is what I recorded what you were thinking?" I asked Rick. He nodded yes.

Because the class was quiet, with very few students wanting to share, I asked the following question, hoping to stimulate discussion and help students build connections between the numerical model represented by the first three strategies and the geometric model represented by Rick's idea. "Using repeated addition, we discovered that we could find the product of eight times seven two ways, by adding eight seven times or by adding seven eight times. Would this also be true of skip-counting?" I asked.

Juan said, "We could skip-count by eights to fifty-six." We tried it and it worked. I recorded on the board: 8, 16, 24, 32, 40, 48, 56.

"We could count by sevens, too," Brooke said.

"In a whisper voice, help me skip-count by sevens eight times," I said.

"Seven, fourteen, twenty-one, twenty-eight, thirty-five, forty-two, forty-nine, fifty-six," the students responded, using their whisper voices. I added this counting sequence to the other ideas listed on the board: 7, 14, 21, 28, 35, 42, 49, 56.

"There are two ways to use repeated addition to help you find the product and two ways to use skip-counting. Do you think there might be another way to use Rick's idea to help you find the product?" The students looked somewhat unsure. "Talk with your neighbor. First one of you can talk for thirty seconds. No interruptions! Then it is the other person's turn to talk for thirty seconds with no interruptions. Then I will ask you to share your ideas with the class."

Carol was eager to share. "My partner and I agree that there is a second way with Rick's idea. You should be able to make a rectangle with eight rows and seven squares in each row. It's the same rectangle but sideways. It would be like a picture of the other ways. At least that's what Krissy and I think." I sketched Carol's idea.

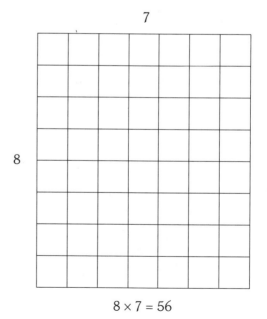

$$8 \times 7 = 56$$

The other students nodded their agreement. I decided to ask for more strategies. Several hands were up.

"You could do eight circles and put seven tally marks in each one or do seven circles with eight tally marks," Conrad suggested. I drew these suggestions.

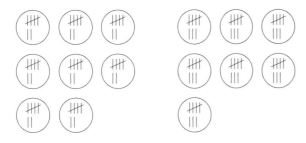

"I thought of using a fact I already knew to help," Brian said. "I knew eight times five equals forty. So I thought, 'All I have to do is add two more groups of eight, then I'll have seven groups of eight!'" I recorded:

$8 \times 5 = 40$

$40 + 8 + 8 = 56$

"That's not exactly how I did it," Brian corrected me. "I did eight times five equals forty. But then I also knew that two eights is sixteen, so I added sixteen, not eight plus eight." I corrected my recording so it read:

$8 \times 5 = 40$

$8 \times 2 = 16$

$40 + 16 = 56$

"That's it," he said, smiling. "I know the first way you wrote it and this way equals the same, but I thought of it the second way."

"Mine is sort of like Brian's because I used a fact I already knew," Jeremiah said. "But I used a different one. I did seven times seven equals forty-nine and then added one more eight to make seven eights, which is fifty-six." I recorded:

$7 \times 7 = 49$

$49 + 8 = 56$

"Well if you knew division, I think you could use division to figure this out," Jasmine suggested. Her classmates looked at her with surprise initially. "Well, fifty-six divided by eight equals seven. The fifty-six is the answer in multiplication. It's like backwards multiplication."

"Oh, it's like fact families, like with addition and subtraction, only this time it is multiplication and division! I get it!" Dana said. I wrote:

$8 \times 7 = 56$

$7 \times 8 = 56$

$56 \div 8 = 7$

$56 \div 7 = 8$

"I did it different than any of the ways up there and I am not sure if it is right," Kim said tentatively. "After I did some other ways, I was looking at my paper and wondered if I could do seven times four equals twenty-eight and then double that?"

I wrote Kim's idea on the chalkboard:

$7 \times 4 = 28$

$28 + 28 = 56$

"Why do you think that would work?" I asked.

"The seven part is the same in both problems but the four in my problem is half of the eight in the first problem so that's why I think I have to double the twenty-eight."

"Why would that be?" I pushed.

"If you use the picture of the rectangle, seven rows of four would be half as much as seven rows of eight," she explained. "Can I show you?"

Kim came to the board and showed us what she meant by circling seven rows of four (see next page). The students nodded quietly, indicating that they were following her thinking.

Students had no more ideas that they were willing to share. "What did you learn today?" I asked as I collected the students' work to study later.

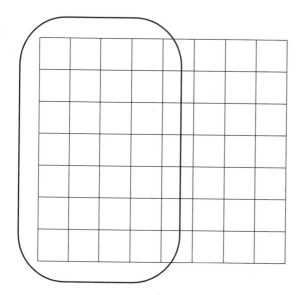

"I learned I better memorize my division facts because it would help me with multiplication," Felicia shared.

EXTENSIONS

One nice way to extend this activity for students who have many correct, well-explained strategies is to ask students to write about how 8 × 7 = 56 is related to 56 ÷ 7 = 8. The relationship between multiplication and division is an important one for students to understand.

Questions and Discussion

▲ **Why is it important to look at students' understanding? Isn't it enough for them to simply memorize the multiplication and division facts?**

While it is important that students develop facility with the multiplication and division facts, it is not enough to simply memorize them. Understanding what multiplication and division are and how they are related will help students tremendously with fractions and algebra, and it is also important to their number sense. Limited understanding or lack of facility hampers students' progress as they move to higher levels of mathematics. Students must have facility with the basic facts as well as understanding.

By asking students to write about their understanding, you can gain insight about their strengths and weaknesses. Asking students to explain their thinking to you as they work can give further clarification about their ideas. Class discussions are also useful to reveal what students already know. You can make instructional decisions that will help students deepen their understanding and build connections between ideas they already understand and new ideas.

▲ **What kinds of response do you hope to see in students' work?**

There are several responses I hope to see. They include the following:

   ▲ Numerical Responses

   repeated addition

      8 + 8 + 8 + 8 + 8 + 8 + 8 = 56

      7 + 7 + 7 + 7 + 7 + 7 + 7 + 7 = 56

   skip-counting

      8, 16, 24, 32, 40, 48, 56

      7, 14, 21, 28, 35, 42, 49, 56

friendly facts

$8 \times 8 = 64$ $8 \times 6 = 48$ $7 \times 4 = 28$

$64 - 8 = 56$ $48 + 8 = 56$ $28 + 28 = 56$

▲ Geometric Representations

rectangles or arrays

▲ Pictorial Representations

circles and stars

▲ Commutative Property

$8 \times 7 = 7 \times 8$

$7 \times 8 = 56$

▲ Connection to Division

$8 \times 7 = 56$ $7 \times 8 = 56$

$56 \div 7 = 8$ $56 \div 8 = 7$

▲ Connections to the Real World

example: There are seven octopi swimming in the bay. How many legs would there be altogether?

As I looked at the students' papers, Cally's work concerned me because she indicated that she relied on a trick to remember the answer to 8×7. Her work showed that her only way of figuring out the product should she forget the trick is to draw a rectangle. (See Figure 1–1.) This is a powerful and useful idea, but it appeared to be her only idea. When I talked with Cally during the work period, she also indicated that there was no other way for her to figure out the product of 8×7.

Joaquin's work showed a very common misunderstanding about multiplication. His picture showed eight birds times seven birds equals fifty-six. His illustration failed to show he understood that multiplication has to do with equal groupings. In fact, his picture showed only fifteen birds rather than the fifty-six it should have shown. Joaquin's work did show that he understood he could use repeated addition to find the product. (See Figure 1–2).

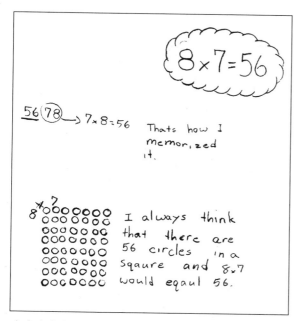

▲▲▲▲▲▲Figure 1–1 *Cally had only one strat-egy besides the trick she used to memorize 8 × 7 = 56.*

▲▲▲▲▲▲Figure 1–2 *Joaquin showed he could use repeated addition to solve 8 × 7. However, his drawing shows he did not understand that multiplication involves equal groups. He drew 15 birds and stated the total is 56.*

Rachelle's paper was stronger because she had several strategies. She showed she could find the product by skip-counting, by using repeated addition, by using the commutative prop-erty, by drawing an array, and by using the multiplication chart. (See Figure 1–3.)

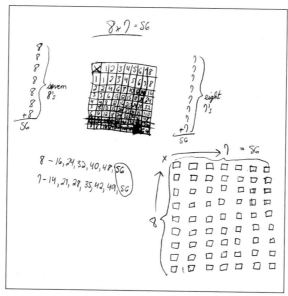

▲▲▲▲▲▲Figure 1–3 *Rachelle showed several strategies to solve 8 × 7.*

Brooke also showed some strong understanding. She used repeated addition and pictures showing equal groups and showed that these two ideas are connected. However, when Brooke wrote a story problem that was supposed to be solved by 8 × 7, holes in her understanding appeared. Her problem was more about addition than multiplication. (See Figure 1–4.)

Matt's paper was interesting. He found the wrong answer to 8 × 7. However, he used tally marks (seven groups of eight and eight groups of seven), indicating some understanding of the commutative nature of multiplication. Matt also used repeated addition. His picture of the two puppies did not show understanding. At the bottom he showed that he was beginning to get an idea that there is a relationship between multiplication and division, but he indicated he was not clear about this. (See Figure 1–5.)

Jeremiah also indicated his understanding was developing. He could find the product by repeated addition by using the commutative property and by using related known facts. For example, he used 7 × 7 = 49 then added one more group of 7 to make 8 groups of 7, or 56. (See Figure 1–6.)

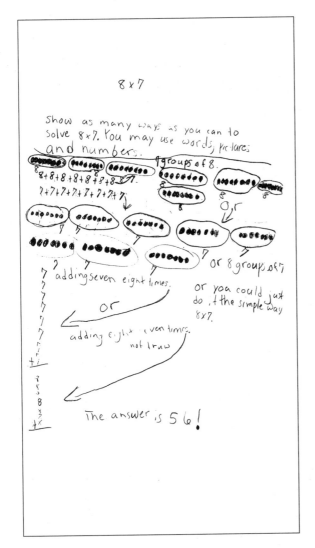

▲▲▲▲▲▲Figure 1–4 *While Brooke used several good strategies to solve 8 × 7, her multiplication story revealed holes in her understanding.*

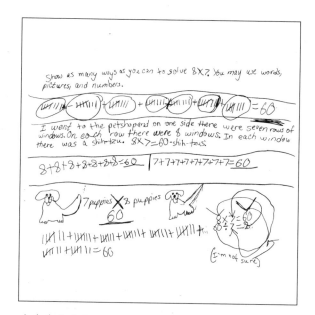

▲▲▲▲▲▲**Figure 1–5** *Matt's paper showed emerging understanding. He solved the problem incorrectly but he showed his understanding of multiplication as repeated addition and equal groupings.*

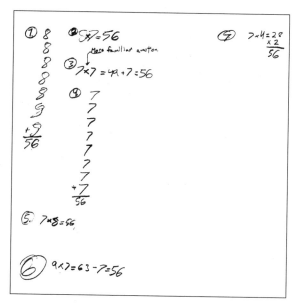

▲▲▲▲▲▲**Figure 1–6** *Jeremiah used several strategies, including using a friendly fact: $7 \times 7 = 49$, plus one more group of 7 equals 56.*

Kirk's paper showed several sophisticated approaches to solving 8×7. He used friendly facts, a more sophisticated application of repeated addition, and an unusual application of a rectangle. (See Figure 1–7.)

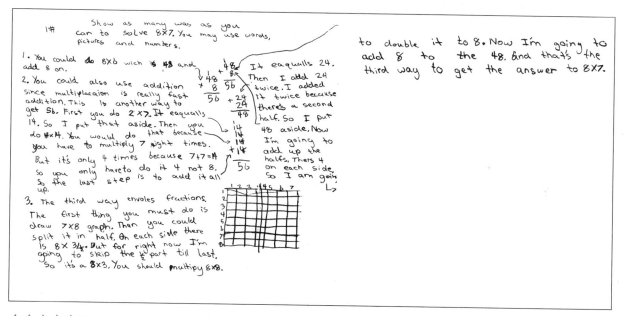

▲▲▲▲▲▲**Figure 1–7** *Kirk's work showed his understanding through the use of several strategies.*

▲ What are common mistakes children make on their individual papers?

The first time children are faced with this type of assignment they tend to give incomplete explanations. This requires that you question them either while they are working on the assignment or at some later time to clarify what they do and do not understand. For example, children often give one repeated addition example for 8×7 such as $8 + 8 + 8 + 8 + 8 + 8 + 8 = 56$ but not the other repeated addition sentence that would also solve the problem. Joaquin did this on his paper. Therefore, the teacher must find out whether this is a lack of understanding or whether the student simply did not feel it important to include the second number sentence.

Common misunderstandings include a student not realizing that multiplication involves combining equal groups. Students may show this lack of understanding by drawing one group of eight objects, then placing a multiplication sign and drawing a second group of seven objects, as shown in Joaquin's work. When this occurs, it is important to help students see why this thinking doesn't make sense. Also, it is important to provide students with concrete experiences that reinforce the concept of multiplication.

Another strategy that is often missing from student work is the use of rectangles or arrays. Even when rectangles or arrays are included, students sometimes make errors in counting, which creates inaccurate pictures and/or products. When students include rectangles or arrays, teaching them to label two sides of the rectangle or array, like Cally and Rachelle did in their work, seems to reduce the number of counting errors.

Other common flaws in student work include omission of any connection between multiplication and the real world. Students are often unaware of the relationship of multiplication to division. Some students may also not recognize the commutative property. Students may come to you knowing their facts but having learned them by using tricks like the one Cally used. Cally had only one other way to figure out this problem besides the trick she had learned. When children are taught little tricks like this, in the moment it might seem useful, but as they have to take the information and apply it to new learnings or use it to problem solve, they are unable to do so. I believe that to ask children to memorize discrete pieces of information with no understanding is to handicap them in future learning, because they will lack the understanding to apply what they have memorized.

▲ How is the information from the students' papers useful?

Knowing where students are strong and weak guides my choices when determining which activities would be most useful for my particular class at any given time. For example, children are often weak at understanding the connection and usefulness of rectangles and multiplication. In this case, time would be well spent exploring rectangles as suggested in Chapter 5, "Related Rectangles."

The ways children look at 8×7 numerically can reveal the sophistication of their level of understanding. The *Silent Multiplication* lesson (see page 37) provides children with an opportunity to look at numbers more flexibly, thus allowing them a greater depth of understanding. It encourages children to see that 8×7 could also be thought of as 4×14 or 2×28 or $2(4 \times 7)$. This kind of flexible thinking will help children be more successful as they move into algebra.

Many students don't realize that they can use what they already know to help them figure out what they don't know. For example, 6×8 could be used to help a student find 8×7 simply by adding one more 8 to the product of 6×8. *Matilda* (see page 113) is a useful exploration for helping students think about this idea of using known information to solve a problem. When Matilda solves 19×14 in her head, students are asked to think about how she did this. She might have solved 20×14 then subtracted one group of 14 or thought of 19 as two groups of 10 and multiplied 10 × 14 and then doubled that product, then subtracted one group of 14 or she might have thought of 14 as one group of 10 and one group of 4, then multiplied 19 × 10 and 19 × 4 then added the partial products to find the product of 19 × 14.

▲ How can doing this lesson periodically be useful?

Using this approach periodically allows you to monitor student growth in understanding over time. As students have experience with this type of activity, I expect to see increasingly clear explanations, more strategies, and a greater sophistication of the ideas included in their writing.

Initially the only tool Antonio had was the use of repeated addition. (See Figure 1–8.)

A few weeks later, he could solve a more complex problem, 12 × 19, using repeated addition, equal groupings, and a rectangular array as well as the standard algorithm. As Antonio's teacher, I wanted to make sure that he understood that he could also solve the problem by drawing a rectangular array that was nineteen down and twelve across and that he could represent the problem with twelve circles with nineteen marks in each. I also encouraged Antonio to think more flexibly about numbers and to make a stronger connection between multiplication and the world around him. (See Figure 1–9.)

▲ How can I help children improve their skill in writing about mathematics?

Giving students many opportunities to write about their mathematical thinking is important. As they are doing their writing, I have found it helpful to walk around and read what students are writing. Reminders about using labels to help clarify their thinking help students. Reminding them to use words, pictures, and numbers to clearly communicate their ideas is also helpful. I have also found that asking questions of students about their work helps guide their writing and the process of sharing their thinking. Once a student has explained her thinking to me, I ask her to make the thinking go from her brain, skip her mouth, go down her arm, out her hand, down her pencil, and onto the paper. This usually brings about a giggle, but it also helps students understand what it is I need from them. I also try to remember to tell them when their explanations have helped me understand, as this kind of guidance is needed as well.

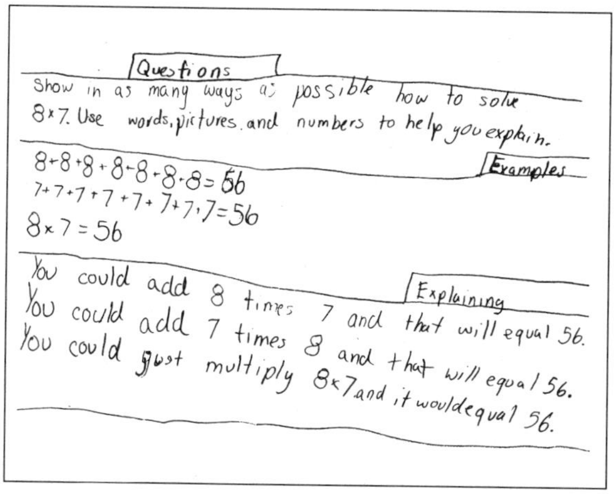

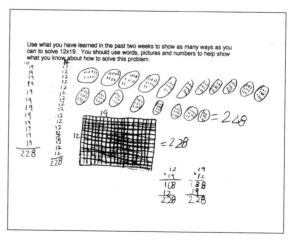

▲▲▲▲▲▲Figure 1–8   Antonio seemed to have repeated addition as his only strategy for solving 8 × 7.

▲▲▲▲▲▲Figure 1–9   A few weeks later, Antonio had added new strategies to his repertoire for solving multiplication problems.

▲ *Why do you record student responses on the board, the overhead, or on a chart?*

Recording student responses on the chalkboard, a piece of chart paper, or the overhead helps students see how their ideas about mathematics can be written. It serves as a good model for students when they are asked to write about their thinking in mathematics. Additionally, writing down students' ideas helps those students who process information more effectively when they can read it, not just hear it. Writing down students' ideas shows that their thinking is valued, which often encourages further, deeper thinking. Students can use the ideas written on the chalkboard, chart, or overhead for later reference.

I always include the students' names with their responses as this gives additional value to their thinking. Students are often reminded they may revise their thinking or ask that their thinking not be recorded.

▲ *If students don't suggest other ways to solve the problem, should the teacher?*

There was a point in the vignette when the students seemed to have no more ideas. Enough information had already been shared that I could ask some leading questions and get the conversation going again, rather than telling the students of other ways to solve the problem. If this hadn't been the case, that is, if the students still had nothing to say, references to previous related activities might have been helpful. Perhaps the teacher could couch an idea in the form of a question. For example, "Would drawing a picture help me solve this problem? If so, how would I draw it?" If these ideas don't work, then the message to me is I need to provide the students with some activities to support them in learning strategies and how to apply and share them with others.

▲ *What do you do about students who seem unable to get started on the written part in the beginning?*

This sometimes happens, especially if students have had little experience with multiplication at the conceptual level. I would ask the student some questions to get thinking going. Some of the questions might be:

Can you think of another way of saying eight times seven? (My goal is to help the student to recognize 8 × 7 is the same as 8 groups of 7.)

Can you draw a picture of what eight groups of seven might look like?

Is there a way you could solve eight times seven using addition?

Can you think of a word problem that could be solved using eight times seven?

If you don't know eight times seven, is there some other fact you do know that you could use to help you?

If the student is not helped by any of these questions, then I know I have to do some work with that child on early concept development of multiplication as described in *Teaching Arithmetic: Lessons for Introducing Multiplication, Grade 3*, by Marilyn Burns.

CHAPTER 2
LEARNING THE MULTIPLICATION CHART

Overview

Through class discussion, students will come to see that the task of learning the multiplication table is manageable. Students discuss the "easy" multiplication facts and what makes them easy, and then eliminate them from the multiplication chart. Through this process, students will eventually find that only twenty-eight "difficult" multiplication facts (twenty-one not including the squares) remain to be learned on a 12×12 multiplication chart or twenty-one "difficult" facts (fifteen not including the squares) on a 10×10 multiplication chart.

Materials

▲ overhead transparency

12×12 multiplication chart (see Blackline Masters)

1–100 chart (optional, see Blackline Masters)

▲ student copies of multiplication chart (optional)

Time

▲ one class period

Teaching Directions

1. Show a chart or overhead transparency of the 12×12 multiplication chart. Ask students to examine the chart, looking for patterns. Teach them how to use the chart to find products if they haven't already learned how.

2. Ask the students which facts are easy. For example, the ones and tens are easy. Because they are easy, cross them off the multiplication chart. (**Note:** You may wish to give students their own copy of the multiplication chart and have them do this process on their own papers as you do it on the overhead chart.)

	1	2	3	4	5	6	7	8	9	10	11	12
1		2	3	4	5	6	7	8	9	10	11	12
2	2	4	6	8	10	12	14	16	18	20	22	24
3	3	6	9	12	15	18	21	24	27	30	33	36
4	4	8	12	16	20	24	28	32	36	40	44	48
5	5	10	15	20	25	30	35	40	45	50	55	60
6	6	12	18	24	30	36	42	48	54	60	66	72
7	7	14	21	28	35	42	49	56	63	70	77	84
8	8	16	24	32	40	48	56	64	72	80	88	96
9	9	18	27	36	45	54	63	72	81	90	99	108
10	10	20	30	40	50	60	70	80	90	100	110	120
11	11	22	33	44	55	66	77	88	99	110	121	132
12	12	24	36	48	60	72	84	96	108	120	132	144

On a 12 × 12 multiplication chart there are 144 facts. After crossing off the ones and tens, ask students to verify that forty-four facts have been eliminated and figure how many are still to be learned.

3. Students will probably agree that the twos and fives are also easy. This eliminates another thirty-six, with sixty-four remaining. (Have students figure this.)

4. Most of the elevens can also probably be crossed off. That means fifteen more can be eliminated, leaving forty-nine.

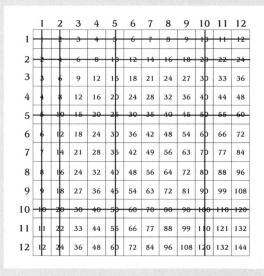 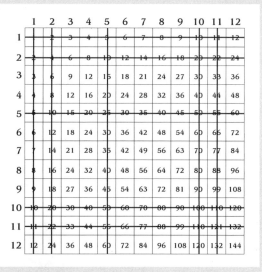

5. Forty-two of the remaining forty-nine facts are commutative, like 3 × 4 and 4 × 3. Point out examples of the commutative property of multiplication and its usefulness for eliminating twenty-one of the forty-two facts. The remaining seven facts are squares. For older students these seem easy to remember, but for younger students these still remain to be learned, bringing the total to twenty-eight.

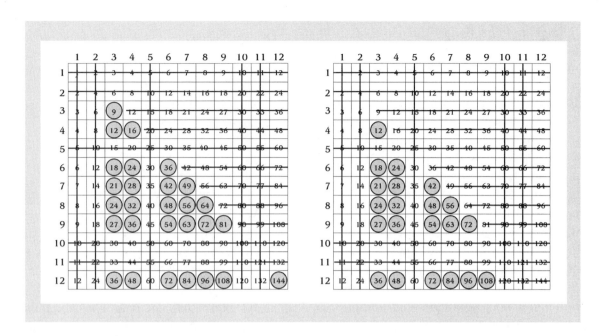

Teaching Notes

To develop a firm foundation in multiplication, students in the fourth and fifth grades need to learn the multiplication table. This can seem overwhelming and often students are defeated even before they start. But facility with multiplication facts is essential for success in multidigit multiplication, division, fractions, factoring, and many key ideas leading to algebra.

In this lesson, students examine a 12×12 multiplication chart that shows 144 products. During a class discussion and through the process of elimination, students will find learning these within their grasp. Eliminating the easy ones, such as multiplying by ones and tens, results in eliminating forty-four facts. Students will probably agree that the fives and twos are also easy facts and those can be eliminated. This reduces the total by another thirty-six facts. So far, eighty facts have been eliminated, reducing the total number of facts to be learned to sixty-four. The elevens, with the possible exception of 11×12, most likely can also be eliminated, which further reduces the total to forty-nine. When the class examines the remaining facts, a powerful discussion can occur, allowing students to develop or reinforce understanding of the commutative nature of multiplication. The commutative property of multiplication states that the product of two numbers does not depend on the order in which they were multiplied, that is, $2 \times 3 = 3 \times 2 = 6$. Of the remaining forty-nine facts, forty-two are commutative pairs, that is, they have duplicates like 3×4 and 4×3. Because of the commutative property, the forty-two remaining facts can actually be split in half, leaving twenty-one to be learned. If students know the squares, these may also be eliminated. However, for younger fourth graders, these facts most likely still need to be learned. There are seven squares remaining, which will increase the total to twenty-eight facts, certainly a more manageable task than the original 144. If using a 12×12 multiplication chart seems too overwhelming, this same process can be used with a 10×10 multiplication chart, with the remaining difficult facts totaling fifteen rather than twenty-eight.

The Lesson

▲▲

I had recently asked my class to solve 8×7 or, if they knew the answer, prove that the answer is 56. Their work indicated they had a strong conceptual understanding of multiplication and could think about 8×7 in several ways. It was clear to me that my students understood what multiplication was, but they needed to work on improving their facility with the multiplication table. I decided to help them see that memorizing the basic facts is not as overwhelming as many of them might have thought. I began by placing a transparency of a 12×12 multiplication chart on the overhead.

"What is this?" I asked the students.

"A hundreds chart," called out several students.

"No it's not; look closer, it's bigger," Jeni said.

"You can tell it's not a hundreds chart because the last number is one hundred forty-four," commented Rob.

"Then it must be a one hundred forty-four chart!" Neal interjected.

"How is this chart different than a hundreds chart?" I asked. I paused for a few moments to allow the students time to think about my question. As hands began to go up, I said, "Share your ideas with your neighbor. One of you will share for thirty seconds while the other listens without interrupting. Then I'll ask you to change and let the first listener share while the first talker listens. Remember, no interruptions." I reminded the students to switch roles at the end of thirty seconds. After the minute was up, I asked for the students to give me their attention once again. Several had their hands up, eager to share.

"It doesn't count by ones like on a hundreds chart," Brooke shared.

"You know how on a hundreds chart, when you go down the column all the numbers in that column have all the same number in the ones place? Well this chart doesn't do it that way," Susanna noticed.

Some students weren't too sure about what Susanna was trying to say, so I quickly put a transparency of a hundreds chart on the overhead. Susanna came to the overhead and chose the column with the 9 at the top. "You see, in this column going all the way down, there is always a nine in the ones place," she explained. The students nodded their heads, indicating that they understood what Susanna was saying.

"Why do you suppose that happens?" I asked. I asked this question because place value had been a struggle for many of these students. I like to take every opportunity to point out to them instances involving place value in hopes of strengthening their understanding and ability to use the structure of our base ten number system as a tool to help them compute efficiently.

"It goes by ones going across, I know," Susanna said. "But I'm not sure about why all the numbers in a column end the same." Susanna and I had struggled all year with place value. She had explored it using hundreds charts, base ten materials, cubes, and beansticks, none of which seemed to make sense to Susanna.

"I think it has to do with adding ten," Hector said. "The difference going down, when you go from one square to one exactly under it, is ten. Actually that's the way it works if you go up exactly one square, too! When you add ten, the ones don't change. That's why I think it works!"

"If you agree with Hector, put your thumb up; if not, put your thumb down," I said to the students. They indicated that they agreed. Had the students not agreed, I would have spent a few moments using the hundreds chart to explore this pattern.

"Does Hector's idea work on this chart?" I asked as I removed the hundreds chart and replaced it on the overhead with the multiplication chart. Again I paused to give students time to look at the chart and consider my question. They were looking a bit perplexed so I decided to ask them to again share their thinking with their neighbors.

"Well, we aren't really that sure, but we don't think so," Calob said. "This chart doesn't seem to follow rules like the hundreds chart. The hundreds chart always does the same rule about adding ten going down or adding one going across and rules like that, but this one changes all the time. Well, at least, that's what we think."

"We noticed that in the first row going across it counts by ones and the first column going down does, too," Alicia said.

"Hey, it counts by twos where the two is on top and it counts by threes where the three is on top!" Ana said. "I think the number on top is what that column counts by."

"How could we test Ana's idea?" I asked.

"You could just pick one and try it," Kasey answered. "It's like the columns are doing skip-counting. I think the rows are doing the same thing too, like in the twos row, it goes two, four, six, eight, and the fours does four, eight, twelve, and like that."

"You can figure out multiplication on it," Kirk said. "I know what it is, it's a multiplication chart and I know how to use it. Say you want to know five times four, you go down five and across four and you move your fingers together down that row and column and when they meet you get the answer, twenty." Gina was watching very closely, balanced on the edge of her seat, intent on Kirk's every word. Conner was also listening very closely, intrigued with what Kirk was

sharing. It appeared that both were on the edge of understanding. I wanted to do one more example in hopes of clarifying what was happening for them. Brooke provided the perfect opportunity with her question.

"Would four times eight work or just that one Kirk said?" she asked.

"How could we find out?" I asked.

"Aaahhh . . . I know, you could go down the side of the chart to where the four is and put your finger there, then go across the top to where the eight is and put another finger there and then move your fingers until they meet," Brooke explained.

"When I do that, what number do you think will be there?" I asked.

"I think thirty-two!" Brooke answered.

I did as Brooke had instructed and sure enough, I landed on 32. Gina let out a little squeal of excitement and declared, "I get it!"

"I told you, it's a chart of all the multiplication facts," Kirk said.

"Kirk is right. How many of you think you understand or already knew how to find the products on a chart like this?" Most of the students raised their hands, indicating they understood. I quickly demonstrated how to find the product of one more fact for those who were uncertain before moving on. "This chart has one hundred forty-four multiplication facts on it. Does that seem like a lot to you?" The students moaned and carried on.

"I don't think I'll ever learn them all!" Melissa said.

"Me either. But I do know some. There are some easy ones," Conner said.

"I agree with Conner. Some facts are easier than others," I said. "Which ones do you consider to be easy?"

"The ones are really easy!" Anthony said. The students indicated their agreement with Anthony.

"Are they easy enough we could cross them off our chart because we know them?" I asked.

"Yes!" the class responded. I crossed them off the chart.

"You could do that with the tens, too. You see, they are like the ones except you add a zero. One times one equals one, one times ten equals ten, three times one equals three, three times ten equals thirty. See?" Kirk explained.

"Can we cross off the tens?" I asked. I did so as the class indicated that the tens were also easy. The discussion continued in this way with students suggesting groups of facts that were easy and why they were easy. Each time we eliminated a group of facts, we figured out how many remained to be learned. The students decided that the ones, tens, twos, fives, and elevens could be eliminated. That left forty-nine to be learned. (Refer back to page 17.)

Miguel said, "I think it is less than forty-nine. Well that's what I think and this is why. If you know four times six, then you also know six times four. Both of those are still on the chart but you only have to learn one and just remember to turn it around and you really know two. The picture would look different, like one is four groups of six stars and the other is six groups of four stars, but both ways it's the same amount of stars."

"Oh yeah!" mumbled several students. If no student had suggested this, I would have pointed it out.

"I have another example that would work. You could do the same thing with three times nine and nine times three," Charlie said. The students nodded.

"I think that's true for all of them," Gina said.

"No, it's not. Look, there is only one place for three times three instead of two like for the others. It's the same with four times four," argued Kirk.

"Oh yeah, my sister says those are square numbers and she's studying square roots. It's like a number times that same number," Gina explained.

"Look, there's like a pattern, the square numbers go down a diagonal," Sandra pointed out.

"Let's look at the diagonal line created by the square numbers. What do you notice about how the numbers are arranged on either side of the diagonal?" I asked. I was hoping the students would notice the symmetry of the multiplication chart, which is a geometric representation of the commutative nature of multiplication.

"Oh wow! They're the same numbers!" noticed several students.

"Why do you think that is so?" I asked.

"I think because they are related like Miguel and Charlie said," Hector offered. "If you look at the twenty-fours and you follow the row going across to the beginning of the row and if you follow the columns going to the top, you will either land on a four or a six. It's because six times four equals twenty-four and four times six equals twenty-four. They both equal twenty-four. If you know one, you know the other, so you only really have to learn one of them and just remember to turn it around."

"This idea that you can turn the numbers around, as many of you noticed, is something special about both multiplication and addition. Mathematicians call it the commutative property. It means that if you change the order, the final amount still stays the same. Since this is true, could we cross out one of each pair that has a duplicate, like cross out either six times four or four times six?" I asked, redirecting the conversation for the moment. The students nodded their heads, indicating I could do this.

I crossed off one of each of the pairs of duplicates. (Refer back to page 17.)

"There are forty-nine facts left. Forty-two have duplicates. Because I have crossed off the duplicates, there are only twenty-one of those left plus the seven that are square numbers. That means you have twenty-eight facts left to learn," I said.

"I can do that, I bet," Anthony mumbled.

"Please take a few minutes and write in your journal about what you learned today," I said as I drew the lesson to a close. Being asked to write about learning helps students think about the lesson more deeply and increases their learning.

Questions and Discussion

▲▲

▲ What are ways to provide practice besides timed tests?

I don't think timed tests help students learn. Timing students leads them to believe that speed is the most important part of learning their facts. This is not true. It is important for students to have recall of their facts so they don't have to constantly figure them out as they do more complex arithmetic, but there are other ways to achieve this.

Time limits also discourage students from thinking about whether their answers make sense or are reasonable. Putting a time limit on students creates a sense of panic and fear for some. This is counterproductive to learning and increases the likelihood students will practice facts incorrectly in the name of doing them quickly. Fear and incorrect practice are not acceptable, nor are practices that promote them.

There are other ways to provide practice for students to improve their recall with the basic facts. Different methods work for different students and variety makes learning interesting. For this reason I believe in providing a variety of ways for students to practice their facts.

The activities in this book provide practice of the facts in interesting contexts while developing and reinforcing conceptual knowledge. In fact, students may not realize that what they are doing is actually practicing and applying their knowledge of basic multiplication facts. The Additional Activities section (see page 161) provides two games that give students practice with the harder multiplication facts. Students gain practice of the basic facts by writing and solving each other's story problems involving the basic facts. Also, there are a variety of games in many teacher resources that provide fact practice.

Once the class has completed this activity, one fact can become the focus for a few days and the class can talk about and consider it in a variety of ways. For example, students could draw a picture representing the fact, write a story problem that could be solved by the fact, or collect and arrange objects in a rectangle or array that matches the fact. They could search for examples of the fact at home. For example, 6×7 could be represented by seven six-packs of soda.

▲ What about flash cards?

This is not a method I liked as a child. However, if a child enjoys using flash cards at home, this is fine as long as it is one of many ways to practice. I feel there are many more interesting ways for children to practice their facts that also develop their understanding than drill with flash cards, which is essentially rote memorization.

▲ *What is wrong with rote memorization?*

Rote memorization is often devoid of understanding. If there is no understanding on the part of the student, there is very little chance that the student will be able to apply the rote learning to a new situation. The memorized material is useless if the student cannot apply it. Multiplication is a key idea in much of what students will do in mathematics in the future. They must understand what multiplication is and how it is related to other ideas in order to meaningfully apply it later when working with division, fractions, and algebra. Children need to memorize the multiplication table, but the memorization must follow understanding, not replace it.

CHAPTER 3
ONE HUNDRED HUNGRY ANTS

Overview

During this investigation, students explore factors of the numbers from 1 to 50. While exploring factors, students gain practice with both basic facts and multidigit multiplication problems. During the investigation and in follow-up discussions, the topics explored by students include the commutative property of multiplication; prime, composite, and square numbers; the number of factors of odd versus even numbers; and what happens when an odd number is multiplied by an odd number, an even number by an even number, and an even number by an odd number. In addition, students strengthen their understanding of the link between multiplication and division. (**Note:** A lesson based on this book is also included in *Teaching Arithmetic: Lessons for Introducing Multiplication, Grade 3*, reinforcing for younger students how multiplication relates to rectangular arrays and helping them think about factors of one hundred and other numbers.)

Materials

▲ *One Hundred Hungry Ants*, by Elinor J. Pinczes (Houghton Mifflin, 1999)
▲ class chart to record the factors of the numbers from 1 to 50 (see below)
▲ 1-inch color tiles (optional)

DIRECTIONS FOR CLASS CHART

I used seven sheets of 18-by-24-inch newsprint for class charts. I folded each sheet to make eight rows, used part of the top row on each to label two columns, and numbered the rows from 1 to 50.

Number	Factors
1	
2	
3	
4	
5	
6	
7	
8	

Number	Factors
9	
10	
11	
12	
13	
14	
15	
16	

Time

▲ three class periods

Teaching Directions

1. Read the first five pages of *One Hundred Hungry Ants* aloud to students. On the chalkboard, record the two ways the ants marched:

1 line of 100: 1 × 100 = 100

2 lines of 50: 2 × 50 = 100

2. Continue the discussion by asking students to predict and explain their predictions for the next way the smallest ant will suggest they march. Record predictions on the chalkboard. Continue reading. Explore with students why the littlest ant did not suggest they march in three lines (because there would be an extra ant, resulting in unequal lines, as 3 is not a factor of 100).

3. Continue reading, discussing, and recording the various ways the littlest ant suggested the ants should march:

4 lines of 25: 4 × 25 = 100

5 lines of 20: 5 × 20 = 100

10 lines of 10: 10 × 10 = 100

4. After finishing the book, ask the students if there are other ways in which the ants could march in equal rows. Possibilities are 100 rows of 1, 50 rows of 2, and 25 rows of 4. Point out that while 25 lines of 4 and 4 lines of 25 each equal 100, they are different when ants march, or when we're thinking of 25 groups of 4 versus 4 groups of 25. However, 4-by-25 and 25-by-4 rectangles are the same, just oriented differently.

Note: If this idea is not clear to students, use a smaller number and 1-inch color tiles to demonstrate. For example, using the number 6, have students build two lines of three tiles. Then have them take another six tiles and build three lines of two. Have students examine how these structures are alike and how they are different. Students in the following vignette had several previous experiences with the idea, so this suggestion was not included in the lesson.

5. Using the information recorded on the board about the various ways the ants marched, introduce the vocabulary words *factor* and *product.*

6. Pose the following situation for students to consider: The story says all the other ants chased after the littlest ant. How many ants were chasing the littlest ant and what ways could they have lined up? Students should know that ninety-nine ants were chasing the littlest ant and students should investigate the factors of 99 to find that the ants could have marched in rows of 1, 3, 9, 11, 33, or 99. Ask for students to explore in pairs and then lead a class discussion about the factors of 99 and why certain numbers are factors and others are not. This sort of discussion not only builds students' ability to think about and use factors but also lays a foundation for understanding the link between multiplication and division.

7. Display the class chart for finding the factors of the numbers 1 through 50. Explain to students that they will be working to find the factors of the numbers 1 through 50 and will record their findings on the chart.

8. Students can work on this individually or in pairs. When students choose a number to investigate, they should write their initials beside that number on the chart to indicate they have chosen it. This system avoids duplication of numbers investigated. (As an alternative, you may stipulate that two students can investigate the same number. This system increases the likelihood of mistakes being caught early.) In the vignette that follows, only one pair of students investigated each number. Students recorded their findings on the class chart as they finished. Those who finished quickly chose a second number to investigate or checked to see if they agreed with the information already posted on the chart.

9. As students work, check the information they record on the class chart for accuracy. You can deal with errors in several ways: (1) ask students responsible to check and/or justify the information recorded on the chart, (2) assign a second pair of students to investigate, then have the two pairs compare and discuss their results, or (3) use the follow-up class discussion as an opportunity for students to think about the work of others and comment about it when they disagree. In the vignette that follows, all three methods were used.

10. After the class chart has been completed, ask students to study the information. Some questions to use to help focus students' thinking include "What do you notice about this information? What do you notice about the even numbers? The odd numbers? The number of factors of some numbers?" After giving students a few moments to study the information quietly, have them discuss their ideas with partners. Then have students write about what they have noticed.

11. After students have written about what they have noticed about the information on the class chart, lead a class discussion in which students share their observations. Record their ideas on the chalkboard or on a large sheet of chart paper.

Teaching Notes

The book *One Hundred Hungry Ants,* by Elinor J. Pinczes (Houghton Mifflin, 1999), provides a nice context for an exploration of factors. The book tells the story of one hundred hungry ants off to a picnic. The illustrations help children visualize some of the ways one hundred ants could march in equal rows, creating rectangular arrays. The arrangements of the ants marching in equal rows, provide the foundation for the development of students' understanding of factors and equal grouping, leading to a further understanding of the connection between multiplication and division. As students find the factors of numbers, they are practicing basic facts and working with multidigit multiplication problems.

Students explored a variety of topics during this investigation. The commutative property of multiplication ($2 \times 3 = 3 \times 2$) was among the topics. The commutative property can be useful for helping students become more proficient with the basic facts. If a student knows $6 \times 8 = 48$, then the student also knows the product of 8×6.

Prime and composite numbers were also discussed because students recognized that certain numbers had only two factors (prime numbers) while others had more than two factors (composite). The number 1 is the exception, as it only has one factor, 1. Several students also realized that most numbers had an even number of factors. The exception to this were the square numbers, which all have an odd number of factors.

A few of the students wondered about the result of multiplying an odd number by an odd number (odd × odd = odd), an even number by an even number (even × even = even), and an odd number by an even number (odd × even = even).

The students in the following vignette had previously explored how to represent the numbers from 1 to 36 as rectangular arrays, as described in the following paragraph. (For a more detailed explanation, see the *Candy Box* activity from *Teaching Arithmetic: Lessons for Introducing Multiplication, Grade 3,* by Marilyn Burns.)

DIRECTIONS FOR CANDY BOXES (OPTIONAL)

Students explore factors by using 1-inch color tiles to make rectangles. Working in pairs, children build rectangles for numbers they draw from a sack that has the numbers 1 to 36 in it. The students cut models of what they build out of grid paper and post them on a class chart. For example, 6 could be represented with rectangles that are 1 by 6 and 2 by 3. The dimensions of the rectangles for 6 are also the factors of 6, that is, 1, 6, 2, and 3 are the lengths of the sides of the rectangles as well as the factors students list on the class chart for *One Hundred Hungry Ants.*

The Lesson

▲▲

DAY 1

I began by reading the first five pages of the story to the students. After the fifth page when the littlest ant suggests the ants march in a line other than a single line of 100, I stopped and asked the students, "What is another way the ants could march in equal lines?"

"They could march in rows of ten, because ten groups or rows of ten would equal ten times ten or one hundred," Neal suggested. I wrote *10 × 10 = 100* on the chalkboard to represent the suggestion that Neal had made.

"They could march in four rows of twenty-five. It would be like four quarters make a dollar; a dollar equals a hundred pennies and a quarter equals twenty-five pennies, so four quarters or twenty-fives equals one hundred!" Jeni shared with enthusiasm. To represent Jeni's thinking I wrote:

1 quarter = 25¢

1 dollar = 100¢

4 quarters = 1 dollar or 100¢

4 × 25 = 100

"If they all just ran they might get there faster," Miguel suggested, giggling.

"Let's see what the littlest ant suggested," I said, then continued to read the next five pages of the story, stopping on the sixth page after the littlest ant says they are moving way too slow. "In the beginning, the ants marched in one line of one hundred and now they are marching in two lines of fifty," I explained as I wrote the following on the chalkboard:

1 line of 100: 1 × 100 = 100

2 lines of 50: 2 × 50 = 100

"Study this information and see if you can guess how the littlest ant will suggest the ants march next," I said, pausing for a few moments to give the students time to consider the information. When about half the students had their hands up, I called on Sandra.

"I think the littlest ant will tell them to march in five lines of twenty-five because that will be a way for one hundred ants to march," Sandra said.

"I disagree with Sandra, because as Jeni said earlier, it takes four twenty-fives to make one hundred, not five," Kasey said.

"Oh yeah! OK, I think the littlest ant will tell everyone to march in four lines of twenty-five," Sandra corrected herself.

"How about ten lines of ten?" Neal suggested again. "You can count ten, twenty, thirty, forty, fifty, sixty, seventy, eighty, ninety, one hundred. Ten lines of ten, it works!"

"I think that what Neal said would work, but I don't agree it's what the littlest ant says next," Brooke said. "There is a pattern. First it was one line, then two lines, three lines won't work because I don't think the lines would be equal if there were three lines, so I think what Kasey and Sandra said would work because it would be four lines of twenty-five."

"How many would be in each line if the ants divided themselves into three lines?" I asked the class. The students stared back at me rather blankly. "Talk it over with your neighbor and see if you can figure it out."

"Can we get a piece of paper to figure?" Kirk asked.

"Sure," I replied. Paper and pencil are important tools for students to use to keep track of their thinking. After three or four minutes, the students seemed to be ready to move on and share their thinking.

"We just skip-counted by three. We skip-counted thirty-three times and landed on ninety-nine and thought we made a mistake so we did it again and landed on ninety-nine again. So we thought we'd better draw a picture. We drew a picture of three tally marks then circled the three tally marks to show it was a group. We got thirty-three groups and only ninety-nine tally marks. We think lines of three won't work because you land on ninety-nine, not one hundred," Hector and his partner, Ana, shared.

"We did it differently. We thought about one hundred and then thought, um, there would be at least twenty-five in each line if there were three lines. Twenty-five plus twenty-five plus twenty-five equals seventy-five. That leaves twenty-five more. I knew that eight times three equals twenty-four, so that means we could put eight more with each group of twenty-five. Each group now has twenty-five plus eight, which is thirty-three. And there is one left over because of the eight times three, which is only twenty-four, not twenty-five," Kirk explained as his partner, Susanna, nodded her agreement.

"I like my idea about ten," Neal explained. "I just made three circles and put tens in the circles until I ran out of tens. There were three tens in each circle and I had one ten left so I divided the ten up into ones and put three ones in each circle. I had three tens and three ones, which is thirty-three, with one left over."

"It's clear that three doesn't work!" Jeni shared. "I think Brooke, Kasey, and Sandra are right, the next way the littlest ant will say is four lines of twenty-five!"

I continued reading the story and sure enough, the next way suggested was 4 lines of 25. As I finished sharing the book with students I recorded on the chalkboard the various ways the littlest ant suggested the ants line up as follows:

1 line of 100: 1 × 100 = 100

2 lines of 50: 2 × 50 = 100

4 lines of 25: 4 × 25 = 100

5 lines of 20: 5 × 20 = 100

10 lines of 10: 10 × 10 = 100

"Are there any other ways the littlest ant could have suggested that the ants march?" I asked as students examined the list of ways suggested in the story. I was interested to know if they would mention such ways as 100 rows of 1 or 50 rows of 2 and whether or not they would see these ways of marching as the same or different. These students had had practice making arrays and had participated in class discussions about such ideas as whether or not 100 rows of 1 was the same or different than 1 row of 100.

"They could have marched in rows of four and that would be twenty-five rows. It would be like twisting the four lines of twenty-five around backward sort of and doing twenty-five lines of four," Rob volunteered.

"Yeah, or you could do twenty rows of five," Susanna added.

"Or fifty rows of two," Jamie said.

"I think you could just do the reverse of the ways listed on the board. With multiplication you can turn the order around and it will still give you the same amount," Kirk explained. "It's the commutative property in action!"

"Commutative means you get the same answer no matter which way you add or multiply, right?" Jeni asked.

"What do you think about Jeni's question?" I asked the class, deciding to take a brief side trip to address the commutative property. "If you agree with Jeni's conjecture, put your thumb up, put it down if you

disagree, and put it sideways if you are not sure."

"What's conjecture mean?" Brooke asked.

"An idea or guess about something," I responded.

"Oh!" Brooke said, putting her thumb up. About half the students put their thumbs sideways, indicating they weren't sure, and about half put their thumbs up, indicating they agreed with Jeni.

"The commutative property means that you can add or multiply numbers in any order and still get the same answer," I explained.

"You can't do that for subtraction, can you?" Ana asked.

"It doesn't work for subtraction because nine minus four equals five and it's not the same as four minus nine. If you do four minus nine you get minus five, which is five less than zero and that is not the same as five, which is five more than zero," replied Hector, who was fascinated with negative numbers. I decided not to correct Hector's use of "minus 5" for "negative 5" but to move on instead.

"Put your thumb up to show me if you remember what the answer is called to a multiplication problem," I said. Quickly, about three-fourths of the students put their thumbs up. "Tell me in a whisper voice what the answer to a multiplication problem is called."

"Product!" was the whispered response.

"I agree. The answer is called the product. Does anyone know what we call the numbers we multiply together to find the product?" I continued.

"The multiplicationers?" Conner suggested.

"I can see where you got your answer. But that is not what mathematicians call them," I responded.

"I think the word is something like *factions,*" Susanna added.

"Susanna's suggestion is close but not quite right," I said. No one else wanted to volunteer an answer, so I continued. "Mathematicians call the numbers multiplied together to give a product *factors.*"

"Oh, so like the numbers one and one hundred multiply together to make one hundred so they are factors of one hundred. That's interesting because one hundred is both a factor and a product of one hundred," Charlie observed. I was impressed with Charlie's observation, but most of the students did not seem to follow his thinking. Rather than pursue his idea at that moment, I decided to wait until the class discussion after the investigation, as I thought this insight would reveal itself to many of the students as they worked and studied the information gathered.

Investigating the Factors of 99

"The story says all the other ants chased after the littlest ant when they finally arrived at the picnic, only to find that all the food was gone. If all the other ants chased the littlest ant, how many ants were chasing?" I asked the students.

Immediately all the students had their thumbs up, indicating that they knew the answer. "Use your whisper voice to tell me." I knew this was not a difficult question for these students. I asked it to give them a different number to consider in order to give them one additional experience with factors prior to having them work with partners on the upcoming investigation.

The whispered response was ninety-nine. "Think in your own brain for just a moment about the following question. If there were ninety-nine ants chasing the littlest ant, what are the ways they could line up if they wanted to chase him in equal lines?" I paused to give the students time to think this over. This problem required them to think about the factors of 99, a number less familiar to them than 100. However, this did not cause any difficulty. Soon thumbs were up, indicating that the students had done some thinking and had

some ideas that they wanted to share. "Talk with your neighbor. You will have thirty seconds to share your thinking while your neighbor listens, then your neighbor will have thirty seconds to share his or her thinking while you listen." The students immediately chose who would speak first and I began timing them. At the end of thirty seconds, I asked the students to switch so the first talker would become the listener and the first listener would become the talker. At the end of the minute, I asked for the students' attention. "Who would like to share?"

"The ants could march in one line of ninety-nine or ninety-nine lines of one," Jamie said.

"I know three would work because when Ana and I were trying to figure out if one hundred ants could march in lines of three, we kept landing on ninety-nine," Hector shared.

"Well ours is sort of like Hector's way. When we were doing lines of three for one hundred, there would be thirty-three in each line when we got to ninety-nine, so thirty-three should work," Melissa added.

I had been recording the students' suggestions for factors on the board. So far I had recorded *1, 99, 3, 33.* I called on Kirk next. "Well, I thought about what I know about my basic multiplication facts. I know that nine times eleven equals ninety-nine, so it was easy. Nine and eleven are factors of ninety-nine. You can think of it another way too. You could think in your brain . . . um . . . what number times nine makes ninety-nine? Then your brain would think and think and then come up with eleven. So you could write blank times nine equals ninety-nine. It's like solving a mystery when you think of it like that!" Kirk explained.

"Ohhhh, you could use Kirk's way for some of the others," Jeni said. "It's like there are pairs of factors. Like nine pairs up with eleven and three pairs up with thirty-three and one pairs up with ninety-nine! If you forget a partner of the pair, then you could think like Kirk did and solve the mystery of the partner you forgot! Cool!"

Meanwhile I added Kirk's pair of factors, 9 and 11, to the list. I asked the students if there were any other numbers they felt should be added to the list of factors for 99. There were no additional numbers they felt should be added. I ended the lesson there for that day.

DAY 2: INVESTIGATING FACTORS OF THE NUMBERS 1 THROUGH 50

I began the second day with a quick review of the list of factors for 99. "Yesterday you discovered that one, three, nine, eleven, thirty-three, and ninety-nine were factors of ninety-nine," I said as I listed these factors on the chalkboard. "How could we prove that these numbers are indeed factors of ninety-nine?"

"If they are factors of ninety-nine, you could skip-count by the number you think is a factor and you should land on ninety-nine. Like eleven, skip-count by eleven and it goes eleven, twenty-two, thirty-three, forty-four, fifty-five, sixty-six, seventy-seven, eighty-eight, ninety-nine," Melissa said.

"You could also think about it sort of backwards, I think. Like start with ninety-nine. And say you want to prove thirty-three is a factor. Well you could see if you could divide up ninety-nine things into equal groups of thirty-three with no leftovers," Alicia shared. Alicia was showing an understanding of the relationship between multiplication and division.

"You can think of it my way that I said yesterday," Kirk explained. "You could choose a number you think is a factor, like nine. Then think . . . what times nine equals ninety-nine. If something times nine, like eleven times nine, makes ninety-nine, then nine is a factor. But if you think something

like . . . what times twelve makes ninety-nine, well nothing does. There is no number times twelve that equals ninety-nine . . . unless it's a fraction, so twelve isn't a factor of ninety-nine. With the numbers listed, they all have a partner on the list that it can be multiplied by to make ninety-nine." Kirk's growing knowledge and fluidity with factors would be a very useful tool to him as he began his study of division and fractions later on.

The students seemed convinced that the numbers on the list, 1, 3, 9, 11, 33, 99, were all factors of 99. I pulled out the class charts listing the numbers from 1 to 50. "Today you may choose to work individually or with a partner. You will be working to discover all the factors of a number you have chosen from the chart. You will each need to record your work on your own recording sheet, even if you have a partner. Please use the number you have chosen to investigate in the title. For example, if I have chosen the number twenty-one, my title would be Factors of Twenty-One. You will need to show how you figured out the factors of your number. Did you skip-count, did you make a rectangle or an array, did you think what times something equals your number, like Kirk has shared? If you try numbers that don't work, please include these on your recording sheet also. When you have chosen a number you would like to investigate, please put your initials on the chart beside that number so we will all know that that number has been chosen. If the number you want has been chosen by someone else, you will need to choose a different number. I have given you a lot of directions. Do you have questions?"

"I don't get how to do the recording sheet," Brooke said. Several other students indicated they were also uncertain.

"I think it might be a good idea to model what I mean. Would that help you?" I asked. Brooke nodded. "I am going to choose the number twenty-one. I will put my initials on the chart to show that I have chosen to work on twenty-one. I need to put my name and date on my recording sheet." I did this as I gave the directions orally. "For my title I will write Factors of Twenty-One. Hmm, I know that one is a factor of twenty-one so I'll write *one* on my paper. I can prove it by drawing one row of twenty-one ants." I drew one row of twenty-one ants on my paper to show that 1 was a factor of 21. "If I can draw one row of twenty-one, then twenty-one must also be a factor, so I could draw twenty-one rows of one."

"Oh, I get it. So three is a factor of twenty-one so I could skip-count by three and land on twenty-one. I would write three, six, nine, twelve, fifteen, eighteen, twenty-one," Brooke said. This quick modeling of how to do the recording sheet helped Brooke and others, as there were no further questions for the moment.

As the students got to work I walked around the classroom, observing what they were doing and listening to what they were saying. Kirk and Jeni were working together and wanted to know if their recording sheets had to look the same. I said they could each choose to organize and record the information in a way that made sense to them. I walked on and noticed that Brooke seemed stuck. "Can I get some tiles?" Brooke asked. "I chose seventeen and I can't think of any other factors of seventeen except one and seventeen, so I thought maybe it would help if I tried to make rectangles and squares out of seventeen tiles." I reminded Brooke that the tiles were on the back counter and she certainly was welcome to use them. As Brooke got up to get the tiles, I moved on, making a note to myself to check back with her to see what she discovered.

"This is really fun! I chose twenty-seven and twenty-seven, one, nine, and three are factors and I know because if I skip-count

by those numbers I will land on twenty-seven. Can I do another number?" Hector wanted to know.

"How do you know that you have found all the possible factors of twenty-seven?" I asked Hector.

"Well, I know that one will work and twenty-seven will work because if I skip-count by those numbers I get twenty-seven. But if I skip-count by two I know I won't land on twenty-seven because skip-counting by twos if you start on an even number means you will always land on an even number and twenty-seven is an odd number. Then I skip-counted by three and that landed on twenty-seven. So I thought three times what equals twenty-seven. I know three times ten equals thirty, so if I subtract one three that would be nine threes and that would be twenty-seven. So three and nine are factors. Four doesn't work because I know four times seven equals twenty-eight so four and seven won't land on twenty-seven because it is only one away from twenty-eight. Five, ten, and fifteen don't work either because I can count by those numbers and they always end with a five or zero, and twenty-seven ends with a seven." Hector continued to explain his thinking in this manner until he accounted for all the numbers from 1 to 27. His thinking showed organization. He applied his knowledge of factors, and he showed understanding of number theory when thinking about why 5, 10, and 15 won't work as factors of 27. This is the kind of explanation I was looking for from students. When it was not forthcoming, I asked questions to guide students' thinking in this direction. I was impressed with Hector's thinking and his persistence.

As the students finished investigating their numbers, they recorded the factors of their numbers on the class chart and chose new numbers to explore until all numbers had been selected. I checked the chart periodically to monitor both the progress of the class and the accuracy of the answers. As I was studying the chart, Rob came over to me and pointed out that he thought 16 was incorrect. The factors that had been listed for 16 were 1, 2, and 16. "What makes you think the factors listed for sixteen are incorrect, Rob?" I asked.

"I know that two times eight equals sixteen. I see the two but I don't see the eight. I think eight should be on the list. I also think four times four equals sixteen so four should be on the list."

"I am glad you are thinking about this, Rob. Go get a sheet of paper and write out your thoughts about what you think is correct about the list and what you think needs to be added and why. Then go show it to Gina, the person who investigated this number, and talk with her about your thoughts and see what the two of you come up with," I suggested. Making mistakes is a natural part of learning. I think students need to be comfortable expressing themselves when they disagree with a response, and I think students need to learn to be sensitive when they express their disagreement. Also, students need to learn how to listen to another student's suggestion for improvement and either defend their original thinking or act to make the suggested improvements. Suggestions for improvements should not always come from adults.

I noticed several other errors in the chart and decided to go directly to the students responsible and suggest they rethink their information. I wanted the information on the chart to be accurate for the writing assignment and class discussion that I had planned as follow-up for the activity.

Meanwhile, I checked back with Brooke, who had used the tiles to investigate 17. She had come to the conclusion that 17 had only two factors, 1 and 17. The students worked with enthusiasm, completing most of the class chart in about thirty minutes. I left the chart posted for the remainder of the day, giving the students a chance to study the information as well as giving the few students who had not yet finished the opportunity to finish and add their information to the chart. Some of the individual recording sheets looked like those in Figures 3–1 and 3–2.

Factors of 15
3 rows of 5
3 5
rows of 3
15 1
1 row of 15
1,2,3,4,5,6,7,8,9,10,11,12,13,14,15
15
15 rows of 1

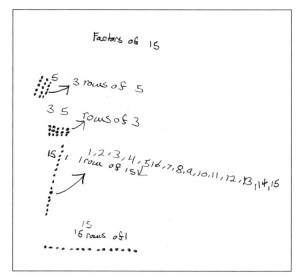

Figure 3–1 *Charlie used arrays to show the different arrangements for 15.*

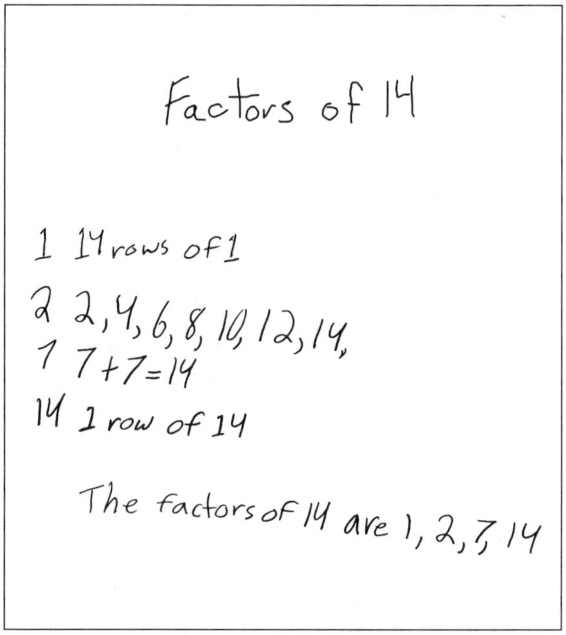

Factors of 14
1 14 rows of 1
2 2, 4, 6, 8, 10, 12, 14,
7 7+7=14
14 1 row of 14
The factors of 14 are 1, 2, 7, 14

Figure 3–2 *Jeni used several ways to find the factors of 14.*

DAY 3

I began the third day by asking the students to take a few moments to look over all the information on the class chart. "As you study the information on the chart, what do you notice about this information? If you find any missing factors or factors that don't belong, think about what made you notice them. Also, what can you notice about the even numbers? The odd numbers? Why do numbers have different numbers of factors?" I said to the students to help them get started in their thinking about the chart.

After giving the students several minutes to consider the information, I asked them to share their thinking with partners. After each person had the opportunity to share his ideas and listen to his partner's ideas, I asked the students to respond in writing to the following prompt: "What do you notice about the information about the factors of the numbers from one to fifty?" Giving students time to think about the question first, then share their ideas and listen to the ideas of others helped all students think of something to write. After fifteen minutes or so, most students were finished and ready to go on.

"Would anyone like to share something they notice about the chart?" I asked to begin the class discussion.

"There's something important about an even number times an even number, an odd number times an odd number, and an even number times an odd number, but I am not sure what it is," Jeni shared tentatively.

"Can you explain a bit more about what you mean?" I encouraged.

"Well I wrote on my paper, *I notice that on some even numbers all the factors are even, and some of the odd numbers all the factors are odd, and the rest that have an odd and even number, like fifty-six, the factors are even and odd,*" Jeni explained. Jeni's thinking was really quite sophisticated and caught me a bit by surprise. As it happened, I was standing beside Jeni as she read her paper and I noticed that her thinking was slightly misguided. While it is true that an odd times an even number will give an even number, Jeni was thinking of the number 56 as being made up of an odd number and an even number. (See Figure 3–3.)

"Jeni has an interesting idea about an odd number times an odd number, an even number times an even number, and an odd number times an even number. We'll investigate her idea further a little later," I said, wanting to keep the discussion focused on what the students noticed on the chart. I recorded Jeni's idea on a chart with her name, giving her credit for having shared the idea. "Who else has an idea you would like to share?" I continued.

"Some numbers only have two factors, like seventeen and nineteen and some other ones," Susanna shared.

"I know what those are called. They are called prime numbers," Hector said. "A prime number means you can just multiply the number and one to make that number and nothing else."

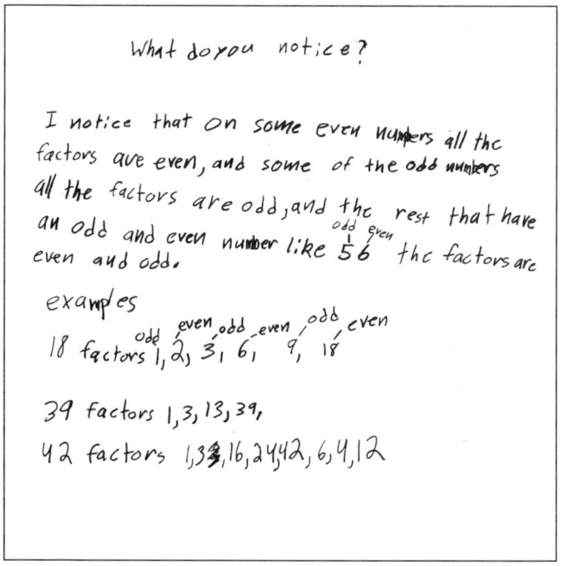
What do you notice?

I notice that on some even numbers all the factors are even, and some of the odd numbers all the factors are odd, and the rest that have an odd and even number like 56 (odd even) the factors are even and odd.

examples

18 factors 1, 2, 3, 6, 9, 18 (odd, even, odd, even, odd, even)

39 factors 1, 3, 13, 39,

42 factors 1, 3, 16, 24, 42, 6, 4, 12

▲▲▲▲▲**Figure 3–3** ***Jeni's understanding of even numbers caused her to make errors when finding patterns in factors of even and odd numbers.***

"I agree. What are some other prime numbers on the chart?" I asked.

"Well ten only has two numbers listed so it looks like it is prime, but I think I disagree. Two and five are listed, but one and ten should also be listed; one times ten equals ten. Ten looks like a prime but it isn't!" Kasey explained.

"Oops! I forgot those two numbers. Can I add them?" asked Sandra, who had investigated the factors of 10.

"Of course," I replied, handing her a pen to make the corrections.

"Forty-one and seven only have two factors so they must be prime," Melissa said, redirecting the conversation to answer my question.

"If numbers with two factors are called prime numbers, what are the other numbers called, nonprime or unprime?" Calob asked.

"Numbers with more than two factors arc called composite numbers," I explained to Calob and the rest of the students.

"Something else I noticed is you can count by one and get any whole number no matter what. One is a factor of all the numbers because you can do that," Melissa said.

"Every even number has two as a factor. See two is even and two is a factor. Four is even and two is a factor of four. Twenty is even and it has two as a factor. But eleven is odd and it doesn't have two as a factor. Same with five and nine. I think only even numbers have two as a factor," Neal explained.

"This is sort of like Jeni's idea. Odd numbers have only odd factors. Like fifteen is odd and its factors are one, three, five, and fifteen. Those are all odd numbers. It's the same with all the odd numbers on the chart," Hector said.

"I noticed that all the numbers that have five in the ones place have five as a factor. Fifteen has a five in the ones place and five is a factor. Thirty-five has a five in the ones place and five is a factor," Brooke added.

"Ohh! My idea is connected to Brooke's!" Neal blurted out in his excitement. "I noticed that the numbers with zero in the ones place have both ten and five as factors! I think that is because five and ten are related, like two fives make a ten, so that is why five is a factor of numbers with five in the ones place and numbers with zero in the ones place . . . I think."

"So five can be a factor of a number with zero in the ones place, but ten can't be a factor of a number with a five in the ones place because it takes two fives to make a ten. Counting by tens skips the numbers with five in the ones place and only lands on numbers with zero in the ones place, but counting by five lands on both. I get it!" Brooke said.

"In all the numbers on the chart, the number itself is a factor because you can multiply it by one," Gina observed.

"I notice that most of the numbers have an even number of factors. But certain numbers like four, nine, and sixteen have an odd number. I wonder why," Miguel shared.

"It's because those numbers can be made into squares. Like if you have four tiles, you can make a two-by-two square. For nine you can make a three-by-three square. The other numbers like eight can't be made into squares, only rectangles. The factors come in pairs, like for eight the pairs are one and eight, two and four, so there are four factors for eight. But for nine the pairs are one and nine, three and three. When you list them you don't have to list three twice, so that is how there gets to be an odd number of factors," Kirk explained. "And you call numbers like four and nine square numbers because you can make them into a square." Kirk's understanding was exceptional, I realize, and I would have offered this explanation if he, or any other student, hadn't done so.

"There's one number on the chart that only has one factor and that's one," noticed Ana.

"Why do you think that is?" I responded.

Ana shrugged her shoulders and then thought quietly for a moment. "I guess the only way to multiply to get one is one times one. It's the only number like that!"

"Ana noticed something very interesting. One is the only number with one factor. Numbers like two, five, seven, and others have exactly two factors. Numbers with exactly two factors are called prime numbers. Numbers like four, six, and eight have more than two factors. They are called composite numbers. One has only one factor. It is neither prime nor composite," I explained.

The class thought quietly for a moment. Then Anthony raised his hand. "Why?" he asked.

I tried to clarify for Anthony and the others. I explained, "Mathematicians made the decision to agree to the definition of a prime number as having two factors and a composite number as having more than two factors. One doesn't fit the definition of either prime or composite, so it is neither."

The chart the students had just created helped them clearly see the prime and composite numbers and how the number 1 did not fit the definition for prime or composite. They seemed satisfied for the moment, but it was a point that would need to be revisited in future lessons for students to solidify their understanding.

Questions and Discussion

▲▲

▲ *During the discussion the students brought up many interesting ideas. What do you do to encourage this?*

Before beginning a lesson, I set a clear purpose for the lesson and carefully consider topics to address during the course of the lesson. As the lesson and the discussion progress, I keep the purpose and topics in mind and use them to guide me as I make decisions about questions to ask and pieces of information to share with the students to spark discussion. I have to constantly decide which ideas from the students to pursue in the moment, which to investigate later, and which to disregard. Occasionally a student will come up with something so interesting that I change the course of the lesson to explore the student's idea.

In this lesson, I wanted students to think about the commutative property, prime, composite, and square numbers, and the relationship between multiplication and division.

▲ *How do you help students understand that 1 is not a prime number? This is confusing for students.*

Some decisions in mathematics aren't based in logical reasoning or principles but are made according to agreed-upon definitions. These definitions clarify conventions that allow everyone to have the same understanding and to standardize how we communicate. There's no logical reason we use the × to represent multiplication, for example; it's a convention that facilitates representation and communication. Similarly, prime numbers are defined as numbers with exactly two factors. With that agreed-upon definition, the number 1 is eliminated from being a prime number since it only has one factor, 1. If the definition were "prime numbers have exactly one or two factors," then the number 1 would be included. But that's not the definition. However, it requires an understanding of factors and products, ideas that are firmly rooted in logical reasoning and principles about numbers, to come to the decision that 1 has only one factor, or that the number 6 has four factors (1, 2, 3, and 6), or that the number 5 has exactly two factors (1 and 5). These are not decisions based on definitions but by the logical structure of the numbers.

▲ *What if students have difficulty with understanding what is the same and what is different about one hundred rows of one and one row of one hundred?*

If the students have not had prior experience with this idea, I would begin by having them build rectangular arrays. I would give them some 1-inch color tiles to use for exploration. Next I would give them a number such as 6 and ask them to use the tiles to build two rows of three tiles. Then I would ask them to use six other tiles and build three rows of two. With both structures before them, I would ask students how they were the same and how they were different, hopefully moving toward the conclusion that while the same number of tiles was being used, two rows of three looks different than three rows of two, although with a rotation the two can be made to be congruent. This line of thinking develops the understanding of the commutative property of multiplication in a very concrete way.

▲ *At one point in the lesson you allowed students to choose to work independently or with partners. Why did you do this? How did you go about assigning partners for those who wanted to work with a partner?*

Giving students the option to occasionally work alone is important. Working with a partner is an important skill and students often do this; however, it is easier for some students than others. For this reason, I decided to give students a choice during this lesson.

I often let students choose their own partners, although I use a variety of ways to assign partners at other times. For this investigation I had decided beforehand that I would assign partners for those who wished to work with a partner by drawing sticks. I have a Popsicle stick with each students' name on it that I keep in a cup. When I need to draw students' names randomly, I simply use the cup of Popsicle sticks. For this activity I asked the students who wished to work independently to each come up to the chart, choose a number, initial it, and start to work. About three or four chose to do this. I quickly pulled their Popsicle sticks out of the cup. For the remaining students, I pulled two names at a time and those students became partners for this activity.

CHAPTER 4
SILENT MULTIPLICATION

Overview

The goal of this activity is for students to explore patterns in factors and products in order to help them develop understanding of the mathematics underlying multidigit multiplication. Students develop strategies to solve increasingly complex problems by using what they already know about simpler related problems. For example, students examine the effect on the product when one factor is doubled, when both factors are doubled, when one factor is halved, when one factor is halved while the other is doubled, and so on. Students also explore the effects on the product when multiplying by 10, and multiples of 10. As students gain facility and confidence with this activity, they can reverse the process by taking a complex problem and solving it by making it into simpler related problems. Skill with computation, number sense, and problem solving are employed and strengthened as students experience this activity. The word *silent* in the title indicates the teaching method used for the lesson, as described in the following sections.

Materials

▲ none

Time

▲ two class periods followed by shorter explorations several times per week spread over many weeks

Teaching Directions

1. Explain to students the rules for a silent lesson:

   ▲ A star drawn on the board or overhead indicates the beginning of the activity and silence by everyone, including the teacher.

   ▲ When a problem is written on the board, students should indicate when they know the answer by putting their thumbs up.

   ▲ When an answer is written, students should indicate agreement with thumbs up, disagreement with thumbs down, or indecision or confusion with thumbs sideways.

2. Draw a star on the board or overhead transparency to indicate that it's time for silence. For an introductory experience, write a multiplication problem on the board or transparency that all students can solve; for example *1 × 2.*

3. Wait for students to show thumbs up.

4. Hand the chalk to a student and indicate that he or she should write the product on the board. Wait for the other students to indicate agreement, disagreement, or indecision or confusion by putting their thumbs up, down, or sideways.

5. Write a second related problem (for example, *2 × 2*) under the first problem. Again wait for the students to indicate when they know the answer with their thumbs. After most students indicate they know the answer, hand the chalk to a volunteer to write the answer on the chalkboard. Have the other students indicate with their thumbs agreement with the answer, disagreement, or indecision or confusion. Erase the star, indicating talking is permitted.

6. Lead a discussion about how the two problems are related and how students can use what they know from the first problem to help them solve the second problem.

7. While steps 1 through 6 model for students the basic structure of this activity, emphasize to the students the need to be silent and think about how to apply what they already know to solve each new problem. Draw a star and continue with the silent lesson for a series of four or more related problems.

8. Erase the star and lead a class discussion about how students used what they knew about one problem to solve another. Pose such questions as the following:

   How are these two problems related?

   What is the same about these problems?

   What is different?

   What happened to the factors?

   What happened to the products?

9. On Day 2, teach the silent lesson again, exploring a new idea such as multiplying by 10. Leave time at the end of class for students to respond to the following prompt: "Something I learned playing *Silent Multiplication* is . . . "

10. Continue on other days with other sequences of problems. See pages 41, 43, 45, 47, and 48 for suggested sequences.

Teaching Notes

This activity works well when used several times a week over an extended period of time. It gives students opportunities to explore and gain understanding about factoring numbers, using the commutative and associative properties of multiplication, using the distributive property, and multiplying by 10, powers of 10, and multiples of 10.

A lesson can focus on just one idea at a time, multiplying by 10, for example. The nature of our number system is such that to multiply a number by 10, you simply need to add a zero, resulting in a zero in the ones place of the product: $10 \times 4 = 40$, $112 \times 10 = 1,120$, and $23,490 \times 10 = 234,900$. Another focus for a lesson might be multiplying by multiples of 10. For example, to solve 20×5, the problem can be thought of as $2 \times 5 \times 10$. When thinking of a problem in this way, the student is developing understanding about factoring numbers and the associative and commutative properties of multiplication. At another time the lesson might focus on what happens to the product when factors are doubled or halved: doubling one factor while the other remains the same results in the product doubling ($4 \times 8 = 32$, $8 \times 8 = 64$); doubling both factors results in the product quadrupling ($2 \times 2 = 4$, $4 \times 4 = 16$); halving one factor while the other remains the same results in the product halving ($8 \times 6 = 48$, $4 \times 6 = 24$); halving both results in a product being divided by four, or one-quarter of the original product ($8 \times 6 = 48$, $4 \times 3 = 12$); halving one factor and doubling the other causes the product to remain unchanged ($18 \times 10 = 180$, while 9×20 also equals 180).

Understandings and insights from these lessons support students as they grapple with the task of efficiently and accurately finding products of multidigit multiplication problems. With time and experience, students learn to solve difficult problems by solving simpler related problems. For example, to solve 240×12, a student might think of 240 as $12 \times 2 \times 10$. With this in mind, the student can then solve 240×12 mentally by multiplying $12 \times 2 \times 10 \times 12$ to get the product 2,880. While the student may not recognize it, the way in which these numbers are actually calculated may involve factoring and applying the commutative and associative properties. Or a student might solve 240×12 by thinking of it as $(240 \times 10) + (240 \times 2)$, and then adding $2,400 + 480$ to get 2,880, an example of the student using the distributive property upon which the traditional algorithm used in the United States is based.

Of critical importance in this activity is the discussion following a series of problems about how the problems are related. By understanding how two problems are related and by using what they already know, students can move forward to solve new, unknown, more complex problems.

An unusual characteristic of this activity is that students and teacher participate silently in some parts. Students indicate when they have solved a problem mentally and their agreement or disagreement with an answer by putting their thumbs up to indicate agreement, down to indicate disagreement, or sideways to indicate indecision or confusion. The silent aspect provides a nice change of pace to typical classroom instruction and prevents blurting out, giving students additional think time. Children also enjoy the opportunity to come to the board to write their responses, and the silent experience provides a basis for valuable mathematical discussion.

When this activity was introduced to the students in the vignette that follows, their experience had been primarily limited to single-digit multiplication, although a few students knew about what happens when any number is multiplied by 10. Thinking about halving and doubling was difficult for these students. As the students became more comfortable with the idea of doubling, they began to incorporate the idea of halving, although the notion of halving was more difficult.

This activity can easily be adapted to the skill level of the students. In some classes, students have asked questions that provided a nice starting point for the activity. When students don't offer a place to begin, a question can be posed for them to explore as they move through the activity. In the following vignette the question posed was "What happens to the product when one factor is doubled?" The vignette illustrates a particular direction this class took. Your students will raise different questions and have different insights. The important ideas on which to remain focused throughout the discussion are the patterns and relationships among the problems and how this information can help students solve more difficult problems.

Additional lessons that support some ideas presented in *Silent Multiplication* are *Related Rectangles* and *Target 300*. *Related Rectangles* links number patterns explored in *Silent Multiplication* with the geometric interpretation of multiplication as rectangular arrays. *Target 300* provides students with additional practice with multiplication by 10 and multiples of 10.

The Lesson

▲▲

DAY 1

I explained to the class, "I'd like to do an activity with you in which you'll look for patterns. I'll start by writing a simple problem on the board that I think you all will know. When you know the answer, show me by putting your thumb up. I will hand someone the chalk and that person may come to the board to write the answer. If I hand you the chalk and you don't want to come to the board, just shake your head no and I will give the chalk to someone else. If you agree with the answer that gets written on the board, put your thumb up. If you disagree, put your thumb down. If you are not certain, put your thumb sideways. Here's the unusual thing about this game: it is played in silence! No one talks, not even me! I will put a star on the board to indicate we must all be silent. I will erase the star when we can talk again." There were no questions, so I decided to start the activity. I made the first round easy so everyone would be successful and become clear about the rules. I began by drawing a star on the board to indicate to all that it was time to be silent. I wrote *1 × 2 =* on the board. Immediately all thumbs shot up. I handed the chalk to Rachel, who shook her head no. I quickly handed the chalk to Alex, who came to the board and wrote *2.* All students indicated their agreement with Alex's answer by putting their thumbs up. Next I wrote *2 × 2.* Again thumbs were up immediately. I handed the chalk to Sam, who wrote *4.* I erased the star, indicating we could talk.

"Who would like to share their thinking about their answer to the first problem?" I began. I wanted the students to see immediately that the problems used for this activity were related. I wanted them to look for the relationship and use that relationship to help them solve move complex problems.

"It was easy. The answer is two. The problem means one group of two, which is two," Sarita responded. Several students nodded, indicating their agreement.

"What about the second problem? What is alike about the two problems and what is different?" I probed.

"Each of the problems has one factor that is two," Nicole said.

"And for the answer you just added the answer from the first problem to itself to get the second answer," Steve explained.

"That's doubling," Allie noticed.

"Oh yeah!" Steve said.

"One factor is the same and the other changes," Shelly added.

"How did it change?" I asked.

"Well, both problems have a two, like Nicole said, but with the other factor, it's like you added it to itself to get the new factor," Shelly explained.

"That's doubling," Allie repeated again.

"So, to get to the second problem from the first one, one factor doubled, one factor stayed the same, and the product doubled," Cori summarized.

"If you agree with Cori, put your thumb up, if you disagree, put your thumb down, if you aren't sure, put your thumb sideways," I said.

Most children indicated their agreement while a few indicated that they weren't sure. I decided to continue the activity and keep a close eye on the students who indicated their uncertainty, hoping that with further exploration, the mathematics would reveal itself.

I put the star back on the board, indicating that silence was necessary. I continued this round with the following set of problems:

4 × 2 =

8 × 2 =

16 × 2 =

32 × 2 =

This series of problems was easily accessible for all students. I erased the star, indicating it was time to talk about what we had just done. "How did the first problem help you solve the second?" I asked.

"Well one times one equals two and so you just add the answer twice to get the answer for the next problem," Jackie explained. "It's that way the whole way. You just add the answer twice to get the new answer." While Jackie showed that she was seeing a pattern in the answers, or products, I was concerned because she indicated no understanding of what was causing this pattern. She seemed to be focusing on the products without looking at the factors or considering why the products were doubling.

"Why do you think the products are doubling?" I asked.

"It's just the pattern I see," she replied.

"I noticed something. One of the factors is always staying the same. The other one is always timesing by two, like Cori said about the first two problems," Juan said.

"I think Juan is right. I noticed that the first factor doubles. It's like if one factor doubles then the product doubles," Rachel shared. The others indicated their agreement with what Rachel and Juan had shared.

"Let's try some more and see if it always works," David suggested.

I used the following sequence for our next round. In the first series, the first factor always doubled. This time I switched which factor doubled so that sometimes it was the first factor and sometimes it was the second.

$2 \times 2 =$

$2 \times 4 =$

$4 \times 4 =$

$4 \times 8 =$

$8 \times 8 =$

$16 \times 8 =$

$16 \times 16 =$

This doubling pattern involved slightly larger numbers than the first series but still was accessible to the students. Taking small steps in the beginning helps ensure success while creating confidence and a greater willingness in students to take risks when the learning gets more challenging.

After the last problem I again erased the star and we had a similar discussion to the first. "What did you notice?" I began.

"It's like you add a factor twice when you go from one problem to the next. Then you add the answer from the first problem twice to get the answer to the next one," David shared.

"It seems like sometimes you used the product from before to get one of the factors in the new problem," Anamaria said. "Like two times two equals four, the product four became one of the factors in the next problem, two times four. But not with two times four equals eight and then four times four equals sixteen. But you could have used the eight and done two times eight equals sixteen instead of four times four equals sixteen!"

"It changes; it's getting bigger," Amy added.

"It's doubling," repeated Allie for the third time, disgusted that her observation was not being understood by her classmates.

"I get it! It's doubling! My hypothesis is that if one factor doubles and one stays the same then the product doubles!" James said, lighting up. Allie rolled her eyes. This reminded me that even though I may tell students something, it does not mean that they hear it in a way that means they understand it or can apply it. I am reminded that each child must make meaning and sense of learning for her- or himself. Understanding is not something that can be gained by simply being told; rather, it is gained through thought and interacting with ideas and experiences.

"Why do you think this is happening?" I asked the students. The students sat quietly, thinking about why.

"How could I represent one times one with a rectangular array?" I continued.

"It would be a rectangle, a square really, that is one going vertically and one going horizontally," explained Sam. I drew what Sam described. I continued the discussion in this fashion, hoping that by giving students the opportunity to look at the geometric representation of what was happening, more would gain understanding of why doubling one factor doubles the product.

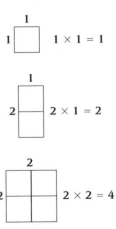

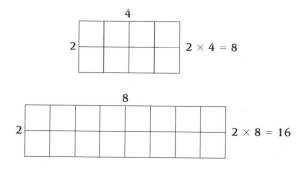

$2 \times 4 = 8$

$2 \times 8 = 16$

"I see what is happening. One side of the rectangle is staying the same and the other side of the rectangle doubles! That's cool!" David said.

"What if you use odd numbers? You have mostly used even numbers. If you used odd numbers and doubled one factor, will the answer still double?" Ben wondered.

"I don't really think odd and even matters. I think it's the doubling part that matters. If you do something in one part of the problem, it changes things in another part. So it's the doubling, not if it's odd or even," Daniel replied after a few moments of thought.

Nicole raised her hand with excitement. "I think I discovered something! I have a hypothesis! Whenever a factor is doubled, odd or even, the product is always even. Like three times three equals nine, but double one of the threes to make six and six times three equals eighteen!"

"Nicole, Daniel, and Ben have some interesting ideas. Let's try a few more rounds of *Silent Multiplication* and see if we can get some information to help them prove or disprove their ideas," I replied.

Cori summarized the discussion and made a request. "Well, Nicole and Ben are sort of the same. Ben is wondering about odd numbers and Nicole is saying that odd numbers when doubled are even. I don't know if she is right. Adding two odd numbers makes an even number, adding three odd numbers makes an odd number. And doubling an odd number is like adding the same odd number twice, which is like multi-

plying by two. Addition and multiplication are related because you can do repeated addition if you don't know the multiplication answer. But I am not sure. Can we use odd numbers this time?" The rest of the students indicated their interest and agreement.

After putting the star on the board to indicate time for silence, I gave the following sequence of problems:

$1 \times 3 =$

$2 \times 3 =$

$4 \times 3 =$

$8 \times 3 =$

$8 \times 6 =$

$6 \times 8 =$

$6 \times 16 =$

$16 \times 12 =$

I erased the star and hands jumped into the air. To give as many students as possible an opportunity to share their ideas, I asked the students to each share their thinking with a neighbor. After each partner had had thirty seconds to share her or his thinking, I asked for the class' attention once again.

"I think my hypothesis was right. If you double any number, odd or even, it will always end up even," Nicole shared with excitement.

"Have you noticed that any number times two is always an even number?" Tom asked. "And doubling is like multiplying by two. That's why Nicole's idea works."

"Hey, I was just thinking. What about multiplying a fraction by two. Then it doesn't always work. Like one-half times two equals one, an odd number, or one-and-a-half times two equals three, another odd number!" Shelly pointed out.

"OK, I see your point. Then any *whole* number times two equals an even number!" Nicole clarified. "And I think two odd numbers multiplied together make an odd number, like three times three equals nine and five times seven equals thirty-five. But doubling an odd number makes an even number, like Cori said, because it's like adding an odd plus an odd, which is an even, it's just you are adding the same odd number twice." Cori nodded her agreement along with most of the other students.

"Let's look at the problems and see how they are related and how knowing something about one can help us solve the next one," I said, turning the conversation in a different direction.

"Let's look at one times three equals three and two times three equals six. What do you notice about these problems?" I asked.

"Well, one factor is the same in both," Tom explained. "That would be the three. And then one factor in the second problem doubled from the first one. One doubled to two. And the products are different, too. Three doubled into six. If you think about rectangular arrays, it is like you had one row of three for the first problem and then you added a second row of three for the second. You doubled the amount of rows and the total number of squares in the array doubled, too," Tom explained. To help the class understand Tom's explanation and to verify that I understood his thinking, I drew the following on the board:

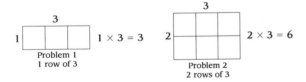

"Is this what you mean?" I asked. Tom indicated that my drawing represented his thinking. (For more on using rectangles with multiplication, see Chapter 5, "Related Rectangles.") "What about the second problem, two times three equals six, and the third problem, four times three equals twelve?" I continued. I called on Jackie.

"I already knew that four times three equals twelve. You can prove it by counting by threes four times or counting by fours three times. Or you can add four plus four plus four or three plus three plus three plus three. Or you could draw a rectangle that was four going down and three going across. Or you could notice that two times three equals six, and four is two times two, so since two was multiplied by two to get four then you could multiply six times two to make twelve!" Jackie's initial understanding concerned me, but here she recognized an important mathematical idea, that is, what you do to one side of the equation, you must do to the other side of the equation.

"What about four times three and eight times three? What is going on there?" I continued.

"It's the same thing; one of the factors doubled so all you had to do was double the last product. Four doubled into eight, so twelve has to double into twenty-four," Cindy answered.

"What about eight times three and eight times six?" I asked.

"It's quite simple really. It's the same thing again. One factor doubled, the three became a six, so the twenty-four had to go twenty-four plus twenty-four to make forty-eight," Shelly replied.

"The next one didn't do anything except switch the order. Instead of eight times six it got switched to six times eight," Daniel said. I had included this pair of problems to give students experience with the commutative property of multiplication. In previous discussions, we had noted that a picture of eight groups of six indeed looks different than six groups of eight, but the final product is the same. Students were familiar with this piece of information because it was useful in helping them learn their basic facts.

"If you look at the next several problems, it's the same thing as doubling one factor, one staying the same, and the product doubling," Steve said. I asked the students to indicate their agreement or disagreement with Steve with their thumbs. They indicated their agreement.

I recorded the students' observations as follows:

$1 \times 3 = 3$

$2 \times 3 = 6$ *double factor × same factor = double product*

$4 \times 3 = 12$ *double factor × same factor = double product*

$8 \times 3 = 24$ *double factor × same factor = double product*

$8 \times 6 = 48$ *same factor × double factor = double product*

$6 \times 8 = 48$ *commutative (order) property = same product*

$6 \times 16 = 96$ *same factor × double factor = double product*

$16 \times 12 = 192$ *same factor × double factor = double product*

"Can we do one more?" David asked. Again, I drew a star on the board to indicate silence was needed. The students immediately were quiet, with their attention on me and the board. I decided for the final series of the day to stick with the doubling pattern we had been exploring, but this time I decided to use numbers that were somewhat more challenging:

4×3

4×6

4×12

4×24

8×24

16×24

32×24

I wrote $4 \times 3 =$. Immediately thumbs went up. I handed the chalk to Alex, who came to the board and quickly wrote *12*. His classmates indicated their agreement by putting their thumbs up.

Next I wrote 4×6 and again thumbs went up quickly. Cindy came to the board and wrote *25*. Her classmates gave her a quick thumbs down. She took another look at her work and immediately revised her answer to *24*, which received a thumbs up from the students.

The game continued with 4×12. The students were not as quick to put their thumbs up on this one, so I gave them a bit more time. When most had their thumbs up, I handed the chalk to Allie, who wrote *48*, to which the students gave a thumbs up.

The next problem proved more challenging still for the students. The child who came to the board got stuck. The problem was 4×24. I handed the chalk to Shelly. She wrote the product of 4×24 as *916*. Most of the other students gave her a thumbs down. She looked puzzled. I drew an arrow from the 12 to the 24 and wrote *same or different?*, to which she wrote *different*. I wrote *How?* Shelly responded *Double* then to the side, she wrote *48 + 48?*, indicating that she knew 48 from the previous problem needed to be doubled. I nodded yes. She then worked the problem on the board, getting the answer of 96. The others indicated their agreement with a thumbs up. Shelly's initial response of 916 was a red flag to me that Shelly was not using number sense and an indicator that class discussions needed to focus more on reasonable answers.

I wrote 8×24 next. Juan came to the board and wrote *192*. The students agreed. The next problem, 16×24, got a wide-eyed response from the class. After a moment to analyze the situation, however, thumbs were soon up, indicating that students thought they had an answer. Ben came to the board and wrote *384*. The students agreed.

The next problem was 32×24. Grinning faces and thumbs up indicated the students were gaining confidence in themselves. Anamaria wrote *768* as the product. A few students indicated they weren't sure by turning their thumbs sideways, but most agreed. The final problem of the series was 24×32. All thumbs were up immediately, as the students recognized I had simply used the commutative property and switched the order of the factors, causing no change in the product. A discussion of how you can use what you know from one problem to help you solve the next followed.

"What did you think of this activity?" I asked after the discussion.

"It was really cool!" James said.

"What made it cool?" I asked.

"Everyone had to think and then someone had to write the answer on the board and then we got to tell if we agreed or not," James explained.

"What did you learn from doing this activity?" I asked.

"We discovered that if you double a factor, the product doubles, if the other factor stays the same," Cori said. "It's like if you do something to one side of the problem, you have to do the same thing to the other side, too. I wonder what happens if both factors double?"

"I don't think the product would double then because that is what it did when only one factor doubled. Now two factors are doubling," James said.

"What happens if you multiply one of the factors by ten?" wondered Tom.

"What if you doubled one factor and multiplied the other one by ten? Then what would happen?" Nicole asked.

I was delighted that the students were curious about these questions. I wrote their questions on the board and told them these were some ideas we would explore another day.

"I was amazed I could figure out such hard problems!" Jeni added with surprise.

"In a way the problems got harder as we went along, but in a way not, because we could use the answer from the problem before and just double it," Sandra said.

"It's just looking for a pattern from one problem to the next and using it," Alan said.

DAY 2: EXPLORING MULTIPLICATION BY 10 AND MULTIPLES OF 10

The enthusiasm of the students from the previous day continued into the second day with the students asking if we could do *Silent Multiplication*. My goal was to give the students the opportunity to explore multiplication by 10 and multiples of 10. Because of the nature of our number system, when a factor is multiplied by 10, the result is that factor with a zero added to the end, or in the ones place. For example, $4 \times 10 = 40$, $432 \times 10 = 4{,}320$, and $6{,}120 \times 10 = 61{,}200$. When one factor is multiplied by a multiple of 10, students can factor and make use of the associative and commutative properties to help them more easily and efficiently solve the problem. For example, 20×56 can be thought of as $2 \times 56 \times 10$. The 20 has been factored into 2×10. The commutative property of multiplication, which has to do with changing the order of the numbers, was used when the 2 was placed at the beginning of the string of factors and the 10 at the end. The associative property of multiplication has to do with how numbers are paired. The student could think $(2 \times 56) \times 10$ or $2 \times (56 \times 10)$. When students understand and apply these ideas, they can become more efficient and accurate in their computation of multiplication. These ideas are also foundations for their later study of mathematics.

I began the lesson with a quick review of what we had done the day before. This benefits both the students who were there as well as those who were absent. I drew the star on the board and used the following series of problems:

$1 \times 10 =$

$2 \times 10 =$

$4 \times 10 =$

$6 \times 10 =$

$12 \times 10 =$

$14 \times 10 =$

$16 \times 10 =$

$23 \times 10 =$

$32 \times 10 =$

Students had no problem with the first four problems. However, 12×10 proved more difficult for some, including the student who came to the board. Tom thought the product was 110. When he received the thumbs down from his classmates, he paused a moment, then began to use his fingers to keep track as he silently counted by ten twelve times. He revised his answer to 120. The students were also somewhat hesitant with 14×10. Cori came to the board and wrote 140. This seemed to reaffirm their somewhat tentative thinking and they seemed more confident for the last three problems, even excited, as they saw the "big" problems they were able to solve mentally.

As shown previously, a double-digit factor multiplied by 10 gave some students difficulty. Thinking of 12 as $10 + 2$ can help students with this difficulty. When students have this understanding, they can think of the problem 12×10 as $(10 \times 10) + (10 \times 2)$, a use of the distributive property. This is foundational for later topics in mathematics and the traditional algorithm. This insight also supports the continued development of students' number sense.

"Yesterday you noticed that you could use what happened in one problem to help you solve the next. What was the pattern we were looking at yesterday?" I asked

after erasing the star and beginning the discussion.

"Yesterday we found out if you double one factor and one factor stays the same, the answer doubles," Anamaria responded. The other students put their thumbs up to indicate their agreement.

"Was that what was happening today?" I asked.

"Sort of. In the first two problems, the ten was the same, but the other factor doubled, so did the product," Tom noticed.

"That's the same thing that happened with two times ten and four times ten," Allie said.

"But I notice something else. The product is the same as one of the factors, only a zero was added at the end," Anamaria shared.

"I noticed that, too. Then I figured out I could just count by tens however many times the other factor was. And then I thought about counting by ten and noticed that if I count by tens, then no matter how many times I count I always end up with a number that has zero in the ones place," Cori said.

"What if you count by tens and begin with thirteen? Then it doesn't work," replied Nicole. "If you start with thirteen then it goes twenty-three, thirty-three, and the ones place always has a three in it."

"Yeah, but if you count by tens mostly you start with ten and then it works," Cori responded.

"It looks like you can figure out some problems two ways. A lot of the problems have a factor that doubled from the one before, so you could just double the product from the one before. Or you could just take the factor that isn't ten and add a zero in the ones place," Shelly summed up.

"If it doesn't double, you had to know about multiplying by ten and adding the zero. If you knew that, it was easy! If not, counting by ten thirty-two times like in the last problem would take a really long time!" Rachel said.

I decided to try one more series with the students since they were picking up new ideas quickly and were engaged in and enjoying the activity. I decided to include the idea of halving and the idea of multiplying by multiples of 10. I used the following problems:

$10 \times 10 =$

$10 \times 5 =$

$20 \times 5 =$

$40 \times 5 =$

$40 \times 10 =$

$80 \times 10 =$

$80 \times 5 =$

The activity proceeded as it had in the past. After a few more series in which we explored doubling, halving, and multiplying by 10 and multiples of 10, I asked the students to quickly write about what they had learned from this activity.

SUGGESTIONS FOR ADDITIONAL EXPLORATIONS AND DISCUSSIONS

Goal: doubling one factor

$3 \times 4 =$

$4 \times 6 =$

$4 \times 12 =$

$4 \times 24 =$

$8 \times 24 =$

$24 \times 16 =$

$32 \times 24 =$

Goal: multiplying by 10

$4 \times 1 =$

$4 \times 10 =$

$40 \times 10 =$

$41 \times 10 =$

$45 \times 10 =$

$451 \times 10 =$

Goal: halving and doubling

$2 \times 6 =$

$2 \times 12 =$

$4 \times 12 =$

$4 \times 6 =$

$8 \times 6 =$

$8 \times 3 =$

Goal: doubling, halving, and multiplying by 10 and multiples of 10 adding one more group

$4 \times 6 =$	$6 \times 3 =$
$2 \times 6 =$	$3 \times 3 =$
$20 \times 6 =$	$30 \times 3 =$
$40 \times 6 =$	$15 \times 3 =$
$40 \times 60 =$	$150 \times 3 =$
$80 \times 60 =$	$150 \times 30 =$
$800 \times 60 =$	$151 \times 30 =$
$801 \times 60 =$	$152 \times 30 =$
$802 \times 60 =$	

Goal: doubling both factors—quadruple product multiplying by 10 and multiples of 10

$3 \times 5 =$

$6 \times 10 =$

$12 \times 20 =$

$24 \times 40 =$

Goal: multiplying by 10 and multiples of 10

$1 \times 12 =$

$10 \times 12 =$

$10 \times 24 =$

$20 \times 24 =$

$40 \times 24 =$

Goal: halving and doubling multiplying by 10 and multiples of 10

$4 \times 20 =$

$2 \times 20 =$

$20 \times 20 =$

$200 \times 20 =$

$400 \times 20 =$

$400 \times 40 =$

$200 \times 40 =$

Note: Halving is difficult for many students. Keep the numbers small at first to increase the likelihood students will more easily see this relationship.

After a great deal of experience, give students a more difficult problem and ask them to change it into easier related problems. One day I put the following problem on the board: *16 × 8*. "How could you solve this problem?" I asked.

"You could think of it as an easier problem like sixteen times ten equals one hundred sixty and then subtract thirty-two because there are two groups of sixteen too many and get one hundred twenty-eight," Shelly shared.

"Another way is to make it into two problems. You could do eight times eight times two. You can think of it that way because the eight times two is sixteen, one of the original factors, and then the other eight is the second factor. It's *Silent Multiplication* going backwards!" explained Anamaria. Anamaria used the ideas of factoring numbers to make a simpler problem as well as applying the associative and commutative properties of multiplication.

"You could also do it by changing the sixteen into ten plus six and then multiplying both the ten and the six by eight. Ten times eight is eighty and six times eight is forty-eight. Eighty plus forty-eight is one hundred twenty-eight," David said. David made use of the distributive property.

This is the kind of flexible thinking and making sense of multiplication I had hoped my students would achieve. We continued to explore other similar problems, such as 14×48.

EXTENSION

In another class that had experience exploring patterns in factors and products through *Silent Multiplication*, I changed the whole class lesson to a small group activity. I said to the class, "We are going to change *Silent Multiplication* slightly. You are going to play with just your table group. One person will write a problem on a sheet of paper and pass the paper on to the next person. The next person will write the answer and write a new related problem and pass it to the third person. The third person will check the answer the second person gave, solve the second person's problem, and write another related problem and so on. If you think an answer is incorrect, you must prove it to your group. Remember you must do this silently," I explained.

I decided to model the activity quickly. I asked the class to gather around a table. I drew a star on the board, indicating everyone needed to be silent, and sat down. I began by writing $4 \times 4 =$ and then passing the paper to Alicia. She answered my problem of 4×4 by writing *16* and then wrote 8×4. She passed the paper to Jamie, who checked Alicia's answer of 16, answered Alicia's problem of 8×4 with *28* and wrote the new problem 8×8. Jamie passed the paper to Gina. Gina checked Jamie's answer of 28 for 8×4 and went on to solve the next problem. Alicia noticed that Jamie had written the wrong answer and Gina had not noticed, so Alicia interrupted Gina by tapping her pencil to get Gina's attention. Alicia pointed to $8 \times 4 = 28$ and shook her head no. Then Alicia wrote on the paper $8 \times 2 = 16$ and $16 \times 2 = 32$. Gina and Jamie did not seem convinced. Next Alicia wrote *8, 16, 24, 32*. Gina, who could be a bit stubborn, still shook her head in disagreement with Alicia, so Alicia drew four circles with eight tally marks in each and finally convinced both Jamie and Gina of her thinking. I decided to stop the activity here, as the other students were getting excited and were eager to return to their seats to get started. I erased the star and said, "I hope you noticed how the girls were able to disagree and justify their thinking. Remember to check each other's work. Are there any questions?" I said.

"Can we get started now?" Conner asked eagerly.

I nodded yes and the students quickly returned to their seats and got to work.

Observing the Students

Watching the students work together was very revealing. By watching closely as the students worked, I was able to gain insights not only about who did and did not understand the mathematical ideas underlying this activity but also about the depth of understanding of many of the students as well as where some of their difficulties were.

Because Susanna and Neal had both had some difficulties with *Silent Multiplication* lessons, I decidcd to pay close attention to them initially. I checked in with Neal and his group. The group started with $5 \times 30 =$ 150. The second person wrote $10 \times 60 =$. Brooke responded with *600* and wrote *40 × 60.* Neal quickly wrote *2,400* as the product and added the new problem of *80 × 120 =* . Charlie responded *9,200.* Neal disagreed with the answer Charlie gave and wrote *12 × 8 = ?? Check the chart.* The chart Neal referred to was the class multiplication chart made of rectangles. Charlie checked the chart and corrected his answer to read *9,600.* (See Figure 4–1.) I was satisfied that Neal understood what he was doing and pleased to see the students use the chart as a way to justify their thinking.

I moved on to Susanna's group. They were having some difficulty in part because of Susanna's confusion. Kirk wrote the first problem, *2 × 3 =,* to which Susanna responded *6.* When Susanna had to write a new related problem, she became frustrated. She wrote *3 × 5,* to which Kirk wrote a long note showing why he felt that 3 × 5

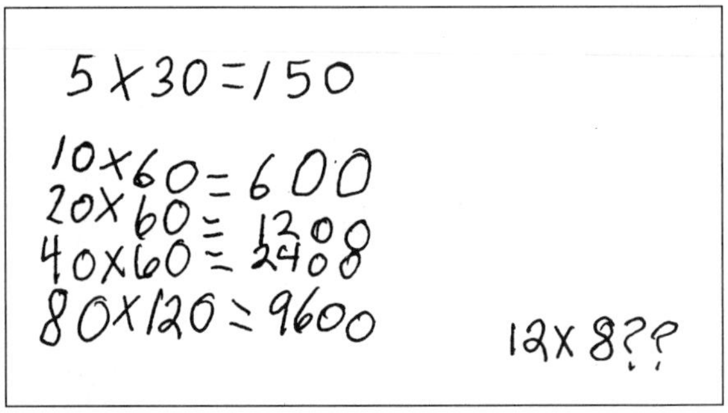

▲▲▲▲▲▲Figure 4–1   *Neal disagreed with an answer and suggested Charlie check the multiplication chart.*

was not related to 2 × 3. Susanna erased her work and stared at the paper a moment. Jeni took the paper and wrote, *You know how to double,* to which Susanna responded by erasing Jeni's comment and writing her own, *I don't know!* Miguel, who had been watching but not getting involved, used his fingers. He showed Susanna one finger on his left hand then showed her two fingers on his right hand and wrote on the paper 1 doubled is 2. Susanna also erased this comment, but she wrote the following related problem, *4 × 6 =,* and passed the paper. I wandered on with the intent of returning shortly to check on progress. I appreciated the way the students made an honest effort to help Susanna and the way Susanna stuck with it and was able to figure it out.

The other table groups were deeply involved and not particularly aware I was observing them. There were few difficulties and the students seemed to be making an effort to create interesting, challenging problems. All students were watching closely and checking the responses of their partners.

I returned to Susanna's group. They had abandoned their first game and started a new one. This game seemed to be running more smoothly and when it was Susanna's turn, she had less difficulty writing a related problem. Their second game went something like the following:

writer: Miguel	$1 \times 5 = 5$	solver: Kirk
writer: Kirk	$2 \times 10 = 20$	solver: Jeni
writer: Jeni	$4 \times 5 = 20$	solver: Susanna
writer: Susanna	$8 \times 10 = 80$	solver: Miguel
writer: Miguel	$12 \times 10 = 120$	solver: Kirk
writer: Kirk	$6 \times 20 = 120$	solver: Jeni
writer: Jeni	$12 \times 40 = 480$	solver: Susanna
writer: Susanna	6×40	

I noticed that another group seemed to be extremely intent on their game. Reasonably certain that Susanna and her group were fine, I went over to see what was going on. A student had written the answer of *38* for the problem 6×7. The group had been trying to convince her that the product should be 42. They had come up with three arguments before they could finally convince her to change her original answer. (See Figure 4–2.)

Gina, Jackie, and Alicia had started a game that seemed to focus on the pattern inherent in our number system when multiplying by 10, 100, and so on. They started off with 5×10 and continued until the four-

teenth problem before making an error with the number of zeros that should be in the product. (See Figure 4–3.)

When I checked back with Neal, his group was intent on solving 160×240. Melissa was the one attempting to solve this problem, which Charlie had written. The other three were pointing to give her clues and supporting her by agreeing as they watched her work out the problem. After patience and support from her group, Melissa successfully completed the problem by writing the product of *38,400*. Watching Melissa work convinced me that her understanding was developing well, she was persistent, and she willingly attempted and

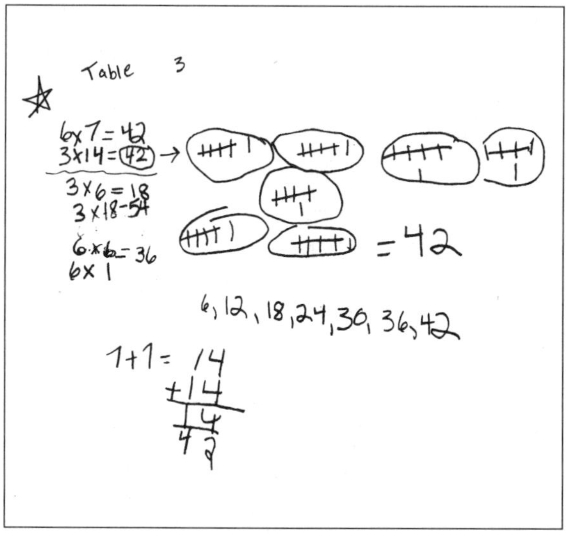

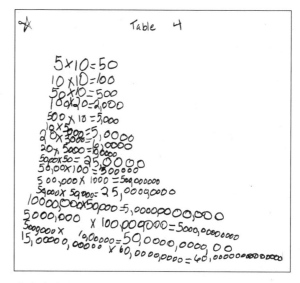

▲▲▲▲▲▲**Figure 4–2** *Arguments to convince a student that the product of $6 \times 7 = 42$. The error was corrected.*

▲▲▲▲▲▲**Figure 4–3** *Gina, Jackie, and Alicia focused on multiplying by 10 and multiples of 10.*

successfully solved a problem I would have thought too difficult. (See Figure 4–4.)

I found it fascinating to watch the children solve the problems and interact with one another during this activity. I was interested to know what they thought they learned from the experience. I asked the students to respond to the following prompt: "Something I learned by playing *Silent Multiplication* is . . . " The students seemed to get a variety of things from this lesson. Jackie wrote that she learned about halving and doubling numbers and gave some examples done correctly, indicating that she understood. (See Figure 4–5.)

Susanna wrote that she understood the effects of halving and doubling on the product and gave a correct example, which really pleased me, as Susanna had had to struggle to make sense of this information.

Alicia also seemed to understand this concept and gave several nice examples as supporting evidence of her understanding. (See Figure 4–6.)

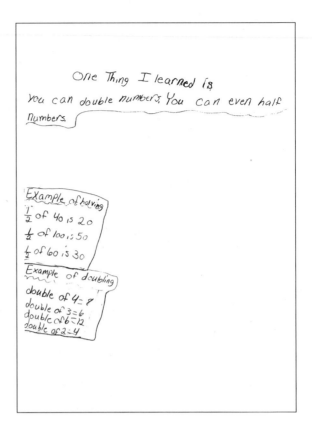

▲▲▲▲▲▲Figure 4–5 *Jackie learned about halving and doubling.*

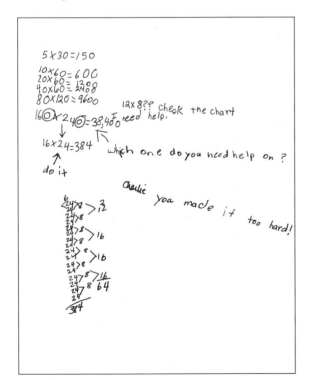

▲▲▲▲▲▲Figure 4–4 *The group helped Melissa solve 160 × 240.*

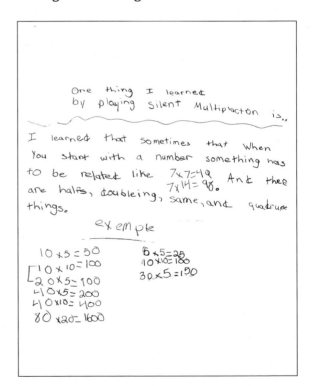

▲▲▲▲▲▲Figure 4–6 *Alicia showed her understanding.*

Melissa really enjoyed this activity. She had figured out three patterns. She wrote the patterns and gave examples of each. And, of course, she wrote about her solution to 160 × 240. (See Figure 4–7.)

Casey's work indicated that he thought he understood doubling. However, his examples did not support this. As his teacher, I needed to go back and talk with him about doubling and then compare it to the pattern he mentioned as an example of his understanding. (See Figure 4–8.)

Calob's work focused on his understanding of adding zeros when multiplying by 10. It was clear he recognized the pattern, but I wondered about his understanding when he explained his second example, 20 × 20 = 400. He indicated that he added two zeros to the sum of 2 + 2. While adding 2 + 2 in this example yields a correct answer because 2 + 2 and 2 × 2 both equal 4, addition will not work in other cases. I needed

to work with Calob to help him recognize a couple of things: first, where the two zeros came from in 20 × 20, that is, 20 × 20 can be thought of as 2 × 2 × 100 or 2 × 2 × 10 × 10, and second, why the 2s are multiplied rather than added, as he thought they should be. (See Figure 4–9.)

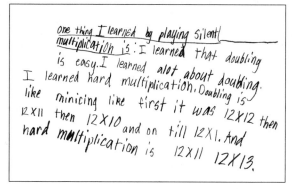

▲▲▲▲▲▲Figure 4–8 *Casey's work indicated he needed help with the concept of doubling.*

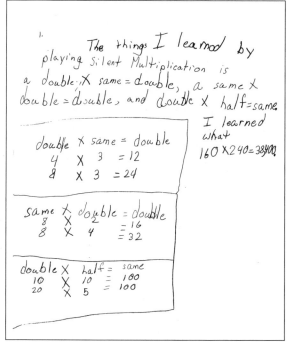

▲▲▲▲▲▲Figure 4–7 *Melissa wrote about solving 160 × 240, a problem her group helped her solve.*

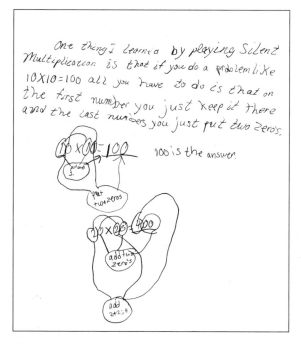

▲▲▲▲▲▲Figure 4–9 *Calob recognized the pattern of multiplying by 10 and multiples of 10 although a misconception appears in his work.*

Silent Multiplication   53

Questions and Discussion

▲▲▲

▲ Why is this activity done silently?

The activity is done silently for several reasons. The silence seems to cause children to focus intently, more so than usual. Perhaps this is because it is different to learn silently. Perhaps it is because only one sense is being used to take in information, or maybe there is some other reason. The important thing is children are very focused. Another benefit of silence is that those children who tend to blurt out aren't as prone to that behavior. The silence seems to slow things down and give students more quality thinking and processing time.

▲ Doesn't the silence make it difficult to correct students?

When correcting students, I can't rely on a quick verbal response that may or may not make sense to the child. Rather, I have to think more deeply and I have found I rely more on making connections between ideas and using pictures. This is using another modality, which often benefits students.

When I have found general confusion that needed a verbal explanation, I have erased the star, indicating that talking was now OK, and we have had a discussion.

▲ Why are the class discussions so important in this activity?

It is during the class discussions that students explore the connections and relationships among the problems. They consider how these relationships can be used to help them solve bigger, more difficult problems. Many students will not make these connections on their own. They need the structure, questioning, and sharing to guide their thinking and develop their ability to use known information to solve a new problem.

▲ How do you know what questions to ask?

The questions I ask vary from situation to situation. My decisions for discussions about this activity are guided by the patterns we are exploring and by the students themselves. For example, if I want students to see the effects on the product of doubling one factor, then the problems I use and the questions I ask remain as focused as possible on this idea. I honor what students have to say, but if their comments are leading down a different path, I will often redirect the class with a question focused on the mathematics I want the students to understand. The key is to keep in mind what mathematics is to be taught while listening carefully to what students are saying and using this information to guide comments and questioning.

There are some general questions that can be used to get a discussion going. Some of these include

> What did you notice?
> What would happen if . . . ?
> What patterns do you see?
> How do you know this information is reasonable?
> What did you learn or discover?
> What are you still wondering about?

Once the discussion gets going, the mathematics to be explored and the students should be the guides for questions and comments.

▲ *What if my students have difficulty with doubling?*

The book *The 512 Ants on Sullivan Street*, by Carol Losi (Scholastic, 1997), provides a context through pictures and a story in which students explore the doubling pattern. In the story, the number of ants needed to take each subsequent item from the picnic basket doubles. To help students make the connection between doubling and multiplying by 2, an addition sentence can be listed representing the number of ants needed to carry away a food item. For example, four ants working in two pairs were required to carry away a chip. The addition sentence would be $2 + 2 = 4$. Next to the addition sentence, you could write a multiplication sentence representing the same situation: $2 \times 2 = 4$. This idea, along with others, appears in the back of the book.

CHAPTER 5
RELATED RECTANGLES

Overview

Related Rectangles builds on *Silent Multiplication* by linking the number patterns explored in that activity to the geometric model of rectangles. This connection gives additional support to the development of students' understanding about relationships between factors and products. Understanding these relationships increases students' number sense, which results in their increased accuracy in computation. Students also use their problem-solving and spatial skills as they work with tiles to explore the numerical patterns from a geometric perspective.

Materials

▲ 1-inch color tiles (about 30–40 per student)
▲ overhead tiles (optional)
▲ centimeter squares grid paper (see Blackline Masters)
▲ overhead transparency of centimeter squares grid paper (optional)
▲ crayons or color pencils
▲ Related Rectangles Assessment Grids (optional; see Blackline Masters)

Time

▲ one class period

Teaching Directions

1. Distribute about 150 1-inch tiles to each table of four to six students. Ask students to cooperate to find possible ways to arrange twelve tiles into rectangles following four rules:

▲ Tiles must be arranged in a square or a rectangle.

▲ Tiles must be laying flat in a single layer.

▲ Complete sides of tiles must match.

▲ The rectangle or square cannot have space inside; that is, it should be a filled-in rectangle.

2. In a class discussion, students share the ways they found to arrange their twelve tiles. Build the rectangles as students suggest them, using an overhead projector and overhead tiles or some other way so that all in the class can see. Have table groups check to see if they have each solution shared as one of their group's solutions. Record the rectangles suggested by the students on the board or on an overhead transparency of centimeter squares grid paper.

3. Play *Silent Multiplication* using the following series of problems:

6×4

12×2

6×2

12×4

6×8

3×4

This series of problems is only a suggestion. The problems work well to help students see halving and doubling patterns. Any series that helps students see this will work. **Reminder:** Odd numbers result in fractions when finding half.

4. After playing *Silent Multiplication,* lead a discussion with the students comparing the relationship of one problem with the next or talking about how students could use information from one problem to help them solve the next problem. For example, with $6 \times 4 = 24$ and $12 \times 2 = 24$, the first factor, 6, doubles to become 12, and the second factor, 4, is halved to become 2. There is no change to the product.

5. After the discussion, ask children to return to the first problem, 6 × 4, and build a rectangle with their tiles to represent it. Build the rectangle on a table with tiles or on the overhead projector using overhead tiles. Using a blank overhead transparency, or on the board, record the rectangle, color it in, and label it.

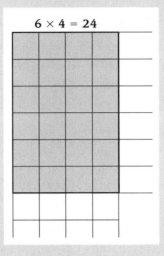

6. For the second problem, 12 × 2, ask students to build a rectangle using tiles. Again, do as students suggest; record, color, and label as before. Discuss how the first and second rectangles are related. Continue in this way building rectangles for the remaining problems or until you are confident that students see the connections between patterns from *Silent Multiplication* and the rectangles that represent the problems.

7. Ask students to use tiles to create their own rectangles, record them on grid paper, and color and label them. Then each group can create a second related rectangle with tiles and again record, color, and label it on their sheet of grid paper. Students write about how their two rectangles are related.

8. As an assessment, give each student a sheet with three rectangles drawn on it: an 8-by-6, an 8-by-12, and a 4-by-24. (See Blackline Master, page 185.) Ask students to explain how the rectangles relate to one another.

Teaching Notes

Prior to the beginning of this activity, these students had had experience with *Silent Multiplication*. I wanted to build on their experience and help them understand the mathematics underlying the patterns we had explored. For example, I wasn't sure they knew why the product doubles when one factor is doubled, why doubling one factor and halving the other results in no change in the product, and so on. Using the tiles to represent multiplication problems gives students concrete, geometric models of relationships between factors and products.

The students in the vignette that follows had had previous experience with arranging tiles into rectangles. This experience is extremely useful as a foundation for *Related Rectangles*. (See Marilyn Burns's *Teaching Arithmetic: Lessons for Introducing Multiplication, Grade 3.*)

The Lesson

BUILDING RECTANGLES WITH TILES

"Please take twelve tiles from your table's bag of tiles," I began. Students were seated in table groups of four students. Bags of about 150 1-inch plastic color tiles had been distributed to the tables prior to the lesson. Because these students had had previous experience with arranging tiles into rectangles, I planned only a short opportunity to revisit this activity. "I would like you to arrange tiles into rectangles. Before you begin, there are some directions I need to review. First, your tiles must be arranged in a rectangle. A square is OK because a square is a special kind of rectangle. Second, they must lay flat on your desk in a single layer with no holes in the rectangle. And complete sides of tiles must touch."

"We did this before," Melissa said.

"Yes," I replied. "But this activity is a little different. There is a third thing I want you to do, so please wait just one moment before you start," I continued. "I want your table group to work together so that each of you has a different way to arrange twelve tiles according to the rules."

"Is three times four the same as four times three?" Conner asked.

"When we explored before we counted them as the same. Today we are going to count them as different ways to arrange the same number of tiles," I explained. "You'll see why soon." The students quickly got to work. As I walked around the room observing the students work, I had to remind a few that the rectangle or square they made had to be solid.

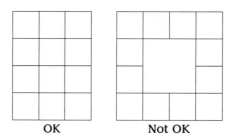

OK   Not OK

After five minutes or so, I could tell from a quick glance around the room that all the table groups had accomplished the task. I called for the students' attention. Using an overhead projector and a transparency of centimeter squares grid paper, I planned to record the various ways the students had arranged their tiles to model for them how to record, label, and color their rectangles using grid paper.

"Who has a way to arrange their twelve tiles that you would like to share with the rest of the class?" I asked. Everyone's hand shot into the air. I called on Brooke.

"You could make a column going down that has six tiles in it, then make another one right next to it," Brooke explained.

Using overhead tiles, I followed Brooke's directions. I made the following rectangle.

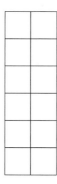

"Is this how you did it?" I asked. She nodded yes. "I am going to record Brooke's arrangement on a transparency of grid paper," I explained as I drew her rectangle on the transparency. "I am going to use a marker to color in Brooke's rectangle so it is easier to see, and right beneath it I am going to label it six times two equals twelve because there are six tiles going down and two going across and twelve altogether." (Labeling the first number as the number of squares going down the rectangle and labeling the second number as the number of squares going across is arbitrary. I did it this way so students would be consistent.) I added Brooke's name to the transparency to show she had been the one to share that idea. "Put your thumb up if someone in your table group has a rectangle like Brooke's," I said. All groups indicated that someone in their group had created a 6-by-2 rectangle.

"Who has another way?" I asked.

"You could do three tiles down and then add three more columns like the first one so you have four altogether, then you would have a three-by-four," suggested Susanna. I used my tiles to build the rectangle Susanna had suggested.

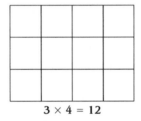

3 × 4 = 12

"Put your thumb up if someone in your table group has the same way as Susanna suggested," I said. All students put their thumbs up. "How could I record Susanna's way on my transparency?" I asked.

"You would draw a rectangle that has three squares going down and four going across, then color it in, and label it three times four equals twelve," Charlie answered. The students indicated their agreement by nodding their heads, so I fol-

lowed Charlie's instructions and added Susanna's name.

"Another way?" I asked.

"Since you said that for today three times four would be a different way than four times three, you could do four times three. It would look a little different, twisted, but it would use the same amount of tiles," Kirk said.

I did as Kirk suggested and built a 4-by-3 rectangle with my overhead tiles.

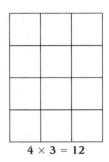

4 × 3 = 12

Then I recorded Kirk's way on the grid as I had done with the others. I continued with this discussion until all six ways of arranging twelve tiles (1×12, 12×1, 6×2, 2×6, 3×4, 4×3) had been built, recorded, and labeled. While this activity was not particularly challenging for this group of students, it provided a good review and a common foundation on which to build the rest of the lesson.

SILENT MULTIPLICATION

"We are going to take a few moments and play *Silent Multiplication* and then we are going to come back to the tiles. So for right now, push your tiles aside and we'll play," I explained. We used the following sequence of problems:

$6 \times 4 =$

$12 \times 2 =$

$6 \times 2 =$

$12 \times 4 =$

$6 \times 8 =$

$3 \times 4 =$

When we completed the game, I began the discussion with the following question: "What happened to get us from the first problem to the second problem?" I asked.

"The six doubled and the four halved so it became twelve times two and the amount was the same, twenty-four," Melissa answered.

"What about from the second to the third problem—what happened there?" I continued.

"The twelve was put into two parts . . . " Ana began.

"Do you mean halves?" I asked to help me better understand her thinking. She nodded yes and continued.

"The twelve was put into half, the two stayed the same, and the answer from the problem before was double from the new problem," Ana said.

While I understood what Ana was saying, her explanation was not as clear as it could have been, perhaps because she was not altogether comfortable with the notion of half. I made a note to myself to check back with Ana during the next work time to assess her understanding of half and if appropriate, help her gain more understanding about half. I continued the discussion with the students until we had completed all six problems, each time asking them how the problems were related or how they could use information from a previous problem to help them solve the new problem.

CONNECTING *SILENT MULTIPLICATION* TO RECTANGLES

After we completed the discussion I asked the children to go back to the first problem, $6 \times 4 = 24$, and build it using tiles according to the same rules we had followed at the beginning of the lesson for building rectangles with twelve tiles.

"Do you mean we build a rectangle with twenty-four tiles or a rectangle that has six tiles going down and four tiles going across?" Neal asked. I worried that Neal did not connect the idea that the factors, 6 and 4, dictated the rectangle he was asked to build and that the rectangle would use a total of twenty-four tiles.

"It's the same thing!" said Kirk, a student with strong mathematical abilities. I took advantage of Kirk's willingness to make this statement and asked him to explain why he thought they were the same.

"Well, it's easy really. If you make a rectangle that is six down and four across and count all the tiles, it doesn't matter if you count them by ones or sixes or fours, if you count correctly, it takes twenty-four tiles to make a rectangle that has four rows of six tiles. So that's why it's the same thing!" Kirk explained.

"Oh yeah!" Neal said.

There were no further questions so I had the students build their 6-by-4 rectangles at their desks while I built one on the overhead projector. On a clean transparency of centimeter squares grid paper I recorded my 6-by-4 rectangle, colored it in, and labeled it $6 \times 4 = 24$. After I did this, I walked around the room to observe how the students were doing. The students were having little difficulty. After a few moments, I noticed that most students had finished, so I asked for their attention.

"Please compare your rectangle with your neighbor's to see if they're the same," I said. The students took a few moments to check. Hector and Calob were waving their hands in the air as they argued with each other about their rectangles.

"Hector's rectangle has four on the side and six going across. Mine has six on the side and four going across. I think mine is right because we have been doing it where the first number in the problem is the number of tiles on the side and the second number tells the number across," Calob said.

"But it doesn't really matter because it uses the same numbers and comes out to twenty-four tiles! It's just twisted around is all!" Hector argued.

"But didn't we say that for this problem the first number would be the number going down the side and the second number would be the number on the top?" Calob asked, looking at me.

Even though we had discussed this as a class, I decided this point was important for everyone to reconsider for this activity and a nice way to introduce the commutative property of multiplication. I asked Hector and Calob if they would be willing to share their discussion with their classmates. Both boys agreed. I asked for the students' attention. "Hector and Calob have been having a discussion I would like the rest of you to think about," I said. I asked both boys to come to the front of the room and build their rectangles on the overhead. "Hector and Calob are having difficulty agreeing on how a six-by-four rectangle should be positioned. I am going to ask both boys to explain their thinking and then we will talk about an important point," I explained to the other students.

"I think mine is correct because we have been saying that the first number is the number going down and the second tells how many tiles go across," Calob said. "So I think the correct rectangle should have six tiles going down, and four rows going across."

"I think it could be either way because you are using the same numbers and you use twenty-four tiles either way. The difference between them is that one is twisted around," Hector explained.

"The reason I asked the boys to share their discussion with you is because the rule they are discussing, about which factor tells the number of tiles going down and which tells the number of tiles going across is not based on a mathematical reason, but rather it's a choice I made. I made that choice to help us communicate more clearly. Both boys are right that six times four could be represented by either rectangle. Mathematicians have a name for this idea. It is called the commutative property of multiplication and it means that six times four equals four times six. But for this lesson, I have decided that we will use the first number to tell how many tiles should be in each column, or going down, and the second number to tell how many tiles should be in each row, or going across," I said. The students nodded quietly, indicating that they understood. I thanked the two boys for sharing their discussion and thinking with the rest of the class.

"Six times four was the first problem in our series, and the answer was twenty-four. The second problem was twelve times two, and the answer was still twenty-four. How could I rearrange my six-by-four rectangle with twenty-four tiles to make a twelve-by-two with twenty-four tiles?" I asked. I paused to give the students a moment to think this over. "Talk with the person beside you about how this could be done and why your idea makes sense. First one person talks while the other listens, then at the end of thirty seconds I will ask you to change so the first listener gets to talk and the first talker gets to listen," I said. After thirty seconds I reminded the students to switch roles and at the end of one minute, I asked for the students' attention, and most students raised their hands, indicating that they wanted to share their ideas. I called on Kasey.

"You could break the four into two parts. It would be like two rectangles side-by-side that were six-by-two. Then you could put them back together again, but this time, instead of putting them side-by-side, you would put one above and one below. When you put them together it would make a twelve-by-two," Kasey explained.

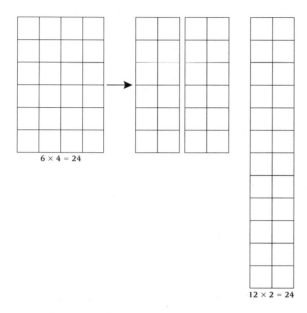

6 × 4 = 24

12 × 2 = 24

Using my overhead tiles, I did as Kasey instructed me to do. "What happened to the sides?" I asked.

"One side got shorter and the other got longer," Susanna shared.

"The one that got longer . . . it doubled," Conner added.

"And the one that got shorter actually was divided into half. You see, two is half of four," Kirk said. The other students nodded their agreement.

"What happened to the total?" I asked.

"It stayed the same," the students said.

"Why?" I asked.

"Hum . . . well you didn't change the number of tiles altogether, you just changed how they were arranged, I think," Jeni explained.

No other students seemed to have anything else to add, so I moved on. "How is the six-by-four rectangle related to the twelve-by-two rectangle?" I asked. Again I paused to give students time to consider this question. When about half the students had raised their hands, I called on Miguel.

"Well, I think they are related because they have the same total number of tiles and the sides are related . . . like doubling and halving. Like two and four are related, but I don't think twelve and six are related in the same way . . . oh it's too hard to explain!" Miguel said.

"I think I know what you mean," Sandra said. "But sometimes it is hard to explain!" The other students smiled.

"Let's use Miguel's idea of the relationship of halving or doubling to see if we can build the third problem, six times two, from our twelve-by-two rectangle," I suggested as I recorded and labeled the 12-by-2 rectangle onto my grid transparency. The students quickly divided their rectangles into half along the side that had twelve tiles.

"What happened to the sides?" I asked.

"The side that was twelve was divided into half. That made the total number of tiles in the rectangle less," Melissa said.

"How much less?" I pushed.

"Six," replied Melissa.

I was trying to get Melissa to recognize that six was half of twelve. "What relationship exists between twelve and six?" I pushed.

"I'm not sure. Can I call on someone else?" Melissa said. I nodded yes. She called on Jeni.

"Six is half of twelve, or twelve is six doubled," Jeni explained. "One of the sides was cut in half, and so the total number of tiles was cut in half."

"How is twelve times two related to six times two?" I asked.

"One is half of the other," Rob said. I recorded and labeled the 6-by-2 on my grid transparency.

The students seemed to be catching on quickly. I decided to have them consider how 6 × 2 was related to 12 × 4. I gave them a moment to think about it quietly, then asked them to each share their thinking with the person sitting beside them. After the students had talked with their partners, I called on Gina to share her thinking with the class.

"Both sides are doubled. At first I thought the total tiles would be doubled, but it wasn't. I know because the total for six times two is twelve and twelve doubled is twenty-four. But twelve times four is forty-eight, which is two twenty-fours, so I guess forty-eight is four twelves?" she said, a bit uncertain of herself.

"Yeah, that's what I think, too," Anthony said.

"If you agree with Anthony and Gina put your thumb up," I said. The other students indicated their agreement. "How could I record twelve times four on grid paper?" I asked.

"Make a rectangle that goes down twelve and across four," Jamie said. I did as Jamie suggested, colored in the rectangle, and labeled it *12 x 4 = 48*.

CREATING RELATED RECTANGLES

"I would like each of you to use your tiles to create a rectangle that is related to twelve times four in some way you can describe," I said.

I observed as the students worked. Most created a 6-by-8 or a 2-by-24 rectangle. After the students had created their related rectangles, I had them share their ideas with partners and then we had a group discussion. Because the students came up with only two possibilities I decided to push their thinking.

"I agree that a six-by-eight and a two-by-twenty-four rectangle are related to a twelve-by-four rectangle. There are others, too. For example, I think that a twenty-four-by-eight is related. Who thinks you know how a twelve-by-four relates to a twenty-four-by-eight rectangle?" I pushed.

"The twelve and four are doubled to become twenty-four and eight," Kirk said.

"What do you think will happen to the total number of tiles in the rectangle when I double both sides?" I asked.

"I'm not sure. I need to try it," Kirk replied.

"Ohhh! What about twelve and twelve? I think that is related to twelve-by-four because the first twelve would stay the same and then the four would be like skip-counting three times by four. I wonder what happens to the product?" Jeni said, excited by her own question.

The students were starting to come up with a variety of ideas. "The rectangles we have been making together with tiles and I have been recording on my transparency of grid paper are related by halving or by doubling or by doing both halving and doubling. Here's what I would like you to do next. I would like you to make a new rectangle out of tiles. Choose a size that you can record on a sheet of grid paper. After you have made your new rectangle out of tiles, record, color, and label it on your grid paper as I have been doing. Then make a second related rectangle. Record this on your grid paper also. Finally, explain in writing how the rectangles are related just as we have been discussing. Are there questions?" I said.

"So, we are going to do what you have been doing on the overhead," clarified Sandra.

"Yes," I said.

"Do we make a different rectangle from the ones we've talked about?" Neal asked.

"Yes," I replied.

There were no more questions for the moment. The students got to work creating their new rectangles from the tiles. As they worked with the tiles, I observed as I handed each student a sheet of centimeter grid paper. Anthony looked up at me as I walked by with a puzzled look on his face.

"I'm stuck!" he said with frustration.

"Tell me what you have done so far," I said.

"I made a rectangle. It's three by nine. I can't make it go in half," he explained. As he talked, he showed me that, indeed, neither side could be divided evenly.

"Why do you think this is happening?" I asked.

Anthony paused for a few moments, recounted the number of tiles on each side and thought some more. "I think because the three and the nine are odd numbers and if you divided odd numbers into halves you have a leftover . . . so I think it doesn't work," he said.

"I understand what you are saying about the difficulty you are having with dividing odd numbers into halves. What other patterns have we been exploring?" I asked, hoping to redirect his thinking. I was hoping he might consider doubling one or both of the sides. But, Anthony did not go down that road. He chose to do something that surprised me. He was intent on dividing sides, so rather than dividing a side into halves, he decided to divide a side into thirds.

He studied his rectangle again with great seriousness. "I know! I could cut it into three parts and then put them together!" Anthony said.

"Show me," I encouraged him. He split his 3-by-9 rectangle into three 1-by-9 rectangles, then reassembled them into a 1-by-27. He immediately got to work recording his idea on his grid paper. When I checked back on Anthony later, he had correctly recorded his first two rectangles along with his thinking about how the two rectangles were related. He had gone on to create a third related rectangle. However, his third rectangle reflected an error in his thinking. He had broken the 1-by-27 into two parts, which he explained he thought were equal. Then he put them together to form a new rectangle, which he labeled as *2 × 13*. When I noticed this, I asked him how many total tiles there should be. He responded that there should be twenty-seven. Next I asked him to count the number of tiles in

his third rectangle. He noticed that there were only twenty-six. Upon this discovery he looked up at me, giggled, and said, "I kept trying to figure out how I all of a sudden had an extra tile. Now I know. I guess I should count everything at least twice!" Anthony also had not connected to this situation his earlier observation that dividing odd numbers by two results in a leftover tile. (See Figure 5–1.)

As I observed the students working, I noticed Calob had chosen to build a rectangle with one odd and one even dimension, 9×6. I watched for a moment to see if he

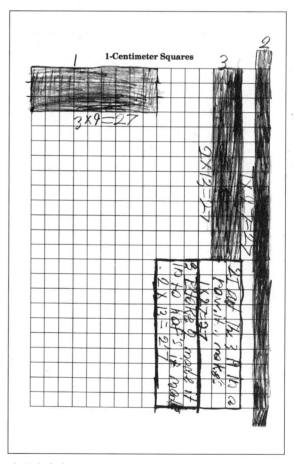

▲▲▲▲▲▲Figure 5–1 *Anthony successfully split a 3-by-9 rectangle in 3 to reform it into a 1-by-27 rectangle. Anthony did not realize his earlier observation that dividing an odd number by two results in a remainder. He split a 1-by-27 rectangle and reformed it into a 2-by-13 rectangle, losing one square in the process.*

would have difficulty dealing with the odd number. He decided to use the same number of tiles, dividing the even side in half, which caused the odd number to double when he reassembled his rectangle into an 18-by-3. (See Figure 5–2.)

I also noticed that Jeni had done the same thing as Calob, only she used a 7-by-6 rectangle. As I walked by, she called me over with excitement. "Look what I found out!" she exclaimed. "I already memorized seven times six equals forty-two. But I found out that when I cut the six side into half and moved it to make a fourteen times three rectangle, I went from a basic problem to a hard problem and I still could solve it! I have math power!" (See Figure 5–3.)

Being able to change factors and know what the results of those changes will be on the product can be a powerful tool, as Jeni discovered when she explored the relationship between $7 \times 6 = 42$ and $14 \times 3 = 42$.

Generally, the students were able to accomplish this task accurately and they found it engaging.

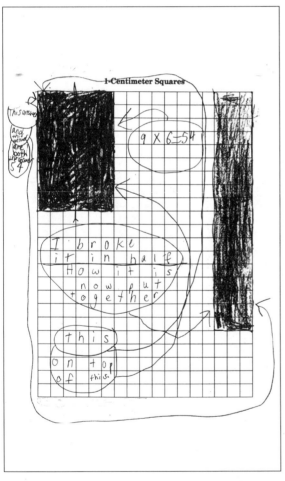

▲▲▲▲▲▲Figure 5–2 *Calob spit his 9-by-6 rectangle into two to create a new 18-by-3 rectangle.*

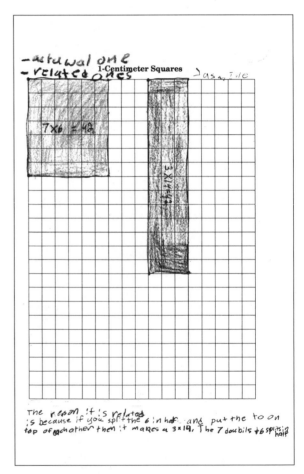

▲▲▲▲▲▲Figure 5–3 *Jeni made a powerful discovery. She discovered she can change factors and know the results of those changes on the product.*

ASSESSMENT

I gave the students a sheet of paper with three rectangles: an 8-by-6, an 8-by-12, and a 4-by-24.

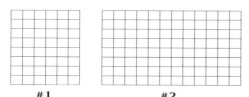

#1   #2

Explain how rectangle 1 is related to rectangle 2.

#3

Explain how rectangle 2 is related to rectangle 3.

I asked how the second rectangle related to the first rectangle, and how the third rectangle related to the second rectangle. I wanted to see if students would notice the effect on the rectangle of doubling and halving sides and if they would be able to write about it. For example, I hoped students would notice that when one side of rectangle 1 was doubled to create rectangle 2, the number of square units also doubled. Kasey's paper was very typical of the responses I got. It was clear that her under-

standing was emerging and with more experience and opportunity to share and listen to other's ideas, she would have even clearer understanding and a clearer explanation. (See Figure 5–4.)

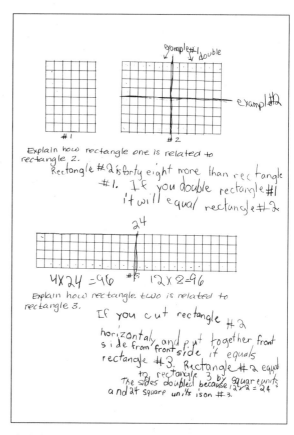

▲▲▲▲▲▲**Figure 5–4** *Kasey's paper was representative of others in the class.*

Questions and Discussion

▲▲▲

▲ *What would you do to help students who did not do well on the assessment?*

I would provide additional opportunities to explore related rectangles. This could be done independently, in a small group, or as a whole class, depending on the needs of the students. Questioning would focus on making the connection from the numbers to the rectangles and how they are related. I would also provide many opportunities to discuss ideas and how to record them in a written form. Describing mathematical thinking can be a challenge.

▲ *Why is it important for students to think about multiplication as rectangles?*

One reason is that the more ways students have to think about something, the deeper their understanding. Some students find it easier to think about multiplication with numbers, some by skip-counting, and some need a tool such as rectangles. Deeper understanding leads to more accurate, efficient computation, better number sense, and better ability to apply knowledge to a problem-solving situation meaningfully.

This geometric model of multiplication as rectangles can be applied to help students understand some beginning concepts of multiplication with fractions. For example, a student could draw a rectangle that was one-half unit by three units as a representation of $\frac{1}{2} \times 3$. The student could use the drawing to verify that the product was $1\frac{1}{2}$. However, it should be noted that using rectangles to represent multiplication of fractions gets tricky for problems such as $3\frac{1}{2} \times 4\frac{1}{2}$.

As students explore multiplication as rectangles, they should also realize that they are working with the areas of rectangles and squares.

▲ *What do you do when students get stuck?*

I ask students to talk and I listen carefully to their responses. These questions and statements work well to get students talking:

> Tell me what you have done so far.
>
> What is it you are trying to do?
>
> What do you understand the task to be?
>
> Is there a way you could draw a picture?
>
> Tell me what you know so far.

Listening to students' responses to questions and statements like these often gives me enough information, and I can ask more specific questions if necessary to help the student move forward.

In this vignette, Anthony got stuck. He built a 3-by-9 rectangle and wanted to divide the sides in half. My initial statement to him was "Tell me what you have done so far." He explained what he had done, what he wanted to do, and why what he wanted to do wouldn't work. It was as if his own verbalizing helped him come up with a solution to his problem.

I have often found that children will find answers to their problems if someone gives them an opportunity to talk aloud and listens carefully to what they have to say.

CHAPTER 6
CALCULATING SQUARES

Overview

Calculating Squares is a problem-solving activity that offers students experiences not only with multiplication but also with measurement and geometry. During the investigation, multiplication is related to the concept of area as students find the number of squares on an $8\frac{1}{2}$-by-11-inch piece of paper ruled into $\frac{1}{2}$-inch squares. Later, based on this experience, students estimate and then figure out the number of squares on a second sheet of paper ruled into 1-inch squares. **Note:** *Calculating Squares* is a useful introduction to Chapter 7, "Covering Boxes."

Materials

▲ paper ruled into $\frac{1}{2}$-inch squares, 1 per student (see Blackline Masters)
▲ paper ruled into 1-inch squares, 1 per student (see Blackline Masters)

Time

▲ one class period

Teaching Directions

1. Show the students a sheet of $8\frac{1}{2}$-by-11-inch paper ruled into $\frac{1}{2}$-inch squares. (See Blackline Master, page 188.) Ask students: "What information do you need in order to figure out the number of squares on this paper?" After students have shared their ideas, ask them to figure out the answer.

2. Observe as students work, offering guidance when needed.

3. When most students have completed the task, lead a class discussion about the number of squares on the sheet of paper and the strategies students used to find their solutions.

4. Hold up an $8\frac{1}{2}$-by-11-inch sheet of paper ruled into 1-inch squares. (See Blackline Master, page 187.) Ask students if there are more or fewer squares on this second sheet. Ask them to estimate first, then figure out the number of squares.

5. Lead a second class discussion about the number of 1-inch squares on an $8\frac{1}{2}$-by-11-inch sheet of paper and the relationship of this information to what students previously found out about the number of $\frac{1}{2}$-inch squares. Have students share their strategies.

Teaching Notes

Computation, problem solving, and number sense are all important elements of this lesson. As students figure the number of $\frac{1}{2}$-inch squares on an $8\frac{1}{2}$-by-11-inch sheet of paper, they are practicing computation through using multidigit multiplication. Because the students in this vignette had had previous experience with multidigit multiplication, many used the distributive property and multiplying by 10 to solve the problem. Problem solving and number sense are called into play when students use what they have learned from figuring the number of $\frac{1}{2}$-inch squares on an $8\frac{1}{2}$-by-11-inch sheet of paper to predict the number of squares on a second sheet of paper ruled into 1-inch squares.

The rectangular grid created when paper is ruled into squares provides a geometric representation of multiplication. When an $8\frac{1}{2}$-by-11-inch sheet of paper is ruled into $\frac{1}{2}$-inch squares, a 17-by-22 rectangular grid is created. The grid can be viewed as 17 groups of 22 squares or 22 groups of 17 squares. This representation reinforces for students that multiplication has to do with equal groups.

A somewhat surprising insight for students is the relationship they discover when they compare the number of 1-inch and $\frac{1}{2}$-inch squares needed to cover the same-size sheet of paper. Students had agreed there were 374 $\frac{1}{2}$-inch squares on the paper. When asked to predict the number of 1-inch squares on the same-size sheet of paper, many students thought it would be half the number of squares (187) because there are two half-inches to an inch. These students were surprised to discover the number of 1-inch squares was actually a quarter of the total of 374 $\frac{1}{2}$-inch squares, or $93\frac{1}{2}$ 1-inch squares. The reason for this is because it takes four $\frac{1}{2}$-inch squares to fill a 1-inch square. So the number of 1-inch squares needed to cover an $8\frac{1}{2}$-by-11 sheet of paper is one-fourth the number of $\frac{1}{2}$-inch squares. Or conversely, it takes four times more $\frac{1}{2}$-inch squares to cover an $8\frac{1}{2}$-by-11 inch piece of paper than 1-inch squares.

The Lesson

▲▲

I gathered the students on the floor so that they could more easily see the sheet of paper I had in my hand. I was holding an $8\frac{1}{2}$-by-11-inch sheet of white paper ruled into $\frac{1}{2}$-inch squares. "As you can see, my paper is covered with squares. What information would I need to know in order to figure out how many squares are on this paper?" I asked, then paused for a moment.

"You would need to know how many squares are going down, vertically," said Anamaria.

"How many squares are going across," Tom added.

"Can you think of a way to figure out how many squares there are without counting the number over or across?" I asked.

"You would need to know the size of one side of the square," Amy said. "You would only need to know the length of one side of the square because if you knew the length of one side then you would know the length of all the sides because a square has all the sides the same."

"I agree with Amy that you would need to know the size of the squares. But you would also need to know how long the paper is," David added. "If you know the size of the squares and the length of the paper going down, you can figure out how many squares it would take to go down the paper. I think you could multiply or divide or something . . . I'm not sure. It probably depends on the situation, but I'm not sure."

"One more thing you should know," Nicole added. "You should know if all the squares on the page are the same size."

"My paper is eight and a half inches across and eleven inches down. Each square is one-half inch on a side and all squares are the same size." I paused and wrote this information on the board. "I'd like you to work with the person who sits beside you. Together you are to find out how many squares are on my paper based on the information and the ideas we have shared."

"Do we record our work?" Tom asked.

"Yes, you will need to talk about and share ideas with your partner, but I want each of you to record your thinking on your own sheet of paper," I responded.

"Do we have to agree or can we talk about it and then decide to put different things on our paper?" Jackie asked.

"You should put whatever makes sense to you on your paper, Jackie," I replied.

"Can I use a ruler?" Amy asked.

"How would you use the ruler to help you?" I asked.

"I'm not sure. Maybe draw all the squares on my paper and then count them," Amy said after some thought.

"I think we're supposed to do it without a ruler and I have an idea of how to do it," said Steve, Amy's partner. Steve and Amy put their heads together and got to work as Steve explained his idea about how many half-inch squares it would take to go across the $8\frac{1}{2}$-inch page.

There were no further questions and the students got to work on the problem.

OBSERVING THE STUDENTS

As I observed the students working, I overheard Tom and Cori counting by halves to figure out the number of half-inch squares it would take to go across the top of the page.

Anamaria and Daniel had concluded that each inch was equal to two half-inches so each inch going across or down the page represented two half-inch squares. Anamaria explained to me, "We figured out the top by deciding first to forget the half-inch in eight and a half inches for a minute. So that left eight inches across. Each inch equals two half-inch squares, so you could go eight plus eight equals sixteen or eight times two equals sixteen. It's the same thing! Then add one more square for the last half-inch. That would make seventeen squares across. Now we are figuring out how many down."

I noticed that Ben was multiplying $8\frac{1}{2} \times$ 11. "Ben, what question are you trying to answer?" I asked him.

"How many squares are on the paper," Ben replied.

"How large are the squares?" I continued.

"One-half inch on each side," Ben said.

"I see you are using the numbers eight and a half and eleven. Why did you choose these numbers to help you figure out the number of squares on the paper? How do the numbers eight and a half and eleven relate to what you are trying to figure out?"

"They're how big the sides of the paper are," Ben explained.

In an attempt to help Ben figure out for himself that he was going down a road that might not get him where he needed to go, I showed him a sheet of paper ruled into 1-inch squares and the sheet I had already shown the class ruled into $\frac{1}{2}$-inch squares. "How many half-inch squares do you think fit along the top of the page?"

"Well for one inch that would be two squares, for two inches that would be . . . two squares and two squares more so that would be four squares, for three inches that would be two squares three times . . . it's a doubling pattern! It takes two half-squares for an inch. So if the paper is eight and a half inches, that would be eight times two, which is sixteen, and then half of a square?"

"Why half of a square?" I asked.

"Because it is eight and a half inches across, no wait, would it be one more square because one square is a half an inch? Would it be seventeen squares? It would be, I get it now!" Ben was busy figuring out the other dimension of the paper as I walked away.

I continued to observe and talk with the students as they worked, and a little while later I returned to check on Ben's progress. He had figured out the number of squares on each side of the paper and was in the process of calculating the total by multiplying 17 by 22. He multiplied as follows:

$$17 \times 10 = 170 \quad 170$$
$$170 \times 2 = 340 \quad 340$$
$$17 \times 2 = 34 \quad \underline{+34}$$
$$544$$

"Ben, talk to me about what you are doing here. I am a little confused," I said, noticing that Ben appeared to have lost track or didn't understand exactly what he was trying to figure out. "I notice that you seem to be trying to solve seventeen times twenty-two. What does that really mean?" I asked.

"It means that I am trying to figure how much is seventeen groups of twenty-two or twenty-two groups of seventeen," Ben explained.

"Seventeen or twenty-two groups of what?" I asked, wanting to keep Ben aware of the actual task of calculating the number of squares on the page.

"It depends on how you turn the paper, but either seventeen groups of twenty-two squares in a column or twenty-two groups of seventeen squares in the rows. Either way it will be the same amount of squares," he said.

Ben seemed to clearly understand the task. His confusion seemed to be in the abstractness of keeping track of the number of groups he was combining. When he added the partial products 170 + 340 + 34, he actually found the total for 32 groups of 17 rather than 22 groups of 17.

"Ben, I see you added one hundred seventy plus three hundred forty plus thirty-four. How many groups of seventeen are in one hundred seventy?" I asked.

"Ten," Ben replied quickly.

"So the one hundred seventy is ten groups of seventeen and you want to figure out twenty-two groups of seventeen. How many more groups do you need?" I asked.

"Uhhmm, twelve, because if I add twelve to the ten I already have, then that will make twenty-two," Ben replied.

"What does the three hundred forty represent?" I asked, returning to the list of partial products Ben had added to solve 17 × 22.

"Well, I think twenty groups because one hundred seventy is ten groups and one hundred seventy plus one hundred seventy is like ten groups plus ten more groups, so three hundred forty is twenty groups of seventeen," Ben said.

"So if I add three hundred forty to one hundred seventy, how many groups of seventeen will I have combined?" I asked.

"Oh, it would be thirty and that's too much!" Ben said with surprise and confusion. "When I multiplied one hundred seventy by two and got three hundred forty, then I didn't really need to think about the first one hundred seventy? Is that it?" Ben wondered. I paused for a moment because Ben will often ask questions aloud and then answer them correctly himself after a bit of thought. "Yeah, I think that's it! So I need to add three hundred forty, which is twenty groups of seventeen, to thirty-four, which is two groups of seventeen, then I will have twenty-two groups of seventeen, which is three hundred forty plus thirty four, which is three hundred seventy-four, yeah, that's it, three hundred seventy-four!" Ben concluded with a smile.

Tom, a student willing to explore his ideas in mathematics, had been waiting patiently for me to finish my conversation with Ben. He had tried his latest idea and wanted to share it.

Tom began, "I know I could multiply seventeen by twenty then add two times seventeen to figure out seventeen times twenty-two. But I thought I could take the two from the twenty-two and put it with the seventeen, then it would be nineteen times twenty instead of seventeen times twenty-two. That's almost twenty times twenty, which is really easy. Twenty times twenty is four hundred, two times two is four, twenty times two is forty, so twenty times twenty is four hundred. But that's one group too many, so I have to subtract one group of twenty from four hundred, which is three hundred eighty. But Ben got three hundred seventy-four. I'm confused. The way Ben did it makes sense but I checked my work for mistakes."

I paused for a moment to consider how to help Tom more clearly understand what was happening. It seemed that Tom was trying to simplify the calculation by changing 17×22 to 19×20, and finally subtracting 20 from the product of 20×20 to arrive at 19×20. However, the answer to 19×20 isn't the same as the answer to 17×22. Tom's strategy would work for an addition calculation; that is, $17 + 22$ is the same as $19 + 20$. But it doesn't work for multiplication.

Thinking through how to respond to Tom in the midst of a busy classroom wasn't easy. I had planned my lesson, but I hadn't prepared for his idea. I asked him, "Tom, what is it we are trying to figure out?" I decided that asking Tom to clarify the task might help him see why his idea didn't work for multiplication.

"How many squares are on the paper," Tom responded.

"What do you know about the grid?" I asked.

"They are half-inch squares and there are seventeen across and twenty-two rows of seventeen," Tom explained.

"In seventeen times twenty-two, what does the seventeen tell you?" I asked.

"There are seventeen squares across the top of the page and twenty-two rows if I hold the paper this way," Tom said, holding the paper so the short sides were the top and bottom. "That's twenty-two rows with seventeen in each row."

"When you changed the problem from seventeen times twenty-two to nineteen times twenty, what did that do to the meaning of the problem?" I asked.

Tom thought for a moment. "Oh, seventeen rows twenty-two times . . . that can be the same as twenty-two rows seventeen times if you turn the paper sideways. But nineteen times twenty would be nineteen rows of twenty or twenty rows of nineteen. Maybe that's why Ben and I got different answers. Maybe nineteen rows of twenty isn't the same amount as seventeen rows of twenty-two. It seems like that should have worked, but it didn't."

"How about you share your idea with the other students during the class discussion and maybe all of us can help you more clearly understand what is happening," I suggested. (Later on, I realized I could have asked Tom to construct a grid that was 19 by 20 and compare it to the 17-by-22 grid.)

Ben and Tom had given me important insights into their understanding. Both boys had misconceptions indicating confusion about the concept of "equal groups/groups of" in multiplication. This insight was important in helping me think about what to listen for as students shared their ideas during the class discussion. I looked around the room and noticed students were finishing. I gave a warning, indicating that they had three minutes to complete their work and then we would have a class discussion about what they found out.

A CLASS DISCUSSION

"What did you find out about how many half-inch squares are on an eight-and-a-half-by-eleven-inch sheet of paper?" I asked to begin the discussion. Most students were eager to share.

I called on Shelly. "I figured out that there are three hundred seventy-four squares on the paper. I know that for every inch there are two squares. One side is eleven inches. There are twenty-two squares on that side because eleven inches times two squares in each inch is twenty-two. The other side is eight and a half inches. Eight inches times two squares in an inch is sixteen. That leaves one-half of an inch, enough for one more square. Sixteen plus one is seventeen. There are seventeen squares on the eight-and-a-half-inch side. That means the grid is seventeen squares by twenty-two squares. Can I come to the board to show how I figured out the total squares?"

I nodded to Shelly. She wrote the following:

$$\begin{array}{ccccc} 22 & 2 & 20 & 10 & 20 \\ \underline{\times 17} & \underline{\times 7} & \underline{\times 7} & \underline{\times 2} & \underline{\times 10} \end{array}$$

Shelly explained her thinking as follows: "First I knew I could take twenty-two and seventeen apart to make twenty plus two and ten plus seven. I multiplied the ones, seven times two and got fourteen. Then I multiplied twenty by seven and got one hundred forty. Next I multiplied the two and ten and that made twenty, and last I multiplied the tens together, twenty times ten, and that equals two hundred. I added all the products up. Fourteen plus one hundred forty plus twenty plus two hundred equals three hundred seventy-four."

"How many thought of it the way Shelly did?" I asked the students. Several raised their hands. "Did someone solve it in a different way?" I asked.

I called on Cindy. Cindy explained, "Cori and I counted by halves. Like we counted one-half, one, one and a half, and so on until we had counted to eleven. Then we figured out how many times we had counted by halves. It was twenty-two. That meant that there were twenty-two squares on one side of the grid because each square was one half-inch and we had to count by half twenty-two times to get to eleven. We did the same thing on the eight-and-a-half-inch side. We had to count by half seventeen times on that side. We figured out that the grid was twenty-two squares by seventeen squares, like Shelly said. Next we had to figure out twenty-two times seventeen to know how many squares altogether. So we multiplied seventeen by ten. That equals one hundred seventy. Ten groups of seventeen is one hundred seventy, but we need twenty-two groups of seventeen. We multiplied seventeen by ten again and got one hundred seventy again. One hundred seventy plus one hundred seventy equals three hundred forty. Twenty groups of seventeen equals three hundred forty. We still needed two more groups of seventeen. That would be thirty-four. Three hundred forty plus thirty-four equals three hundred seventy-four."

Ben said, "I did mine sort of like Cindy and Cori, but I got confused and ended up figuring out the answer for thirty groups of seventeen instead of twenty groups by doubling one hundred seventy to get three hundred forty and then adding three hundred forty and one hundred seventy."

"I am still kind of confused by why my way didn't work," Tom added. "I thought that I could make twenty-two into twenty and add the extra two to seventeen to make nineteen. Then I could multiply twenty by twenty, which is really easy, and subtract one group of twenty to make nineteen groups of twenty. That didn't work and I don't really get why not."

The students thought for a few moments about what Tom had shared. Cori raised her hand. "What if we made a smaller problem. Maybe that would help us figure out why Tom's way didn't work." The students nodded their agreement with Cori's suggestion.

"You could get some tiles and you could try it with a smaller problem, like three times six," Rachel suggested.

"Tell me what to do with the tiles and why," I replied.

"First make three rows of six. You do that because of the three, which means three groups of, or it could mean three rows of. Then you put six in each group or row because of the six. That tells you how many in each group," Rachel explained. I did as Rachel had suggested, creating a rectangular array of tiles that was three tiles going vertically and six tiles going horizontally.

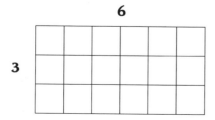

"Now what?" I asked.

"I'm not very sure," Rachel replied after a few moments of thought.

James had his hand up. James suggested that we think of another problem similar to 3×6 because that is what Tom had done when he changed 17×22 to 19×20. He suggested moving a 1 from the 6 to make 5 and move the 1 to the 3 to make it 4, which would change the problem from 3×6 to 4×5.

"How should I show James's idea using the tiles?" I asked.

"You could take the last column of three and move it to the bottom of the rectangle to change the problem from six rows of three to four rows of five," suggested Nicole. "I don't think it will work, though, because you will only have three tiles and there will be five columns, so two columns would not get another tile and then it wouldn't be a rectangle anymore."

Several students nodded, indicating that they agreed with what Nicole had shared. I did as Nicole had suggested and verified that indeed it did not work, as Nicole had predicted.

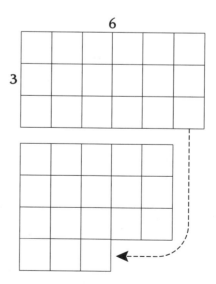

"Do you think we should try another example and see if the same thing happens?" I asked. The students agreed we should. We explored this time using 5×7.

Several students asked for tiles to help them think about this problem. Some talked with their partners about their ideas and some did their thinking using numbers but no concrete materials. Several students started with 5 × 7 and moved a 1 from the 7 to make the 7 a 6. They added the 1 to the 5 to make it a 6 also. They knew 5 × 7 was 35 and were still a bit surprised to find that changing the problem to 6 × 6 gave a product of 36. Others moved 2 from the 7, adding it to the 5 to change the problem from 5 × 7 to 7 × 5, which did give the same product. Students recognized, however, that while 5 × 7 and 7 × 5 will give the same product, the actual problem looks different; that is, 5 groups of 7 look different than 7 groups of 5. A few students even tried 3 × 9 and 4 × 8. I called the students back to order to discuss what they had found out. I listed the various problems they had investigated on the board for all to see.

Anamaria was the first to share. "I think the only way that Tom's idea will work is if when you move numbers around you move them so it's the reverse of how you started. For example, five times seven and seven times five."

"Why do you think this is so?" I asked the students.

"I think it has to do with groups. When we moved one group of tiles around it didn't fit exactly because when we did four times eight instead of five times seven, we moved the last group of five and there weren't enough tiles to put one in each group that was left," David shared.

Jackie said, "I sort of agree with David and sort of not. We did four times eight too, but we moved the bottom group of seven and not the last group of five. We discovered we had three tiles left over. We moved seven tiles and that was enough for each row of the four rows left to get one more, but not enough for each row to get two more. We gave each row one tile and had three tiles left over."

David's way

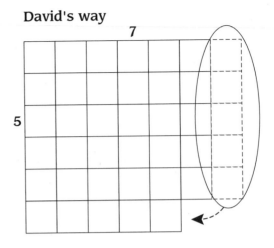

Jackie's way

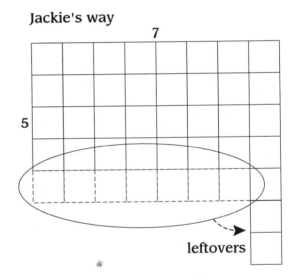

leftovers

Tom raised his hand. "I guess my idea doesn't work because it messes up the idea of how many groups and how big the groups are. If I move the numbers like I was doing, then I am changing the number of groups and their sizes and making a different problem. Hmm!"

This had been a useful discussion and exciting for me as a teacher to observe.

The students sat quietly, appearing to reflect upon what Tom had just said. "Does anyone have anything else you would like to add?" I asked. No one seemed to have anything further to add so I decided to move on.

"We have found out that there are three hundred seventy-four half-inch squares on an eight-and-a-half-by-eleven-inch sheet of paper." I paused and held up a second sheet of $8\frac{1}{2}$-by-11-inch paper, this one divided into 1-inch squares. "Are these squares larger or smaller than the squares we were just thinking about?" I asked.

"Larger," responded the class quickly.

"Do you think there will be more squares or fewer squares on this paper than the first?" I asked.

"Fewer because the squares are bigger. That means one square takes up more space so less of them can be on the paper," Daniel explained.

"I agree with Daniel. Just looking across the top, on the first paper, there were seventeen squares, and on this one I can see there are eight and an extra part of a square," Amy said.

"Eight and some is less than seventeen!" piped in Allie. "That makes me think there will be less squares altogether!"

"How big do you think the squares are?" I asked.

"I think an inch because it looks like there are about eight and a half across the top and I know the paper is eight and a half inches across," Cori explained. "That probably means there are eleven going vertically because the vertical side of the page is eleven inches." Cori paused to count the squares to check her thinking. "Yep, I counted eleven."

"If there are three hundred seventy-four half-inch squares on an eight-and-a-half-by-eleven-inch sheet of paper, how many one-inch squares do you think there are on an eight-and-a-half-by-eleven-inch sheet of paper?" I asked.

"One hundred!" Daniel quickly replied.

"Eighty-nine," Jackie said.

"Eighty-five," Cori said.

"Why?" I asked as students shared their estimates.

Cori explained, "I think there are less than one hundred, but near one hundred, because it seems like four little squares could fit in one larger square. Three hundred seventy-four is close to four hundred and four hundred divided by four is one hundred. There would have to be less than one hundred because I rounded up. There are really less than four hundred half-inch squares, so there has to be less than one hundred one-inch squares."

"Work with a partner to find out how many one-inch squares are on this paper. Even though you will be working with a partner, I would like each of you to use your own recording sheet to show me how you thought about this problem," I explained. I asked the students if they needed the paper ruled into 1-inch squares to help them solve the problem. They indicated they did not. I decided to respect that and chose to save the paper for later in the lesson as a way for them to verify their thinking. I quickly assigned partners and the students got to work.

Initially students approached the problem in one of two ways. They either wanted to divide 374 by 2, explaining that on each side of a large square it took two small squares to equal a large square, or they wanted to divide 374 by 4, explaining that four small squares could fit inside a large square.

They didn't seem to recognize something that was obvious to me and that I assumed they would notice. Even though the size of the paper and the size of the squares had been discussed, it was not readily apparent to some students that the grid was $8\frac{1}{2}$ by 11 inches and $8\frac{1}{2}$ by 11 squares. I had also assumed that students would choose to solve this problem using multiplication rather than division. I had assumed that this would be easy for students to see and was surprised that they didn't realize this. Once the relationship between the size of the squares and the size of the paper was realized, students quickly noticed that they could get the total number of squares by multiplying. Some still chose to divide, however.

When most students seemed to be finished, I gave the class a two-minute warning, indicating that they needed to finish, as we were ready to begin discussing what they had found out.

I called on Steve to share. "We think there are eighty-eight and a half squares because the grid is eight and a half by eleven squares. We multiplied the eight times eleven and got eighty-eight and then added the one-half to get eighty-eight and a half."

Rachel said, "We thought what Steve said at first. But then we thought really, really hard. There are really eleven groups of one-half, not one, like Steve said. There is a half-square in each row and there are eleven rows. That's why we think there are eleven halves instead of one. It should be eleven times eight, which is eighty-eight and then eleven times one-half, which is five and a half. You put those together and that equals ninety-three and a half squares."

The students looked puzzled and uncertain of either explanation. I decided to have them investigate and verify the correct number of 1-inch squares using the 1-inch grid paper.

"You look confused and not certain which explanation makes sense. I would like you and your partner to use a piece of paper ruled into one-inch squares to verify the correct number of squares," I explained. After giving the students a short work period, I called them back together.

"What did you find out?" I asked.

"I didn't agree with either Steve or Rachel. I thought the total number should be one hundred eighty-seven because I thought I should divide three hundred seventy-four by two. Boy was I surprised when I checked my answer using the one-inch paper!" Shelly shared.

"I thought like Shelly, too," Amy shared. "First it took seventeen squares to go across the top, then eight and a half. Eight and a half is half of seventeen, so I thought I just had to divide by two. It didn't work!"

"I think it partly worked. You did one side, but you forgot the other side of the square. You forgot to think about the vertical side. Half of seventeen is eight and a half, but the other side was twenty-two and now it's eleven, so you have to remember about both the vertical and the horizontal sides," Nicole said.

Anamaria shared, "When we did it the first time we divided three hundred seventy-four by four and it equaled ninety-three and a half. Then when we verified it using the paper, it still equaled ninety-three and a half. With the paper we did eleven times eight. The eleven was for the vertical side and the eight was for most of the horizontal side. There was an extra half-square in each row we had to come back to. Eleven times eight equals eighty-eight. Then the eleven half-squares were easy. We put two half-squares together to make a whole square. There were five pairs of halves that made wholes and one half-square left over. That made five and a half squares to add to eighty-eight. Eighty-eight plus five and a half equals ninety-three and a half."

I called on Ben next. "I knew it took four small squares to equal a large one. I started by dividing three hundred seventy-four by two and got one hundred eighty-seven and a half. Then I divided one hundred eighty-seven and a half by two again, because I needed to find out how many groups of four because it took four small squares to equal a large one and the first time when I divided I only found out how many groups of two. I got ninety-three and three-fourths. The three-fourths seems wrong because half of a half should equal one-fourth, not three-fourths. When I look at the grid, the three-fourths part just doesn't make sense."

I could see where Ben had made his error. When he divided 374 by 2 he somehow came up with an extra half. "What could you do to double-check your division for three hundred seventy-four divided by two?" I asked.

"Um, you should be able to add one hundred eighty-seven and a half plus one hundred eighty-seven and a half and get three hundred seventy-four," Ben responded.

"Try it, " I suggested.

"Oops! I see what happened. It should be one hundred eighty-seven not one hundred eighty-seven and a half. So half of one hundred eighty-seven is ninety-three and a half. I can see where the extra half would be on the grid. I get it," Ben said with a smile.

Cori and Rachel were eager to share their thinking. They thought they had a way of proving that four little squares equaled a large square. I asked them to come to the board and show the class their thinking. Cori drew a square on the board and labeled it on all sides as equaling an inch. Cori explained, "I am pretending my square is an inch on all sides. I labeled it to remind you it is supposed to be an inch. The small squares were one half-inch. I could put two half-inch squares inside the larger square along the top. It would take two to go across the top. Now think about the vertical side. One square is already there, but you would need a second one to fill in the side. So far, that is three squares. I need to add

one more to fill it in. That would equal four squares altogether."

"I just took my pencil and did this," Rachel said, dividing the larger square Cori had drawn into four smaller squares.

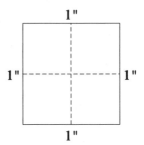

"Each of the smaller squares is one-half inch and it took four of them to fill up the large square. Simple, don't you think?" she asked her classmates. They giggled and seemed convinced.

EXTENSIONS

1. For more experienced students, present a third problem: "How many squares would there be on a sheet of paper ruled into three-quarter-inch squares?" Have students estimate first and then figure out the total. The fractions involved are an added challenge in this extension.

2. You probably won't have a student in your class suggest changing 17×22 to 19×20. But consider telling your students about Tom's idea and giving them the opportunity to grapple with it. The experience can be useful for enhancing their understanding of multiplication.

Questions and Discussion

▲▲▲

▲ *The class in the vignette had had many experiences in multiplication prior to this lesson. Does that mean a less experienced class should wait to do this activity?*

No, this exploration is appropriate for less experienced students as well. Less experienced students would be more likely to use strategies such as repeated addition or skip-counting. The students in the vignette did not use these strategies. As the result of many experiences and many class discussions involving multiplication, these students had developed more efficient methods of figuring, such as using the distributive property and multiplying by 10.

▲ *Why do you allow children working together to write different answers on their papers? Shouldn't partners agree?*

Students worked together in this activity to help each other think through the problem. As the students worked together and shared their ideas, they often did reach agreement. There are times, however, when students can't or won't agree. Demanding that partners come to the same conclusion runs the risk of forcing children to acquiesce to something they don't agree with. If encouraged to talk and share and then write what makes sense to them, they remain more engaged and open to other's ideas. This increases the student's learning and confidence.

▲ *In the vignette, you allowed Ben and Tom to struggle with their ideas. Why not just tell them the answer or what to do?*

When students are allowed to grapple with ideas with guidance and support from their teacher, they often will arrive at a correct solution. As a result, the learning is more likely to be long term than if the information is simply handed to them. Also, when students figure something out for themselves, the understanding is deeper and they are more likely to be able to apply their insights to new situations.

It is important to monitor student frustration. In the vignette, both Ben and Tom were willing to persist. Both were curious and wanted to know about their ideas. To have told them rather than to let them discover would have taken away a wonderful learning experience and the confidence that comes from accomplishing something that was challenging.

▲ *How could you explain to a student why it's not correct to change 17×22 to 19×20?*

One way might be to help the child think about the problem with simpler numbers. You might say: "Suppose the problem was three times five and you didn't like multiplying by three. You found it easier to multiply by two. So you changed the problem from three times five to two times six. That may make the problem easier, but it wouldn't produce the same answer!"

This shows that it doesn't work to change factors but doesn't explain why. Let's still think about 3×5. One way to show what that means is to draw three groups with five circles in each. If, however, you decided you only wanted two groups, then you'd have to take the third group and spread out those five circles, putting two and a half circles in each of the other two groups. (Remember that multiplication always has to have equal-size groups.) Dividing up the circles this way would change the problem to $2 \times 7\frac{1}{2}$, which produces the same answer. Changing the problem to 2 × 6, however, gave each group one more circle, leaving out the three other circles. And you can't just do that.

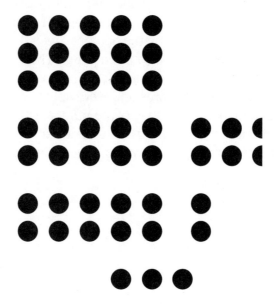

It might also help to think about 3 × 5 as a rectangular array. A 3-by-5 rectangle has an area of fifteen squares. Rearranging those same squares into a 2-by-something rectangle calls for adding two and a half squares to each of the two rows to make a 2-by-$7\frac{1}{2}$ array. A 2-by-6 array has only twelve squares in it.

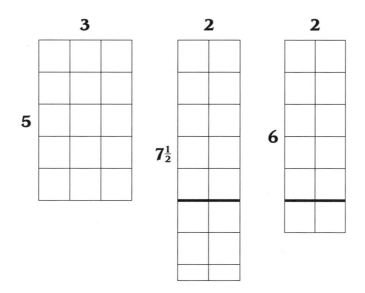

OK, back to 17 × 22. That's 17 groups of 22. If you take 2 from each of the 17 groups of 22 to make 17 groups of 20, that results in removing 34. Then, if you add two more groups to make 19 groups of 20, that results in adding 40 more. Removing 34 and adding 40 results in a net gain of 6, so the answer to 19 × 20 of 380 is too large by 6.

▲ *Why did you think it was valuable for children to estimate and explain their estimates?*

I asked the children to make estimates and explain them throughout this lesson. I did this to strengthen and build their number sense by giving them opportunities to make guesses, then verify the accuracy of their estimates by finding the actual answer. I began by asking students to estimate the number of squares on a sheet of squared paper. Their initial estimates were not particularly accurate because of a lack of prior experience. Once students made their initial estimates, they found the actual number of squares and were able to compare their estimates with reality. This experience helped them gain a sense of the number of $\frac{1}{2}$-inch squares on the grid. If this lesson is used as an introduction to *Covering Boxes,* then estimating and checking estimates lays the foundation for students to make sense of the larger numbers encountered in *Covering Boxes.*

CHAPTER 7
COVERING BOXES

Overview

This lesson presents students with a problem-solving investigation that provides experience with estimation, multidigit multiplication, and relating multiplication to finding the area of rectangles. Using boxes they bring from home and paper ruled into $\frac{1}{2}$-inch squares, students work in pairs to figure out the number of squares that would cover the surfaces of boxes. The activity engages students not only with multiplication but also with geometry and measurement.

Materials

▲ boxes, 1 per pair of students

▲ 18-by-24-inch newsprint, 1–2 sheets per pair of students

▲ paper ruled into $\frac{1}{2}$-inch squares, 5–7 sheets per pair of students, depending on box size (see Blackline Masters)

Note: About one week before starting this lesson, ask students to bring in an empty box from home. Boxes that work well for this project include those of the size of cereal boxes, cake mix boxes, and cracker boxes.

Time

▲ two class periods

Teaching Directions

1. If you have not done the *Calculating Squares* lesson with your students (see page 69), before continuing with this lesson, it is important to do at least steps 1–3 of *Calculating Squares* to introduce the class to calculating the number of squares in a grid. This supports students' ability to make sense and check for the reasonableness of the calculations they do as part of *Covering Boxes*.

2. Hold up a box for students to see and ask them to estimate the number of $\frac{1}{2}$-inch squares it will take to cover all faces of the box.

3. Explain and model what the students are to do as follows:

1. Trace one face of the box onto the squared paper, matching the edges of the face as closely as possible with the lines on the paper. If the face of the box is larger than one sheet of paper, tape sheets together until you have a sheet that is large enough.

2. Use the closest line when it is not possible to get all edges on a line exactly.

3. Cut out the paper face you traced and glue it to a large sheet of newsprint.

4. Explain to students that they are to trace all of the faces of their boxes onto squared paper, cut out their tracings, and glue them on newsprint. Then they are to figure the total number of $\frac{1}{2}$-inch squares it took to cover their boxes. Have students use a second strategy to verify their initial results.

5. After students have completed the assignment, lead a class discussion for students to share strategies, compare results, and reflect on the activity.

Teaching Notes

While students had experience representing multiplication as geometric arrays prior to beginning this lesson, they had not had much experience multiplying larger numbers. Most of the students were still in the process of learning the multiplication table. Some of the students had discovered that the pattern of adding a zero when multiplying by 10 could be a useful tool. A few had even recognized that this pattern of adding a zero could be extended to adding two zeros when multiplying by 100. Other strategies students were routinely using to multiply included using repeated addition, breaking a larger rectangle into smaller, more manageable rectangles in order to find the area of the larger rectangle, and relying on friendly, or landmark, numbers. A few students had started to make use of the distributive property. These same ideas were among the approaches children used to find the number of squares needed to cover their boxes.

Computation, problem solving, and number sense are all essential components of this activity. Computation practice is embedded in the problem-solving context of the activity. When students are engaged in finding the number of squares on the grid paper, then finding the area of each of the faces on their boxes, and finally figuring the total number of squares needed to cover their boxes, they are practicing computation with addition and multiplication. Not only are the students practicing computation, but they are also applying their number sense skills. The context of the problem keeps students constantly focused on making sense of the mathematics and checking for reasonableness of outcomes.

A valuable aspect of this lesson was for students to have a common problem-solving experience and then hear other students' approaches. The way the investigation is structured, going from a relatively easy situation to a somewhat more difficult situation, gives students access to the problem initially, then provides them with support to deal with increasingly difficult problems. This support is provided through class discussion of strategies, the use of concrete materials, and opportunities for students to make conjectures and then check them against reality. Additionally, asking students to solve a problem in more than one way encourages them to try new strategies, and they are supported through sharing ideas with fellow students and the use of lists of strategies made during class discussions. The chance to listen to other students' strategies allows children to consider methods of solving a problem that might be more efficient, leaving behind strategies that become cumbersome when working with larger numbers. Such potentially cumbersome strategies include skip-counting, making tally marks, and using repeated addition. Also, asking students to explain and justify their thinking encourages the development of understanding.

In the vignette that follows, children worked in pairs, sharing one box and recording their thinking and solutions about figuring out how many $\frac{1}{2}$-inch squares would cover its surface. In a concluding class discussion, students shared the strategies they used to figure the total number of squares needed to cover their boxes.

The Lesson

▲▲▲

DAY 1

I began by showing the students a sheet of paper ruled into $\frac{1}{2}$-inch squares. "Who remembers what we did with this paper?" I asked. We had previously worked on the problem of figuring out how many squares there were on one sheet of paper. (See page 69.) Students recalled the activity and many remembered that we had found out there were 374 squares.

I then held up a small cereal box for the students to see. "If I were to cover my cereal box with this squared paper, knowing there were three hundred seventy-four squares on each sheet, about how many squares do you think it would take to cover the whole cereal box?" I asked.

The students each talked this over with a partner for a few moments. Several were eager to share their estimates with the class. Kirk said, "Alicia and I think it would be about one thousand. One sheet has about four hundred squares. You'd use one sheet for the front, another for the back, and you could use a third sheet for the two side

faces. That's three sheets of four hundred, which is twelve hundred, but there would be some left over, so we think about one thousand squares."

"But there are six sides on the box. You didn't do the top and bottom," Jeni said. "Rob and I think it is about fourteen hundred. We thought the same thing as Kirk and Alicia, except we thought we would need another paper for the top and bottom." Most students nodded their heads, indicating that they thought this was reasonable.

Jeni made a very common error when she used the word *side* to describe the face of her box. Using correct mathematical language is important. I have found that reminding children gently of correct language encourages its future use.

"When we talk about this part of the box," I said as I pointed to a face of my box, "it is really called a face rather than a side. Often people call it a side, but the correct mathematical name is *face*."

Next I modeled how to trace the faces so that the edges of each face lined up as closely as possible with lines on the grid. I instructed the students, "Use the closest line when it is not possible to get all edges on a line exactly. Be sure to trace all faces." I decided to wait to give them the rest of the directions about cutting their tracings out and gluing them onto newsprint because this class had difficulty following more than a couple of directions at a time. I answered the few questions the students had and they got to work tracing the faces of their boxes onto squared paper. The students worked well together. Most pairs took turns tracing the faces and holding the boxes in place.

When several of the pairs had completed tracing, I asked the students to stop their work and gather on the rug so I could give them additional instructions. I had cut out a 22-by-15 tracing from one face of my box and glued it to a large piece of newsprint.

"Once you have finished tracing all the faces of your box, cut out what you traced and glue them onto a large sheet of newsprint, as I have done. Then figure out how many squares it took altogether to cover your box. What are some strategies you might use to figure this out?" I asked.

"I think you could just count them," Sandra said.

"You could count by how many there are in each row, like skip-counting," Brooke suggested.

"Could you show me what you mean?" I asked.

Brooke came to the front and counted one row. The row had twenty-two squares. "You could count by twenty-twos, but that seems like it might be sort of hard!"

"How many times should I count by twenty-two?" I asked.

Brooke paused and studied the array carefully. "Could I call on somebody to help me?" I nodded yes. She called on Conner.

"I think fifteen because there are fifteen rows of twenty-two," Conner explained. He came to the front of the room, counted the number of rows to verify his answer and to show Brooke and her classmates what he meant.

"So one strategy would be to count by twenty-two fifteen times," I said as I listed Brooke and Conner's suggestion on the chalkboard.

Hector posed the following thought: "I have another idea. It would be hard to count by twenty-twos, so could each twenty-two be broken into two tens with two leftover and then count by tens fifteen times and then count by tens fifteen more times then count up the leftovers?"

"What do the rest of you think about Hector's ideas?" I asked the class.

"I don't get it!" Jeni said with a bit of frustration. "Where did you get the tens and why do you have to count them fifteen times and then fifteen times again?"

"I think you could break twenty-two apart so the numbers would be easier. Twenty-two would be two tens and two ones. If I counted by twenty-two I would have to do it fifteen times, but there are two tens in twenty so if I count by tens, which is easy, then I would have to count them fifteen times twice because I broke the twenties into halves," Hector explained. Several of his classmates indicated they were following his thinking by nodding their heads. Jeni still did not seem convinced.

"It's sort of like counting a bunch of fingers. Like maybe you wanted to count the fingers on three kids. You could count by ten three times, three kids with ten fingers, or you could count by fives six times, three kids with two hands each, or six hands, and then count by fives six times," Kirk clarified.

Jeni seemed to want to think about this for a few moments, so I decided to move on and check back with her later.

"Maybe another way you could do it is by making 10-by-10 squares, which is a hundred. Then you could make rectangles from the leftover squares and multiply them like when we figured out how many squares were on the paper," Kasey said.

"Can you show us your idea?" I asked.

Kasey came to the front and, using a marker, drew two 10-by-10 squares on my grid. With the remaining squares, she drew two 5-by-10 rectangles and one 2-by-15 rectangle.

10×10	10×10	2×15
5×10	5×10	

"To find the total number of squares, what would I have to do next?" I asked Kasey.

"Oh, you would add up the number of squares in each of the rectangles."

I added Kasey's idea of making smaller rectangles to the list of strategies the students could use to solve the problem.

"I think you could just use multiplication. Count up how many on the side, then how many across the top, and then multiply those numbers together," Melissa said. I added Melissa's suggestion the list.

"Those are big numbers! Can we use calculators?" Calob asked.

"Calculators are an important tool. You may use them, but you must do three things: clearly explain what numbers you used and why, show where you got those numbers by clearly labeling your work, and show at least one other way to find the answer. Remember, part of your job when finding out how many squares it will take to cover your box is to explain clearly in writing how you got your answer, step-by-step." Calculators are an important tool and children should have access to them, but I also wanted the students to use what they knew to solve this problem. That is, I wanted them to use strategies such as repeated addition, making smaller rectangles then adding them together to find the total, using the distributive property ($22 \times 15 = 20 \times 15 + 2 \times 15$), using landmark, or friendly, numbers, or whatever made sense to them. After my explanation about the use of calculators, I added Calob's suggestion to the list of strategies.

The students were eager to get back to work. This problem was challenging enough to keep them very interested, but not so difficult as to overwhelm them. The cutting and pasting aspect of the lesson was especially valuable because having each face cut out of grid paper provided students a concrete way of figuring the area of each face as well as the total surface area of the box.

As I observed the students, I reminded them about labeling their work and clearly explaining their thinking. Students used a variety of strategies. Hector and Kasey had made some discoveries that they were using to help them solve the problem. They realized that opposite faces of their box were congruent, so once they knew the area of the front face, they also knew the area of the back face and simply had to double the area of the front. They also realized that they could put congruent faces together to form a larger rectangle and use the dimensions of the larger rectangle to find the combined surface area. For example, two of the faces were each 10-by-16 square units. Kasey and Hector made the two 10-by-16 rectangles into one larger 32-by-10, then applied what they knew about multiplying by 10 and found the area of 320 square units. Kasey and Hector understood each other so well that as they were recording their explanation, one child would write a few words, then the other child would write the next few words and somehow it came out to be a coherent explanation.

As students completed their figuring, I asked them to verify their work using a second strategy. I reminded them to refer to the list of strategies we had generated during our class discussion.

DAY 2

Students had worked hard on their solutions and had come up with a variety of interesting approaches, and I planned to have a class discussion for them to share their thinking with their classmates. Pairs of students showed the class their boxes, reporting the total number of squares it took to cover each box and the approaches they used to figure this out. In addition, the students shared various discoveries they had made during the course of the investigation. As the students explained, I listed the strategies they had used on the chalkboard.

Kirk and Alicia discovered that opposite faces of their box were congruent. They found the square units of the front face, then doubled it, then found the area of a side face and doubled it, then found the area of the top face and doubled it, then added this information together for the total.

Conner and Sandra had a box with a height of 25 units. The method they chose was specific to the situation and numbers involved. Recognizing that 25 was an easy number to count by, they figured out how many columns it would take to go around the box, then counted by 25 that number of times. They added in the area of the top and bottom, which they figured by multiplying the length times the width.

Jeni and Rob chose a large box and ran into numerous difficulties calculating with larger numbers. Rather than change to a smaller box, they persisted and eventually were able to figure out the number of squares needed to cover the box with the help of a calculator. They were especially proud that they got the largest answer!

After the students had shared, I asked them to reflect for a few moments on this investigation. "What did you like about this problem?" I asked the students.

"I liked working with big numbers," Anthony said.

"I thought drawing the faces was neat. I guessed it would only take about a couple of hundred squares to cover my box, but boy was I wrong! It took like over a thousand, or something like that!" Ana shared.

"It was a challenge but it didn't damage my brain or anything because I got it!" Kirk said.

"I think it would be interesting to see if someone else covered my same box, if they would get the same answer," Susanna said.

"It is interesting but not too hard, and it has big numbers," Rob said.

EXTENSIONS

1. This lesson makes an excellent follow-up or independent activity. To adapt the lesson in terms of skill level, using grid paper with larger squares will make the problem easier because the numbers will be smaller. Conversely, using grid paper with smaller squares will generate larger numbers and will increase the difficulty of the problem. Also, varying the size of the box will produce different challenges.

2. Students could use the same box, cover it with different-size grid paper, and compare the results. For example, have students cover a box first with $\frac{1}{2}$-inch grid paper and then predict and investigate what would happen if they covered the same box using 1-inch grid paper. Then ask students to predict what would happen if they covered the same box a third time using $\frac{1}{4}$-inch grid paper. Also, grid papers with different-size squares each give another experience, as done in the beginning part of the *Calculating Squares* lesson (see page 69).

3. After students have covered their boxes, you could hold a class contest. It would be like guess the number of jelly beans in a jar, but instead of jelly beans, students would make guesses about the number of squares that would cover a particular box. When students gain confidence with this activity, you could follow it with a more challenging activity. Put out a box and ask students to estimate the surface area of the box using a different-size grid paper. An additional twist would be to present students with a cylindrical box, such as an oatmeal box, and have them make estimates about the number of squares required to cover it.

Questions and Discussion

▲▲

▲ *Why do you think it is valuable for children to estimate and explain their estimates?*

I asked the children to make estimates and explain them throughout this lesson. I did this to strengthen and build their number sense by giving them opportunities to make guesses, then verify the accuracy of their estimates by finding the actual answers. If students have no idea of how many squares are on one sheet of grid paper, they will have no idea of how many squares it would take to cover one face of their box and they certainly will have no idea of how many squares would be needed to cover the entire box. When students have no idea what to expect, this exercise can become a meaningless manipulation of numbers. When children have a sense of what to expect, the likelihood of accurate, thoughtful work increases.

▲ *How did you decide what was the appropriate use of calculators in this activity?*

In this lesson, only a few students chose to use calculators. The students that used calculators had already shown one solution they had used to find the number of squares to cover their boxes.

There are some important issues to keep in mind regarding calculator use with children. To begin with, calculators are a tool used by adults to facilitate computation in everyday life. Before the calculator can be a useful tool, students must know what operation to use and what numbers to use, and they must have some idea of the approximate answer in order to decide if the answer generated by the calculator is reasonable.

Finding different answers to the same problem is a result that sometimes occurs when children use more than one approach to find the answer. When the calculator is one of the approaches, children often assume that the calculator answer is the correct answer. This is not always the case. Giving children the chance to experience this kind of situation is a useful example of why it is so important for them to make sense of the situation and to constantly check to see if their answers, whether generated by a calculator or some other means, are making sense.

▲ *It seems you rely on class discussion and recording to teach. How does this help children learn?*

In class discussions, students have the opportunity to share their own ideas as well as listen to the ideas of others. Recording on the chalkboard or on class charts provides a reference that students can refer to later in the lesson.

In the preceding vignette, Alicia is a good example of how this works. As I watched the students working to find the number of squares on the faces of their boxes, I noticed that Alicia was using groups of tally marks to represent the rows of squares on the grid. She drew sixteen circles with fourteen tally marks and counted them up to find the total. The use of tally marks is a strategy that was familiar and comfortable to Alicia and one she frequently used. For this problem, however, the use of tally marks was time-consuming and not very efficient. I reminded Alicia that while she was successful in finding the actual number of squares using tally marks, she needed to solve the problem a second way and compare the answers. At first Alicia was puzzled, then she remembered about the list of strategies I had recorded, chose one that was new for her, and again met with success, this time using a new and more efficient idea.

▲ *Why did you ask the students to solve a problem using two different strategies?*

Solving a problem using two different strategies encourages children to try new ideas and become more flexible in their approach to computation. Typically students will begin with a strategy that is comfortable for them. Because the student is comfortable and confident with the first strategy chosen, she is usually successful, which builds her confidence. If the student makes an error, it is easier for her to find it as a result of her comfort level.

When students solve a problem the second way, they are typically moving into more unfamiliar territory. The lists of strategies provide direction and choice, which helps prevent students from getting stuck. Monitoring and carefully posed questions from the teacher can provide guidance when needed.

Sometimes students get two different answers. This is a wonderful opportunity for students to investigate why they found different results when the situation calls for the same results.

▲ *Why did you have students work in pairs for this activity?*

There are many advantages to having students work in pairs. In this case, one advantage was practical: it made it easier to handle the materials. One student could hold the box firmly in place while the other student traced carefully around a face. This helped create accurate tracings of each face and greatly reduced the frustration that can occur when students work alone on this sort of activity. Having accurate tracings increases the likelihood students will make such discoveries as the opposite faces on a rectangular prism are congruent.

Another advantage is that when students work in pairs, there is a greater chance that while solving the problem at hand, each student's understanding will be strengthened and enriched as he listens to his partner's thinking and explains his own. This was a complex problem for these students and having another person to talk to helped keep students moving forward rather than getting bogged down and stuck, as often happens when students work alone on challenging tasks.

▲ *You have students working in pairs. When do you have students work individually so you can monitor how each is doing?*

When assessment is my primary purpose, I have students work independently. Also, there are learning situations when I give students the choice of working independently or with a partner. It is important for students to know how to do both. This lesson was not an assessment. In fact, students were exploring, conjecturing, and engaging in the act of learning. Additionally, there were practical reasons, such as handling the materials, that I chose to have the children working in pairs.

▲ *How do you support the use of correct mathematical language, such as the correct use of* side *and* face*?*

I make a focused effort to model and use correct mathematical language in all situations. I often say things like, "Mathematicians call this a face," or "This cube has six faces." I encourage children to use the correct language both in their discussions and in their written work. When appropriate, I gently correct students when mathematical language is misused or missing.

Another method I use is to keep mathematical vocabulary posted in a prominent place in the classroom. The words are listed along with a picture or short written meaning of the word. I encourage students to use this list in their writing and speaking. I add words to the list as they come up in lessons or discussions.

CHAPTER 8
THE GAME OF TARGET 300

Overview

Target 300 is a game that engages students in developing their number sense, computing, and problem solving. Students use the underlying place value structure of our number system as they multiply by 10 and multiples of 10. While multiplication is the focus, computational practice using addition and subtraction also occurs throughout the game. Students are involved in problem solving and applying their number sense when they make choices about the numbers to use to reach the target amount of 300.

Materials

▲ 1 die per pair (or some other way of generating the numbers 1–6, such as spinners or small pieces of paper numbered from 1 to 6 and placed in a bag)

▲ optional: rules for *Target 300* to distribute to students (see Blackline Masters)

Time

▲ one class period to introduce the game, then additional time for playing and discussion

RULES

You need:

a partner

1 die

The object of the game is to be the player whose total is closest to 300 after six rolls of the die. This means that the total can be exactly 300, less than 300, or greater than 300. Each player must use all six turns.

1. Each player draws a two-column chart on a recording sheet as shown, one column for each player.

Player 1	Player 2

2. Player 1 rolls the die and decides whether to multiply the number rolled by 10, 20, 30, 40, or 50, keeping in mind that each player will have six turns and the target amount is 300.
3. Both players write the multiplication sentence representing the first player's choice and product. For example, Player 1 rolls a 2 and multiplies it by 20, and both players write the multiplication sentence *2 × 20 = 40.*

Player 1	Player 2
2 × 20 = 40	

4. Player 1 hands the die to Player 2 and Player 2 follows the same steps as Player 1.
5. At the end of each turn, the player adds his or her new amount to the previous score to keep a running total.
6. At the end of six turns, players compare scores to see whose score is closest to 300 and record underneath the chart:

_____ won.

_____ was _____ points away from 300.

_____ was _____ points away from 300.

Teaching Directions

1. Using an overhead projector or the chalkboard, introduce the game by modeling with a student how to play.

2. Then have students play the game in pairs. Allow time for them to play several games.

3. Have a class discussion about students' strategies.

4. The next day, have students play again with a target of 600. Have them discuss how their strategies changed.

Teaching Notes

Previously, the students in the following vignette had had many experiences with *Silent Multiplication* and the pattern created when multiplying whole numbers by 10. The nature of our base ten number system is such that when one factor is 10, adding a zero to the right-hand side of the other factor produces the product; for example, $10 \times 4 = 40$ or $112 \times 10 = 1,120$. Class discussions and written work from students that emerged after participating in *Silent Multiplication* indicated that students were beginning to grasp this idea. This is a powerful pattern for students to be able to recognize and apply. Understanding this pattern allows students to be more efficient when computing multidigit numbers, and it helps them evaluate the reasonableness of their results.

While many students quickly recognize that $9 \times 10 = 90$, students who don't might use strategies such as counting by 10 nine times. A few students might recognize that $9 \times 1 = 9$ and add a zero to the first partial product of 9 to get a final product of 90. When solving a slightly more difficult problem such as 20×4, a student might count by 20 four times, or think $2 \times 4 = 8$ then multiply the partial product of 8 by 10 to get the final product of 80. In an even more complex problem such as 480×20, a student might think 480 doubled is 960, $960 \times 10 = 9,600$, or 48 doubled is 96, $96 \times 10 = 960$, 960×10 again equals 9,600. Or a student might realize that rather than multiplying by 10 twice, multiplying by 100 would accomplish the same thing: $96 \times 100 = 9,600$.

Target 300 encourages children to think about the strategies they use when multiplying and the choices they make when aiming for a target amount. The game reinforces thoughtfulness in problem solving and estimation. Also, because both partners keep a written record of their own choices as well as their partner's choices, each student is continually engaged not only with her own thinking but with her partner's as well.

The Lesson

▲▲

"Today I would like to share a game with you," I began. The students responded with interest, eager to hear more. "In this game you will be multiplying by ten, by twenty, by thirty, by forty, or by fifty." As I explained this, I wrote the following on the board for later reference by the students:

$\times 10$

$\times 20$

× 30

× 40

× 50

I continued with my explanation: "You will play with a partner. The goal of the game is to be the player closest to three hundred. You could get exactly three hundred, or you could get less than three hundred or more than three hundred, but the goal is to be the closest."

Allie had a question. "Does that mean that one person could have two hundred eighty, which is twenty away from three hundred, and the other person could have three hundred ten, which is ten away from three hundred, and the person with three hundred ten would win because they were closer to three hundred?"

"Allie asks a good question," I responded to Allie and the rest of the class. "Based on the goal, which is to be the player closest to three hundred, what do you think is the answer to Allie's question?" After a moment's thought, hands went up.

I called on James. "Even though the player with three hundred ten went over three hundred, that player would still win because they were ten closer to three hundred than the other player, who had two hundred eighty. That's what I think!"

"At first I thought the player with two hundred eighty would win because the other player went over three hundred," Rachel said. "But you said it was OK to go over three hundred, so I agree with James. The player with three hundred ten wins,"

The other students were nodding their agreement with Rachel and James. "You're both right. According to the information I have given you so far, the player with three hundred ten wins," I said to confirm their thinking. There were no further questions on this point, so I moved on.

"You will each have six turns," I continued to explain. "You must take all six turns; that is, you may not skip any. When it is your turn, you will roll one die. You must decide if you will multiply the number you rolled by ten, by twenty, by thirty, by forty, or by fifty. Remember, you want to have the score closest to three hundred and you must take all six turns."

"Oh, this will be easy and fun!" Steve said. "Do we have to write?"

"Good question, Steve," I responded. "Yes, you will have to write to record how the game goes. First, before I show you how to do that, I would like to have a partner to help me play the game and show all of you how to do the recording part." Hands immediately shot into the air. I called on Ben because I knew he had a good grasp of his multiplication facts and how to multiply by 10. I did not want the other students to have to wait as my opponent struggled to figure out the basic facts, nor did I want to subject a child to this struggle in front of the class.

"When you play this game, each of you will need your own recording sheet," I said as I drew two two-column charts on the board, one for me and one for Ben. "I will put Ben's name on one side of the chart and mine on the other," I said as I labeled my chart. Ben did the same on his.

Ben	Mrs. Wickett

"It is a good idea to put the chart in the middle of your paper so you will have enough room to write," I added.

I decided to go first so I could model out loud my thinking process as well as how to record my turn. I rolled the die. "I rolled a one," I said to Ben and the rest of the class. "My goal is have the score closest to three hundred. I will have six turns. One is not a very large number. If I multiply one by ten that will only give me ten. I will still have two hundred ninety to go in five turns. That seems like a lot. Maybe I should multiply by thirty: one times thirty equals thirty. Thirty is closer, but I still have two hundred seventy to go. I think I will multiply the one I rolled by fifty: one times fifty equals fifty. That is closer still and it means I am only two hundred fifty away from three hundred. That's better! Do you agree that one times fifty equals fifty?" I asked Ben. Ben nodded his agreement. I recorded my turn on my side of the chart as shown.

Ben	Mrs. Wickett
	1 × 50 = 50

Once Ben had recorded my turn on his chart, I handed him the die, indicating it was his turn.

Ben rolled a 2. "I am going to multiply the two I got by ten. That gives me twenty. I don't want to get too close to three hundred early in the game in case I get big numbers at the end," Ben shared with the class. We both recorded his turn on our own charts and checked each other's work for accuracy. Ben handed the die back to me.

This time I rolled a 4. "I am going to multiply the four I just rolled by twenty. That will give me eighty for this turn," I said. "Do you agree that four times twenty equals

eighty?" I asked Ben. He nodded his agreement. "This time when I record my turn, I will record four times twenty equals eighty, then I will add the fifty from my first turn to the eighty I just got, for a running total of one hundred thirty," I explained as I wrote my score on my chart.

Ben	Mrs. Wickett
2 × 10 = 20	1 × 50 = 50 4 × 20 = 80 ─────── 130

"How come you didn't multiply four times fifty?" wondered David. "That would have given you two hundred. Add the two hundred to the fifty from your first turn and that would be two hundred fifty. You could almost win on your second turn."

Several students put their hands up in response to David's thoughts. I was interested in what the students were thinking. Rather than respond to David myself, I decided to let a student respond. I called on Cindy.

"Each player has to take six turns. This is Mrs. Wickett's second turn. That means she *has* to take four more turns. If she got two hundred fifty by the end of her second turn, then she could only get fifty more to get exactly three hundred, which is as close to three hundred as you can get! To do that she would have to always roll really low numbers and multiply by ten. She probably wouldn't get four low numbers, like one or two, for four turns in a row. She would probably get some low, some medium, and some high, which would mean she would get way over three hundred and would lose. That's what I think!"

Most students nodded their agreement as Cindy explained her thinking. There were a few who did not seem convinced. I decided that rather than continue to discuss this point I would move on, hoping that observing the game as it was played would clear any remaining confusion. "I think the point Cindy is trying to make is one that will be clearer to you after you have had the chance to watch the rest of this game and play for yourself," I said. I handed the die to Ben, indicating it was his turn. Ben rolled a 1.

"I am going to multiply one times thirty to get thirty," Ben said as he recorded his turn on his chart. I did the same on my chart. "I had twenty on my first turn and now I have thirty more so the total is fifty." Ben and I looked over what each other had written and then he handed me the die.

"I rolled a six!" I said.

"You could multiply six times fifty and get three hundred!" Mario said. "Too bad you have to take six turns!"

"Mario is right. I could get three hundred by multiplying six times fifty. But that would be too big. What would work better?" I asked the class. Hands immediately went up. I called on Allie.

"I think ten because if you multiplied six times ten that would be sixty," Allie shared. "If you add sixty to the one hundred thirty from your other turns you'll have one hundred ninety. Subtract one hundred ninety from three hundred and that means you still have three turns to get . . . one hundred ten? Yeah, one hundred ten more points."

"If Allie's thinking makes sense to you and you think I should take her advice, put your thumb up, if not, put your thumb down. If you are not sure or you are confused, put your thumb sideways," I said. I wanted to check quickly on the students who had seemed confused earlier. I was pleased to see all students indicated that Allie's thinking made sense. The discussion seemed to be helping.

Ben and I recorded my turn on our charts. I handed the die back to Ben. He rolled a 5. His eyes lit up!

"Look, I can win!" he said. "I just multiply five times fifty. That equals two hundred fifty. Two hundred fifty and fifty is three hundred! I win unless you get three hundred too, then we would tie," Ben explained.

Several students moaned. Ben looked a bit surprised by their reaction.

"Ben, you still have three more turns! You have to take them," Leigh reminded Ben.

"*Oooops*!" Ben said, giggling. "I made a mistake! I forgot I had to take all six turns. Can I change my turn?" he asked.

"Sure," I said. "What are you going to do differently?"

"Multiply five by ten. That only equals fifty, which makes my total one hundred. That's way better," Ben said as he recorded his turn on his chart and handed me the die.

I rolled a 5 and multiplied 5 by 10 to get 50. My total so far was 240. Ben and I recorded my turn and checked each other's work. I gave the die back to him.

"I rolled a three," Ben said. "That's good for me. Let's see, if I multiply three by thirty that's ninety so I would have one hundred ninety altogether. If I multiply three by twenty that would be sixty. I would have one hundred sixty altogether if I did that. I still have two turns." Ben paused for a moment to think this over further. "I think I will multiply three by twenty and get sixty." Ben wrote the multiplication sentence on his chart and added the 60 to his previous total of 100 for a new total of 160.

"Look, Mrs. Wickett has two hundred forty and Ben only has one hundred sixty. I think Mrs. Wickett is going to win," Michelle said. The students discussed this among themselves briefly as Ben handed me the die and I rolled.

"Uh oh!" I said, "I got a five. I had better multiply it by ten. That means I get fifty for this turn and my running total is two hundred ninety. I still have one more turn."

"I think you're in trouble!" James said. Several students nodded their agreement with James. Ben looked pleased with the situation. We recorded my turn and I handed the die to Ben.

Grinning, Ben rolled the die. He rolled a 2. The students chatted excitedly with one another about what Ben could do.

"I know what to do," Ben told the students as they gave him unwanted advice. "I am going to multiply two by fifty for one hundred. One hundred sixty from before and one hundred more gives me two hundred sixty," he said as he filled in his chart. "I am in much better shape than Mrs. Wickett!"

"What do you think about Ben's statement that he is in better shape than me?" I asked the excited students.

"Well, you have to roll a one and multiply it by ten to get exactly three hundred. That's going to be unlikely," Steve said.

"Why do you think it is unlikely?" I asked.

"Well . . . I don't know, it just doesn't seem like that will happen," Steve said, shrugging.

"Does anyone else have any ideas about why Steve's idea of rolling a one might be unlikely?" I asked.

"I think all the numbers on the die have the same chance of being rolled. There are six sides on a die. One is on only one side of the die so it has one out of six chances of being rolled," Rachel explained. If the students had not realized this, I would have shown them a die and explained this idea to them.

"Mrs. Wickett can only get exactly three hundred one way, by rolling a one," Tom added. "But Ben can get exactly three hundred in more than one way. He needs forty points. He could get forty by rolling a one and multiplying by forty, or getting a two

and multiplying by twenty, or getting a four and multiplying by ten."

"That means that he could win by rolling three of the six numbers on the die." Cindy observed.

"Yeah, I think that's right, because he could roll a one, a two, or a four and be able to get exactly three hundred," Leigh said.

"I see what Ben means by he is in better shape than me!" I said. "I'll roll the die and let's see what happens."

"I got a three," I said with disappointment. Ben looked delighted at my situation.

"Well you just have to make the best of it and multiply the three by ten," Cindy said.

"That gives me a final total of three hundred twenty," I said as I took Cindy's advice and recorded my turn on my chart. As Ben completed his chart I handed him the die. Giggling with delight and anticipation of getting exactly 300, he rolled. He got a 3.

"Oh!" he said with a surprise. "I didn't get a one, a two, or a four." He paused for a moment to think the situation over. His classmates sat quietly, waiting to see what he would do.

"Ben, you can still win," Rachel said.

"I know, I could multiply three by ten, which is thirty, so my total would be two hundred ninety," Ben said. "Then I would be ten away from three hundred and Mrs. Wickett is twenty away." The class began to cheer and Ben did a little victory dance to celebrate his win. I waited for a few moments for the students to settle down. "When you finish your game, there are a few things I want each of you to write on your recording sheet," I said. "I want you to write who won and how far away from three hundred each player was." I wrote the following on the board under my chart to remind students:

Ben won.

Ben was 10 points away from 300.

Mrs. Wickett was 20 points away from 300.

Ben	Mrs. Wickett
2 × 10 = 20	1 × 50 = 50
1 × 30 = 30	4 × 20 = 80
50	130
5 × 10 = 50	6 × 10 = 60
100	190
3 × 20 = 60	5 × 10 = 50
160	240
2 × 50 = 100	5 × 10 = 50
260	290
3 × 10 = 30	3 × 10 = 30
290	320

Ben won.
Ben was 10 points away from 300.
Mrs. Wickett was 20 point away from 300.

I also wrote the following prompts on the board for students who might need them:

_____ won.

_____ was _____ points away from 300.

_____ was _____ points away from 300.

"Are there any questions?" I asked.

"Can we choose our own partners?" Chris asked.

"This time I want you to play with the person next to you. Next time you will be able to choose your own partner," I said. "I will bring you paper for recording your game and a die. Be sure to put your name on your recording sheet. Record both your turn and your partner's and be sure to check each other's work for accuracy," I reminded the students as I passed out the materials. I chose to pass out the materials myself and assign the partners to save time. Normally I like to give children the responsibility of getting their own materials and at times I like to give them a choice about who their partners will be, but because of the various discussions, the remaining time was short.

The students played the game with great enthusiasm and involvement as partners participated in every turn. Students could be overheard developing strategies and making observations about efficient ways to multiply. Jeni spent some time explaining ideas about this to her partner,

Susanna. "If you look at five times fifty, there is a basic fact in there. Do you see it? It's five times five. Well, five times five makes twenty-five. Then there is a zero after the five in fifty so you have to add a zero to twenty-five to make two hundred fifty."

Susanna responded to Jeni's explanation with, "Why?"

Jeni thought for a moment and shrugged her shoulders. "I have no idea, really. It just works. I think it is like counting by tens. You know, like counting by one five times is five and counting by ten five times is fifty . . . "

I paused and thought for a moment, wondering if I should intervene or let the girls grapple with this problem for a bit. Because they seemed to be making forward progress with their thinking, I decided to let them grapple with it for a while.

"I know that I can count by fifties. So if I did that five times, it would be fifty, one hundred, one hundred fifty, two hundred, two hundred fifty, but I don't get that other part, Jeni," Susanna said.

"Let's try another problem and see if it still works," Jeni suggested. "Let's try thirty times four. Three times four equals twelve and add the zero and it's one hundred twenty. Counting by thirty four times is thirty, sixty, ninety, one hundred twenty. That one works, too! It just works, Susanna! I don't know why!"

Cori, another member of the table group, had been listening to the girls. "It just works because when you count anything ten times, it ends with a zero. You count one ten times, it makes ten, one with a zero, you count two ten times it makes twenty, a two with a zero. You count ten ten times it makes a one hundred, which is a ten with another zero. And thirty is like counting by ten three times so multiplying by thirty is like multiplying ten by three."

After listening to Cori explain it, I decided I was glad I had not interfered with the conversation, as I think she had a nice way of explaining this idea. More importantly, it seemed to help Susanna.

For the students that finished their games quickly, I asked them what they learned from playing the game, then I suggested they play a second game. Once all students had completed at least one game, I asked for their attention. "What is one strategy that you found useful in this game?" I asked.

"It's better to multiply the bigger numbers, like five or six, by ten, especially earlier in the game," Michelle observed.

"If your total gets too big too early, you go too far over three hundred. It's harder to control where you end up," Tom added.

"Multiplying most of the numbers by either ten or twenty was usually a pretty safe thing to do," Leigh said.

Thinking back on the conversation I had overheard involving Susanna, Jeni, and Cori, I decided to ask the following question: "Is there any way knowing your basic facts could help you with this game?"

"Actually if you know your basic facts and how to multiply by ten, this is a very easy game, at least the multiplication part," Jeni shared. "In all the problems we made, there was a basic fact in the problem. Like in three times forty, for example, three times four is twelve. And if you multiply twelve by ten you get one hundred twenty, which is what three times forty equals. You could check to make sure by counting by forty three times: forty, eighty, one hundred twenty. See! It works!"

"That's what we figured out, too," James added. His partner, Tom, nodded his agreement.

"You had to use some strategy in this game. Like you had to be careful about how many turns you had left and how close you were to three hundred. Sometimes I had to solve a couple of problems before I chose the one I thought was best for that turn," Rachel shared.

"There was subtraction in the game, too," Mario said. "I had to subtract how many points I had from three hundred to see how far away I was."

"We did addition when we figured out our total points," Steve said.

No one had anything else to add. I said, "Tomorrow we are going to play again. The rules and how we record will be exactly the same. The one thing that will be different is that instead of trying to reach the target number of three hundred, our target number will be six hundred. Do you think the strategies you used today will be the same or different?"

"I think different because we will be trying to get a larger number so we should multiply by forty or fifty or we won't get enough," Ben shared.

"I don't think you should always multiply by bigger numbers, but I think you should more often than in *Target Three Hundred*," Cindy said. Most students indicated their agreement with Cindy by nodding their heads.

"We'll find out tomorrow!" Rachel added.

Questions and Discussion

▲▲

▲ *What do you do about tie games?*

A tie game such as Cindy's and Julie's is fine in our classroom (see Figure 8–1). Students simply go on to play another game as they would if there were a winner. If you and your students would prefer games not to end with a tie, each player could take one additional roll as a tie breaker when needed. Or, before play begins, students could discuss their ideas about how a tie should be broken and then decide together.

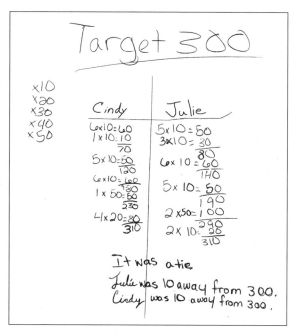

▲▲▲▲▲▲Figure 8–1   *Cindy and Julie's game.*

▲ How can this activity be adjusted to meet the needs of different levels of students?

Target 300 is very versatile. By changing the target number, you also change the arithmetic that students practice. For example, changing the game from *Target 300* to *Target 200* gives students increased practice multiplying by 10. The small target number of 200 encourages multiplying by 10 while discouraging multiplication by multiples of 10. Because the students in the vignette had had practice multiplying by 10 and multiples of 10 when participating in *Silent Multiplication*, I chose to have them play *Target 300* rather than *Target 200*.

Target 600, the game the students in the previous vignette played the following day, encourages students to multiply by the larger multiples of 10.

If you wish to give students practice multiplying by 100 and multiples of 100, change the target number to 2,000 (for practice multiplying by 100), 3,000, or 6,000 (for practice with multiplying by 100 and multiples of 100). My experience has been that the students especially enjoy the larger target numbers. (See Figure 8–2 on page 102.)

▲ What about the child who still doesn't know the multiplication facts?

There are several ways a child in this situation can be supported. First of all, the student can use addition or skip-counting to solve these problems. For example, if a child is trying to solve 3×40, the student could add $40 + 40 + 40$. Or the student could count by 40 three times: 40, 80, 120. Or the student might notice that 3×4 is 12 and count by 10 twelve times.

A multiplication chart can be used for reference to solve problems such as 3×4. Then the student could apply the pattern of adding a zero in the ones place when multiplying by 10, a pattern that reveals itself in *Silent Multiplication*.

▲ Why do students have their own recording sheets?

When children are actively involved, in this case by recording all turns on their own recording sheet, learning increases. There is no downtime. Students' work is more accurate because

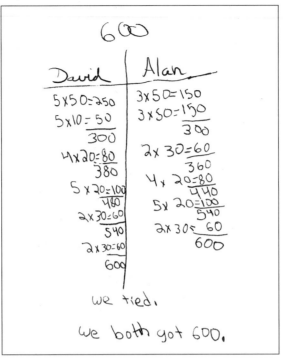

▲▲▲▲▲Figure 8–2 *David and Alan's game.*

two students are considering the computation. Communication is encouraged as students talk to one another and work together. Discipline problems are close to nonexistent because children are involved and learning. With little or no discipline, I have the opportunity to observe and give additional challenges to those that are ready or help students individually as the need arises.

▲ *What is the purpose of making a player wait until the die is handed to her or him?*

Asking players to wait until the die is handed to them is a way of slowing the game down so both players are in the same place at the same time. It prevents situations in which one player hurries another by grabbing the die. This kind of behavior is common and results in frustration and arguments, ultimately interfering with the mathematics and learning.

▲ *What is the value of playing games in math class?*

Games provide a good opportunity for students to practice skills. In this case they are practicing basic facts and multiplying by 10 and multiples of 10. I make it a practice to ask students about the mathematics involved in games, as I did toward the end of the vignette. I find this practice especially helpful because the student can then explain to the parent where the math was in the game he played in school or brought home for homework. This helps everyone more clearly see that learning is, in fact, taking place and there is a valid educational reason for the game.

▲ *Could this game be used for homework?*

Absolutely. The rules for the game are simple and the game is interesting enough to engage both students and an older sibling or parent. The experiences and insights students gain by playing at home can be the foundation for a rich class discussion involving additional strategies discovered. Also, the game is an opportunity for students to explain what math is being used. If dice are not available to students at home, have them put six slips of paper numbered 1 to 6 in a paper bag and draw a slip on each turn.

CHAPTER 9
TWO WAYS TO COUNT TO TEN

Overview

This lesson is based on the book *Two Ways to Count to Ten,* retold by Ruby Dee (Henry Holt, 1990). The story provides a context for students to explore ways to count to 10, thus finding the factors of 10. Later, they go on to investigate the factors for (or ways to count) the numbers from 1 to 50, creating a class chart listing what they find. Besides allowing them to investigate factors, this lesson provides students with the opportunity to think about patterns found on the class chart, prime and composite numbers, and square numbers.

Materials

▲ *Two Ways to Count to Ten,* retold by Ruby Dee (Henry Holt, 1990)
▲ paper bag containing small paper squares each labeled with a number from 1 to 50
▲ class chart numbered from 1 to 50 (see below)

Number	Factors	Number	Factors
1		26	
2		27	
3		28	
4		29	
5		30	
6		31	

Time

▲ two class periods

Teaching Directions

1. Tell the story of *Two Ways to Count to Ten*. If you'd like, show the children the illustrations from the book. **Note:** I tell the story rather than read it to avoid the outdated and sexist references to the king's desire to give away his daughter in marriage as part of the prize awarded to his successor. I begin by explaining to the students that the king of the jungle was looking for a successor, or someone to take his place, and wanted to find the cleverest animal in the jungle. I leave out the part about the king giving away his daughter in marriage as part of the prize but tell the story much as it is written after that reference. I use the illustrations in the book to guide my storytelling.

2. After telling the story, ask students to share other ways to count to 10. Record their ideas on the chalkboard, a chart, or an overhead for later reference. Introduce the idea that numbers you can use to skip-count and land on a target number are factors of that number. Record the factors of 10 on the board: *10: 1, 2, 5, 10.*

3. Discuss with the students the factors of 12. Record *12: 1, 2, 3, 4, 6, 12.* Point out that factors come in pairs. Record again to show this: *12: 1, 12, 2, 6, 3, 4.*

4. Post the class recording chart and show the class the paper bag of numbers. Tell them: "Working in pairs, you'll draw a number from the bag and figure out its factors. After checking results with me, you'll record the factors on the class chart."

5. After the class has posted the factors for the numbers from 1 to 50, have students work in pairs to explore patterns they notice on the chart. To initiate this, describe the pattern of the number of factors starting with 5 and doubling: 5 has two factors, 10 has four, 20 has six, 40 has eight, and so on. Doubling in this way increases the number of factors by two each time.

6. Lead a class discussion for students to share the patterns they noticed. Discuss with students the definitions for prime and composite numbers and why only square numbers have an odd number of factors. Also, discuss what happens when you multiply two even factors, two odd factors, and one even and one odd factor.

Teaching Notes

In the story, the king of the jungle holds a contest to choose the cleverest animal to be his successor. The animal who can throw the spear into the air and count to 10 before it falls to the earth again will be declared the next ruler of the jungle. Many animals try and fail, until the antelope counts by 2s rather than by 1s, as the previous animals had done, and wins the contest. This story introduces counting to 10 by 1s and 2s. Students think about how else to count to 10, thus identifying the factors of 10 to be 1, 2, 5, and 10. While students in the vignette explored a variety of mathematical ideas, the focus throughout the experience remained on factors, factor pairs, and multiples, important knowledge for multidigit multiplication as well as for division, fractions, and later, algebra. Students also investigated square, prime, and composite numbers, and learned why the number 1 is neither prime nor composite. They also explored patterns and relationships among multiples of different numbers, such as 2, 4, 8, and 16 or 5, 10, 20, and so on.

The Lesson

▲▲

DAY 1

As the students sat on the floor so they could easily see the illustrations, I told the story of *Two Ways to Count to Ten*. I explained to the students that the king of the jungle was looking for a successor, or someone to take his place. The successor would be the cleverest animal in the jungle. I left out the part about the king giving away his daughter in marriage as part of the prize, telling the story much as it is written after that reference. The students enjoyed the story and appreciated the cleverness of the antelope who won the contest.

After I finished telling the story, I asked students, "Besides counting to ten by ones and by twos, are there other ways to count to ten?" I paused a moment, giving the students a chance to think. Hands went up quickly. To give as many students as possible the opportunity to share their ideas, I asked the students to take a moment and each share their thinking with a neighbor. After a few moments I asked for the students' attention.

Most students had their hands up, eager to share their thinking. I called on Daniel. "You could count by tens. You would count zero, ten!" Daniel said, pleased with his answer.

"Ten is a multiple of ten," Jackie said.

I was uncertain of Jackie's use of the word *multiple*. Students frequently confuse multiples and factors. While it is true that 10 is a multiple of 10, in this context she should have used the word *factor*. I was not certain if she simply got the two words mixed up or if she was confused about the concept of multiple and factor. "The multiples of ten are ten, twenty, thirty, and so on," I explained. As I explained this I wrote the word *multiple* on the board along with listing some multiples of 10. "If we are thinking about ways to count to ten, we aren't really thinking about multiples."

"Oh, a multiple is sort of like a 'counting by' number. Multiples of ten are numbers you get when you count by ten. That's not what I meant," Jackie replied.

"Maybe she meant factor. You multiply factors to get a product," said Steve, who was using a math-related vocabulary chart, which was always posted in the room.

"Oh yeah," Jackie said as she checked Steve's suggestion for herself on the vocabulary chart.

Rachel redirected the conversation when she shared, "You could also get to ten by fives: five, ten."

"What about threes?" Allie said.

"Try counting by threes and see if you land on ten," I responded.

"Three, six, nine . . . uh oh! I don't think that works!" Allie said.

"What if you did something like four, eight, skip some, ten?" David asked.

"What do you think about David's idea?" I asked the rest of the class.

"I think you have to skip-count by a number that lands on ten. Otherwise, why bother? You could just do anything!" Cori said.

"I agree with Cori. Threes didn't work for Allie because counting by threes doesn't land on ten. So 'skip a few' shouldn't work," Anamaria shared. "Besides, what does that mean? A few could mean anything!"

"It sounds like multiplication. You have to have equal groups. It's sort of like factors in a way," Tom explained thoughtfully.

"Yeah, Tom's right! It is factors. You can count to ten by ones and land on ten. One is a factor of ten . . . and everything else. You can count by twos and land on ten. Two is a factor. Three doesn't work and three is not a factor of ten. There is no number you can multiply three by to make ten . . . unless it's a fraction or something," Shelly said, clarifying her thinking.

"If what Shelly said is right, then if you can count by two and land on ten, then you should be able to count by five and land on ten because two times five is ten. And you can count by five and land on ten, so it works!" Nicole said.

If the students had not made this observation about factors, I would have explained to them that when it is possible to skip-count by a number and land on the target number exactly, in this case 10, then the number used to skip-count is a factor of the target number.

In order to summarize the discussion so far, I asked the following, "We know factors are numbers we can use to skip-count and land on a target number exactly, in this case ten. What are the factors of ten? Or another way to think about it, what numbers can we use to skip-count and land exactly on ten?" Because most of the students had their hands up, I asked them to list the factors together using whisper voices.

"One, two, five, and ten," they responded.

I recorded this information on the board as follows:

10: 1, 2, 5, 10

"Let's think about a different number. What about twelve? What are the factors of twelve?" I continued. I asked the students to confer with their neighbors.

"What did you decide?" I asked after a few moments.

Amy began, "Well, because twelve is an even number, Jackie and I decided that two had to be a factor because two is a factor of all even numbers, right Jackie?" Jackie nodded her agreement. Amy continued, "Like as an example, four is an even number and there are two twos in four. And eight is an even number, too, and you can go two, four, six, eight. See, it works. Two must be a factor of all even numbers."

The students listened carefully to Amy's explanation and nodded their agreement as she spoke. I recorded Amy's suggestion on the board as follows:

12: 2

"I know two more factors of twelve," Ben shared. "Three and four. I know because three times four equals twelve. And I know I can skip-count by both three and four and land on twelve. Three times four means three groups of four or four groups of three."

"Ohh! Ohhh! I get it!" Juan said. "The factors are in pairs; it's like the multiplication facts! Three and four are factors and they are a pair of numbers that make twelve. That's cool. Amy said two is a factor, so I think there must be something that goes with two. But I am not sure what. Can I call on someone?"

Juan called on David. "It has to be six because two groups of six, or two times six, equals twelve."

"Oh yeah!" Juan said. "I knew that!"

I added 3, 4, and 6 to the list of factors of 12.

"You forgot a pair," James noticed after serious study of the list.

"How do you know?" I asked.

"Well, it's quite simple really. You forgot one, which can go into any number evenly, and twelve. There is always exactly one group of whatever number you are doing. So we are doing twelve, there is one group of twelve, so one and twelve are factors of twelve."

I added James's suggestions to the list, which now read as follows:

12: 1, 2, 3, 4, 6, 12

I listed the numbers as above and then asked the students if they could think of a better way to list them so that they would have a way of knowing when they had all the factors.

"Instead of listing them in order, if you listed them in pairs, it might be easier to keep track," Cori suggested.

I wrote the following: *12: 1, 12, 2, 6, 3, 4.* "Like this in factor pairs?" I asked Cori. She nodded her head. "Does anyone else have a suggestion for a way of recording the factors that would help you organize and keep track?" I asked. There were no further suggestions. If Cori had not made her suggestion, I would have made it to the class myself.

I taped the class recording chart the students would be using during the next part of the investigation on the chalkboard and held up a paper bag that held fifty small paper squares. Each square contained a number from 1 to 50. "For this activity, you will need a partner. I will tell you more about that in just a moment. But first I need to share some directions with you. In this bag I am holding, there are fifty small pieces of paper. Each piece of paper contains a number. The numbers go from one to fifty. You and your partner will draw one number from the bag. Together you will figure out the factors of your number. You will need to keep track of this on your recording sheet. When you think you have all the factors and you have a way to prove it, call me over. When you, your partner, and I all agree you have all the factors, you will record your information on the class chart. You may use my way of recording the factors or the way Cori suggested. Are there any questions?"

"Do we each need our own recording sheet or do we just need one?" asked Daniel.

"For this activity you may use just one recording sheet if you wish," I explained.

"What if we can't prove we have all the ways?" James asked.

"Good question, James. What do the rest of you think about James's question?" I asked, throwing James's question out to the class.

"For some of the lower numbers it would be easy. Just think of the multiplication facts that could equal that number," Jackie suggested.

"Or you could just start with one and see if that worked, which of course it does because one is a factor of all numbers, then go to two and see if you can skip-count by two and land on your number, then try the same thing with three, and so on," Nicole said.

"I think you could think of it as division, too," David suggested. "Like, you could decide what you could divide the number into and have equal groups. Like you can divide four into twos with no leftovers, but you can't divide four into threes without having leftovers. So for four, two would work and three wouldn't."

"I get it," James said.

As I called on partners, they came up, drew a number from the bag, and got to work. As the students worked, I observed, asking questions and giving guidance when needed. I was interested to see what strategies students would use. Possible strategies included using basic facts, skip-counting, and using division. Once a pair of students had finished and convinced me that they had found all the factors of their number, I asked them to record their information on the class chart and draw a second number. When the chart was finished, I called the students back to the rug, where everyone could easily see the chart.

A Class Discussion

"What do you notice about the information on the chart?" I began.

"All numbers have at least one way to count to that number. Really, only one has one way, all the rest have two or more," Shelly shared.

"All of them have one as a factor," Cori said.

"Two is always a factor of even numbers," Tom observed.

"When you double five to ten, two factors are added. Five has two factors, ten has four factors, twenty has six factors, forty has eight factors. I think eighty should have ten factors," Nicole noticed. "Can I take this home and work on it tonight? I want to know if you double any number it adds two factors like doubling five did," explained Nicole, who truly enjoyed investigating ideas.

"That will be fine, Nicole," I replied. "We will come back to this tomorrow. You can tell us then what you find out."

DAY 2

Before class, I checked with Nicole to see if she had investigated her question at home as she had asked to do. I didn't want to put her on the spot if she hadn't done this, yet I wanted to give her the opportunity to share if she indeed had taken the time to think about her idea. As it happened, she had explored her idea and was eager to share with the class. Had Nicole not done this, I would have asked the class to investigate the number of factors for 5, 10, 20, and 40 and describe the pattern.

"Yesterday, Nicole was trying to figure out if there was a relationship between doubling numbers and the number of factors. She found that when she doubled five, two factors were added, when she doubled again, two more factors were added, and so on. Based on this pattern, she predicted that eighty would have ten factors. What did you find out about that?" I asked Nicole.

Nicole explained, "I found out for eighty there are ten factors, like I thought. They are one and eighty, two and forty, four and twenty, five and sixteen, and eight and ten.

They were all easy to figure out except for the sixteen. I was pretty sure there should be ten factors, but I only had nine and sixteen didn't seem like it should work. But I knew five was a factor because eighty ends in a zero and when a number ends with a zero, you can count by fives and land on it. I didn't know what number should go with five, so I skip-counted by fives and it took sixteen times so I knew sixteen had to be the last factor."

"Did you find out about if that works for other numbers?" Daniel asked.

"Nope, I got tired and went to bed!" Nicole said.

"That is one question you could investigate today," I said. "I am going to give you and your partner time to examine the chart to look for patterns. Perhaps you want to find out about the question Nicole raised or maybe there is something else on the chart you find interesting."

I hoped as a result of investigating the information on the chart that students would, in addition to finding out more about Nicole's idea, learn about prime and composite numbers, the relationship of the numbers of factors between square and non-square numbers, and the relationship of the factors of related numbers such as 4, 8, and 16 or 3, 9, and 27.

The students were very engaged in this problem. There was little need for assistance from me, so I watched and listened carefully as they worked. After a short time, Ben called me over. "Can we use a calculator to test some of our ideas?" he asked.

"Tell me more about how you want to use a calculator," I said.

"Well, we think we have an idea that works and we want to skip-count past the numbers on the chart and it would be faster if we used a calculator," Ben explained as his partner, Alex, listened.

"Sounds like an excellent way to use the calculator," I said.

"Will it work if we put in what we want to skip-count by and just keep pushing equals?" Alex asked.

"Let's try it," I said as I reached for a calculator. "Tell me which keys to push and we'll see what happens."

"We are counting by eleven, so push eleven and then equals," Ben said.

"Nothing happened. It still says eleven," Alex said with a bit of surprise.

The boys were silent for a few moments. "Did you tell the calculator what to do with eleven?" I asked, hoping my question would get them moving again.

"Oh, push eleven plus and then the equals button a few times," Ben said.

I did as Ben suggested and the calculator gave the following sequence of numbers: 11, 22, 33. "It works!" Ben and Alex said. They went off to investigate their idea.

Some calculators work differently than others. The calculators in our class will do repeated addition, subtraction, multiplication, and division if you enter a number, enter the operation sign, and press the equals button. Your calculators may work differently.

A Second Class Discussion

I called the students back to order for a class discussion. "What patterns did you notice?" I asked.

Many students were eager to share. I called on Rachel and James. "We checked Nicole's rule about when you double a number does it always add two factors. It didn't work for some numbers. Like we tried two. Two has two factors, double two to make four and four has three factors, one, two, and four. We doubled four to make eight and eight has four factors. We don't think it works when you start with two."

"Hey, that's what we did," Shelly and Cori said with excitement. "We found out the same thing, only we started with one and doubled one to two and then kept going to two hundred fifty-six. Can we write what we got on the board?" I nodded yes and the two girls came to the board (see below).

The students watched carefully as Shelly and Cori wrote their idea on the board. "What do you notice?" I asked.

Tom shared, "The factors increase by one and the one factor it increases by is the new number when it was doubled. When one doubled to two, one was a factor of one and it is a factor of two and the new factor is two. It works the same when two is doubled to four. One and two were factors of two and when two doubled to four, the factors are one, two, and four. Four is the new factor."

"But that doesn't always work," interjected Rachel and James. "Sometimes Nicole's pattern about adding two factors

number	number of factors	factors
1	1	1
2	2	1, 2
4	3	1, 2, 4
8	4	1, 2, 4, 8
16	5	1, 2, 4, 8, 16
32	6	1, 2, 4, 8, 16, 32
64	7	1, 2, 4, 8, 16, 32, 64
128	8	1, 2, 4, 8, 16, 32, 64, 128
256	9	1, 2, 4, 8, 16, 32, 64, 128, 256

each time you double works. Three is like that. Three has two factors, one and three. Double it to six and six has four factors, one, two, three, and six. Double six to twelve and the same thing happens. Six has four factors and twelve has six factors, one, two, three, four, six, and twelve," Rachel said.

"Five, six, seven, eleven, and twelve we think are this same pattern. That's about as far as we got though," James added.

"Most numbers have an even number of factors," Cindy said after a few moments. "A few like four, nine, and sixteen have an odd number of factors. I wonder why?"

The students thought about this quietly for a few moments. Slowly a few hands went up.

I called on David to share his thinking. "Well two times two equals four, and three times three equals nine, and four times four equals sixteen. I think they have an odd number of factors because they have two of the same factors. Twenty-five would work the same way, five times five, and twenty-five does have an odd number of factors."

While David's thinking made sense to some students, I decided to take things a step further. I asked the students the ways they could represent 4 as an array. Immediately they suggested a 1-by-4, a 4-by-1, and a 2-by-2. I drew each of these suggestions on the chalkboard.

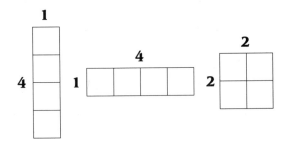

I asked the same question about 9 and added the suggested arrays to those already on the board.

"Look, four and nine can be made into squares," Anamaria said. "I remember,

those are called square numbers because they can make squares!"

"Is that true for sixteen? Can sixteen be made into a square?" I asked.

"Yes," came the response from the class.

"What about twenty-five?" I pushed.

"Yes," they again responded.

"What can we say about numbers that have an odd number of factors?" I asked.

"They must be square numbers and can be made into squares, or someone goofed and left out a factor!" Cindy said.

"I am wondering something," Cori said. "Isn't it possible for a number to be both a multiple and a factor?"

"Explain a bit more about what you mean or give me an example to help me understand a little more about what you are thinking," I said.

"Well someone said that if you count by tens, you go ten, twenty, thirty, and those are multiples of ten. The factors of ten are one, two, five, and ten. So isn't ten both a factor and multiple of ten?" Cori explained.

"Yes, ten is both a factor and a multiple of itself, and that is true for all numbers," I replied.

"I noticed something," Daniel said. "When you count by four, all the numbers you land on, like eight and twelve, have four as a factor."

"There's something really easy," Amy added. "All the numbers have themselves as factors." Amy paraphrased Cori's idea, something children often do to make an idea their own.

"A lot of numbers only have two factors. Eleven and thirteen are like that," Alex said.

"What do you notice about all the numbers with just two factors?" I asked.

"They all have one as a factor," Anamaria said. "Also they have themselves as a factor."

The other students nodded their agreement with Anamaria's observation. "Does anyone know what we call numbers with exactly two factors, one and itself?" I asked. The students were silent, so I took this opportunity to introduce them to the vocabulary of *prime number*. "Mathematicians have a special name for numbers with exactly two factors: prime numbers," I explained.

"Do the others with more than two factors have a name?" Amy wondered.

If Amy hadn't asked, I would have been sure to explain that numbers with more than two factors are called composite numbers. As I explained these ideas to the students, I wrote *prime* and *composite* on the board and made a mental note to add them to the list of math vocabulary posted in the classroom.

"What do you notice about one?" I asked.

"Hey, it doesn't have two or more than two factors! It just has one! What is it?" Nicole asked.

"One is tricky! It is not prime and it is not composite. It is neither," I explained. I didn't want to get too bogged down with this idea, but I did want to be clear about it. To help clarify, I repeated, "A prime number has exactly two factors, itself and one. Three and five are examples." I pointed to these numbers on the chart. "A composite number has more than two factors. Four and ten are examples. One has only one factor so it doesn't fit the definition of either prime or composite."

"Juan and I noticed something else," Steve said. "The even numbers seem to have mostly even factors, but a few odd ones sometimes, like ten has five as a factor

and five is odd. But there are no odd numbers with even factors."

"Why do you think that is?" I asked. Several of the students discussed this among themselves.

"We think it's because odd times odd equals odd," Steve said after talking it over with Juan.

"Put your thumb up if you agree with Steve and Juan," I said.

I paused to make sure everyone had a chance to think this over. Most students put their thumbs up. "Can someone give me an example of an odd number times an odd number that equals an odd?" I asked in an attempt to convince the few students who still weren't sure.

"Five times seven equals thirty-five," Rachel suggested.

"Nine times one equals nine," Daniel said.

"Eleven times eleven equals one hundred twenty-one," Cori offered.

"Does anyone have an example of an odd number times an odd number that equals an even number?" I asked.

After a few moments Anamaria said, "That just doesn't happen. If someone multiplies an odd number times an odd number and gets an even number, I think they have made a mistake!"

The students seemed to have run out of ideas to share. They sat quietly for a moment, looking at the chart and considering the ideas that had been shared. "Does anyone else have something to add?" I asked. There were no additional comments.

Questions and Discussion

▲▲

▲ *In this lesson you let students choose their own partners. How do you avoid hurt feelings if someone doesn't get to work with whom he or she wants?*

First of all, the method I used to have students choose partners in this lesson is one I would not necessarily recommend for all classes. Early in the year I assign partners. Before doing this,

I always remind students that this is not a marriage, merely a short time spent working with someone to solve a problem or accomplish a task. I have also clearly established a climate in which it is accepted that all students have unique, valued attributes to offer our class. Displayed on the front wall of the classroom over the chalkboard are the following words: "We are a community of teachers and learners." Early in the year we talk about the negative impact of moaning and groaning when we don't like the partner who is assigned to us. Students learn quickly this is unacceptable behavior.

This class had become very accepting of the idea of working with anyone. Because of this, I felt they could appropriately handle opportunities to make choices from time to time about whom they would work with. Before allowing them to do this the first time, I talked with them about the right to say no and how to do it politely. We also talked about reasons people might say no that aren't intended to hurt feelings. This kind of experience is real-world experience and helps children learn good coping skills.

▲ *The class chart is an important part of this lesson. In the midst of a busy classroom, how did you check the accuracy of the chart?*

As the students finished finding the factors for their numbers, I asked them to talk to me about how they knew they had all the factors. During the course of these quick discussions, I could check their work as they explained their thinking. If they were missing factors or had incorrect factors, I could redirect them at that point and ask them to check back with me again. Once I was satisfied with their work, they wrote it on the chart. I did check the chart over quickly before the discussion in case someone had inadvertently recorded incorrect information.

▲ *What about students who finish when there are no more numbers left?*

This situation will happen with this sort of activity. To avoid having students with nothing to do and to lay the foundation for the discussion that would follow, I asked students who were finished to look at the information on the chart to find patterns and perhaps make predictions about missing information. When students were unable to do this without guidance from me, I would point out a series of numbers such as 2, 4, 6, 8, and 10 and ask students what they noticed about the series of numbers I pointed out and their factors. Other questions I might ask students to consider would be: "What is different about one and all the other numbers?" and "What do you notice about four, nine, sixteen, and twenty-five that is different from the other numbers?"

CHAPTER 10
MATILDA'S MENTAL MULTIPLICATION

Overview

"Miss Honey," a chapter in Roald Dahl's *Matilda* (Penguin USA, 1998), provides the context for this lesson. Miss Honey is amazed by Matilda's facility with multiplication and asks her to solve 14×19. Matilda mentally solves this problem with ease and accuracy. Students are asked to explain how Matilda might have done this, thus providing them with experience thinking about efficient methods for performing mental computations. Students also represent their thinking using paper and pencil. This experience deepens students' understanding about double-digit multiplication and their number sense.

Materials

▲ *Matilda* by Roald Dahl (Penguin USA, 1998)

Time

▲ one class period

Teaching Directions

1. Begin reading the chapter entitled "Miss Honey" in *Matilda*. Stop to discuss the solutions to the math problems in the chapter—2×28 and 2×487. Ask students to explain the processes they used to arrive at answers to these problems. Continue reading until Matilda states the solution to 14×19.

2. Record on the board how students solved smaller problems such as 2×28 and 2×487. This can serve for student reference later in the activity.

3. Ask students to consider and record on paper how Matilda may have mentally solved 14×19.

Teaching Notes

Prior to this lesson, the students in the following vignette had had some experience examining patterns when multiplying by 10 and multiples of 10 through the *Silent Multiplication* lessons. This prior experience helped students think flexibly about efficient ways to do computations such as 14×19.

One of the important mathematical ideas that I hope to see children using in this lesson is the distributive property. For example, to multiply 14×19, some think of 19 as $10 + 9$. They then distribute the multiplication by 14, multiplying 10×14 and 9×14 to find the partial products of 140 and 126 and ultimately adding those together to find the product of 266. Or, as another example, they can think of 19 as $20 - 1$, multiply 20×14 to get 280, and then subtract the extra group of 14 (1×14) from 280 to get 266.

Often when we solve problems mentally, we compute in much more efficient ways in our heads than we might when performing the paper-and-pencil algorithm. Also, when we solve problems mentally, we are more mindful of the characteristics of the particular numbers to use and of our results. We rely on our understanding of numbers, not merely on an algorithm we've learned to apply. The situation in *Matilda* in which she is able to so easily solve problems mentally offers students the opportunity to closely examine these phenomena.

While a focus of this lesson is to encourage children to think about ways to solve this problem in their heads, it's also appropriate for them to use paper and pencil to keep track of their thinking.

When sharing *Matilda*, I combined reading the story with storytelling it. I found the children especially enjoyed it when I told them the story, more so than when I read it. Also, I used only the first nine pages of the chapter. Several of the children read the entire book independently as a result of this activity.

The Lesson

▲▲

The students gathered around me on the floor to hear "Miss Honey," a chapter from *Matilda,* by Roald Dahl. Matilda is a young girl whose existence is often forgotten by her parents. Matilda, left on her own, teaches herself to read. The chapter "Miss Honey" tells the story of the meeting of Matilda and Miss Honey and the beginning of Matilda's school career. On the first morning of the first day of school, Miss Honey, the teacher, explains to the students the importance of learning the times tables. Miss Honey quickly discovers that Matilda knows her times tables through the twelves. Miss Honey then gives Matilda a series of increasingly difficult problems,

ending with 14×19. Matilda mentally solves all the problems with ease. The focus of this lesson is how Matilda could have solved 14×19.

"How many of you have read *Matilda*?" I asked. About one-third of the students raised their hands. "How many have seen the movie?" I continued. Most raised their hands to this question. "What do you recall about *Matilda*?"

"Matilda's parents are not interested in her," Nick said.

"They ignore her, like she's not even there," Becky added.

"She learned how to read when she was really little. But her dad didn't believe her;

he always thought she was lying about stuff," Joshua said.

"Matilda could read any book. The librarian was always helping her. She was smart in math too," Mia said.

"Do you remember who Miss Honey is?" I asked.

"Her teacher," the students replied.

"Today I am going to share part of the chapter with you in which Matilda and Miss Honey meet," I explained. I started by telling the first page or so of the chapter, then I read the descriptions of Miss Honey and Miss Trunchbull, the headmistress. As I read the part where Matilda recites her two times tables, the children joined in chanting as I read. "Miss Honey has asked Matilda to solve two times twenty-eight. What is it?" I asked the class.

After waiting a few moments until most students had their hands up, I called on Cally. "I think fifty-six," she replied.

"How did you get fifty-six?" I asked.

"I thought of it as twenty-eight plus twenty-eight. Eight plus eight equals sixteen. You put the six down and carry the one. Two plus two plus the one you carried is five, so that makes fifty-six," Cally explained, having solved the problem in her head without using paper and pencil.

I wanted to see if Cally understood what she had done when she shared her strategy, the algorithm typically taught to students. "When you added the eights, what did each eight stand for?"

"They stood for eight ones," she explained.

"What about the twos, what did they stand for?" I continued.

Cally paused for a moment to consider my question, not quite sure of how to respond. I let her struggle for a few moments in the hopes that she would figure out how to proceed on her own. Because she was beginning to get flustered and I didn't want to make her feel uncomfortable

or fearful of sharing her ideas again, I asked her a question that I felt would guide her thinking in such a way that she would be able to get unstuck. "If the eights represented eight ones, then what would the twos represent?"

Her face lit up. "Oh I think I know now! The twos really mean two tens, so I was really adding two tens plus two tens plus the ten I carried."

"Why did you carry?" I continued to probe her understanding, hoping to gain more insight for myself about her thinking and to give the other students something to consider.

Again she paused to consider my question. "I think I carried it maybe . . . maybe because it really stood for one ten and needed to go with the other tens?" she replied tentatively. I nodded to her to indicate her answer made sense.

I recorded Cally's thinking on the chalkboard as follows:

$$
\begin{array}{r}
28 \\
+28 \\
\hline
(8+8) \quad 16 \\
(20+20) \quad +40 \\
\hline
56
\end{array}
$$

"I know another way," Jeannie said. "I just thought in my head that twenty-eight is almost thirty, thirty times two is easy, it's sixty, but that is too much, so I subtracted two twos to get fifty-six." I recorded Jeannie's thinking as:

28 is almost 30

$30 \times 2 = 60$

$2 \times 2 = 4$

$60 - 4 = 56$

"Why did you subtract two groups of two?" I asked.

"I had thirty groups of two and I only needed twenty-eight so I had to subtract out the extra ones," she explained.

I called on Brett next. "Twenty-five is a number that is easy for me to double. It's like two quarters in money. Twenty-five plus twenty-five is fifty. But twenty-eight is three more than twenty-five. Because there are two twenty-eights, I have to add three plus three, three for each twenty-eight, which is six. I add six to fifty and get fifty-six." I recorded Brett's thinking as follows:

25 + 25 = 50

25 + 3 = 28 (a difference of 3)

3 + 3 = 6

6 + 50 = 56

I continued to tell the story, stopping again when Miss Honey asked Matilda to solve 2 × 487. I paused for a moment to allow the students to mentally calculate the answer. When most hands were raised, I asked the students to respond together using a whisper voice. Because I was interested in encouraging students to listen to one another and to try other students' ideas, I asked the students to raise their hands if they solved this problem using a different strategy than they used for the last problem. Many raised their hands, indicating they had tried a different idea. Next I asked the students to indicate if they had used one of the ideas listed on the board from the previous problem or if they used an idea that had not yet been listed.

I called on Jasmine. "I sort of used the same idea as Jeannie. Jeannie rounded up to an easier number. I did the same thing. I rounded four hundred eighty-seven to four hundred ninety. Then I took the zero off of four hundred ninety to make it forty-nine. I know fifty plus fifty is one hundred. Forty-nine is one less so forty-nine plus forty-nine is ninety-eight. If forty-nine plus forty-nine equals ninety-eight, then four hundred ninety plus four hundred ninety equals nine hundred eighty. Well four hundred eighty-seven is really three less than four hundred ninety, so I have to subtract out three twice, because

there are two four hundred eighty-sevens, that is six, so nine hundred eighty minus six equals nine hundred seventy-four."

I recorded Jasmine's thinking as follows:

487 is almost 490

drop the zero to make 49

50 + 50 = 100

49 + 49 = 98

490 + 490 = 980

490 – 487 = 3

two groups of 3 is 6

980 – 6 = 974

"Why could you drop the zero?" I asked Jasmine.

"Well, it's in the ones column and zero plus zero is zero and it just seemed easier to remember the problem if I took the zero off for now and then put it back at the end, since I wasn't changing the ones at all," Jasmine explained.

"I think it has to do with multiplying by ten, but I am not sure," Dana added.

"How many of you thought of the problem like Jasmine did?" I asked.

Several students raised their hands.

"I tried Cally's way, but I got messed up with all the numbers in my head," Greg shared.

"It was hard to keep track of all the numbers in my head when I tried to carry. I could have done it that way with paper," Mia added.

"Were you able to solve the problem another way?" I asked.

"I knew that eighty-five and eighty-five is one hundred seventy. I knew because eighty plus eighty equals one hundred sixty and ten more is one hundred seventy. Then I knew to add four more because the problem was really four hundred eighty-seven. One hundred seventy plus four equals one hundred seventy-four. Then I added four hundred two times, which is eight hundred.

Eight hundred plus one hundred seventy-four equals nine hundred seventy-four," Mia explained. I recorded Mia's solution:

$$80 + 80 = 160$$

$$85 + 85 = 170$$

$$2 + 2 = 4$$

$$170 + 4 = 174$$

$$400 + 400 = 800$$

$$800 + 174 = 974$$

"Is your solution like any of other solutions shared so far?" I asked.

"I don't think so," Mia said.

"How does it seem different to you?" I asked.

"I started sort of in the middle and did the tens, then the ones, and then the hundreds," Mia replied.

I continued reading and telling the story, stopping this time when Matilda correctly solved 14×19. "How do you think Matilda did this? She did it in her head with no paper and pencil and no calculator. What must her thinking have been?" I said.

The students weren't too sure about how she did it. I gave them time to think quietly. "Turn to you neighbor and discuss what strategy she might have used," I instructed after several hands had gone up. "Remember, one of you gets to talk for thirty seconds uninterrupted while the other listens. When I tell you to switch, it becomes the first listener's turn to talk and the first talker's turn to listen," I reminded the students. At the end of thirty seconds, I asked the students to switch, then thirty seconds later, I asked for their attention. This proved to be a challenging problem for the students. Having quiet time to think followed by partner sharing and then whole group discussion helped students find new directions and ways to think about this problem that they might not have otherwise had.

"I would like you to work independently to write about at least one way Matilda may have mentally solved this problem in the story. Remember, you should use words, pictures, and numbers to help you explain your thinking. Are there any questions?" I said as I wrote the directions on the chalkboard.

"Can we use an idea we heard from our partner?" Joshua asked.

"Yes, if you understand it and can explain it clearly on your paper," I responded.

"What about the ideas on the board—can we use them? Or can we use an idea that no one has shared yet?" Mia asked.

"Yes, you may use any ideas you find useful in solving this problem as long as you clearly explain your thinking," I replied.

"What about a calculator? Can we use one?" Krissy asked.

"This time I am going to say no because the story leads us to believe that Matilda figured this out without using a calculator. My question to you is: Without paper and pencil or a calculator, how might Matilda have done this?" I explained.

I know that paper and pencil are useful tools for keeping track of thinking when calculating. My goal for this particular lesson was to help students become flexible in their approaches to calculation, paying attention to the particular numbers at hand and strengthening their repertoire of strategies. Having students record their ideas helps them see that they can use paper and pencil to keep track of their thinking, not merely apply a procedure they have learned.

The students got to work. Some were still uncertain. I answered their questions, then observed as the students worked. Many students immediately used the standard algorithm to solve the problem. When I saw this happening, I asked, "Do you really think Matilda did all these steps in her head?" and then I suggested that these students show me a second way Matilda might have done the problem mentally.

After fifteen minutes or so, I asked for the students' attention once again. Some students had some excellent ideas and some were really struggling. A class discussion seemed a good way to help students gain understanding. Because I wanted students to listen to and think about their classmates' ideas, I told the students they could add other ideas to their papers during the discussion as long as they included the name of the person who shared each idea and the idea was one that made sense to them. I began the discussion by asking, "Is there someone who is willing to share a strategy that Matilda might have used to solve this problem mentally?" Several hands went up immediately. I paused a bit longer to give the more reluctant students time to look over their work and join in the discussion. I called on Rick.

Rick came to the board and wrote the following as he explained, "I think Matilda could have timesed it in her brain by doing this . . . ":

$$
\begin{array}{r}
{\scriptstyle 3} \\
14 \\
\times\, 19 \\
\hline
126 \\
\underline{140} \\
266
\end{array}
$$

126   (9 × 4 = 36, put down the 6, carry the 3. 9 × 1 = 9 plus 3 carried equals 12)

140   (Put a 0 to hold a place, 4 × 1 = 4, 1 × 1 = 1)

266   (Add 6 + 0 = 6, 2 + 4 = 6, and 1 + 1 = 2)

"It would be 266," Rick explained.

"We call this process that Rick used an algorithm," I explained to the class. "An algorithm is a set of steps used to solve all problems of a particular kind. What Rick did is correct, but all those steps would be a lot for Matilda to keep track of in her head. I think she might have needed paper and pencil to help her remember.

"Who has another way?" I continued. I called on Carol.

"I thought of fourteen as ten plus four. Then I multiplied nineteen times ten, which equals one hundred ninety, then I multiplied nineteen times four by doing two times nineteen, which is thirty-eight, and then thirty-eight plus thirty-eight, which equals seventy-six. I had to remember the one hundred ninety from the first part, which was really hard, and add it to the seventy-six from the second part, and it added up to two hundred sixty-six. And I could do it in my head, even though it was reeeaaally hard! Trying to remember parts makes it hard," Carol said.

Carol's reasoning explains the role paper and pencil can play. Often we think of mental computation as using only our brain and nothing else. In fact, using paper and pencil can be an extremely useful tool for keeping track of thinking when solving problems mentally. The hard part for Carol was not the computation but remembering the partial products as she solved the problem.

"I did it by thinking of nineteen as twenty," explained Becky. "The problem is now twenty times fourteen. Then I thought in my trusty brain, hmm . . . I can multiply two times fourteen, that's easy, it's twenty-eight! Then I can add a zero, which is two hundred eighty, but that is twenty groups and I only need nineteen, so I have to subtract out one group of fourteen, so that would be two hundred sixty-six."

As Rick, Carol, and Becky shared their ideas, the other students were comparing their own ideas with those shared. Some nodded in agreement as they noticed they had the same idea and several added ideas not already on their papers. (See Figure 10–1.)

Several students had their hands up. I called on Jake. "I divided the fourteen by two and it equaled seven. Then I multiplied nineteen times seven, which is one hundred thirty-three. Then because I divided the fourteen by two, to make it back to the original problem, I have to multiply one hundred thirty-three times two, which is two hundred sixty-six."

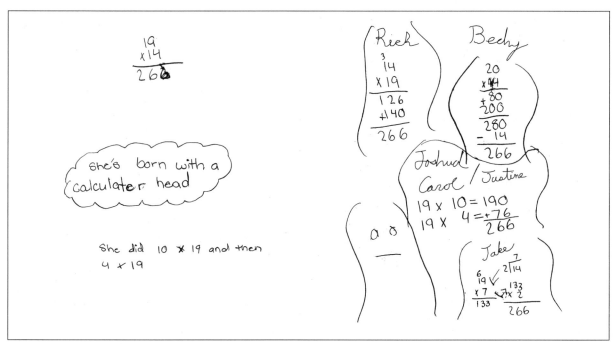

▲▲▲▲▲▲Figure 10–1 *Justine showed her thinking during the work period, then added other students' ideas.*

"I think my idea is like Carol's only different in one way," Brett shared.

"Carol broke apart fourteen, but I think you could break apart the nineteen so it would be ten plus nine and then multiply ten times fourteen equals one hundred forty and nine times fourteen, which is like ten times fourteen minus one fourteen so it is . . . one hundred twenty-six, so the answer still comes out to two hundred sixty-six."

The students seemed to be out of ideas to share. Krissy raised her hand. "The only way I could think of this problem at the beginning is to add fourteen nineteen times and my brain couldn't do that. It helped me to write down other people's ideas. I think I could even use a few of them to solve a different but sort of the same problem . . . like . . . twenty-one times fourteen."

Questions and Discussion

▲▲

▲ Why isn't the algorithm enough?

An algorithm refers to a rule or procedure used to solve all problems of a particular type. When students are taught a set of steps with no understanding of the underlying reasons why they work, the risk is that students are simply performing procedures mindlessly. This is typically the result of teaching that focuses only on paper-and-pencil skills. However, when people solve problems mentally, they often use very different procedures than the standard algorithms, depending on the skills of the individual and the numbers involved. This mental calculation isn't mindless but relies on number sense, understanding of place value, and knowledge of numerical relationships. The value of students considering methods Matilda may have used to mentally solve 14 × 19 is that it asks them to go beyond the paper-and-pencil algorithm many of them know and make sense of the numerical problem in other ways.

Greg's work was like some other students'. His initial thought related to using repeated addition. But then he went on to generate two more powerful ideas, both of which were on his paper prior to the class discussion. (See Figure 10–2.)

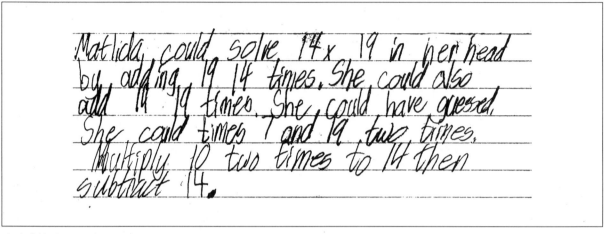

▲▲▲▲▲▲Figure 10–2 *Greg's work showed several powerful ideas about how to solve 14 × 19.*

▲ *Why did you encourage the students to add other students' ideas to their papers?*

These students were not particularly confident or competent about writing in mathematics. They were having trouble in a couple of areas, such as thinking about the mathematics and expressing what thinking they were able to do in an understandable written form. By encouraging them to add other ideas to their own, I was keeping them engaged in the lesson because they had to compare their ideas with others'. I was also modeling for them how to represent mathematical ideas in writing by recording student ideas on the board as they were shared with the class, and I was hoping to broaden their thinking and understanding about the actual mathematics involved. Also, writing down an idea helps children make it their own.

▲ *What is the role of paper and pencil in mental calculation?*

In this activity, the book clearly leads us to believe that Matilda did not use a calculator or paper and pencil to help her solve the problem of 14 × 19. She solved this problem in her head. Mental calculation is often thought to be an act that requires no additional tools. However, paper and pencil can be very useful tools for keeping track of calculations done mentally.

In the vignette, Carol made the statement that doing the problem in her head was very difficult. She explained that she had to remember the answer to one part of the problem while figuring out the second part. This can be very difficult and frustrating. Had Carol used a piece of paper to jot down the first partial product while she figured out the second partial product, this problem would have gone from a difficult problem to a reasonably easy problem. The difficulty for Carol was not the actual computation but remembering the various partial products. In this case, the use of paper and pencil would have aided Carol with remembering and would have taken nothing away from the mental processing she was doing mathematically. Carol's written work in this way would have also been an efficient way to calculate. The standard algorithm looks like this:

$$
\begin{array}{r}
14 \\
\times\ 19 \\
\hline
126 \\
140 \\
\hline
266
\end{array}
\quad \text{or} \quad
\begin{array}{r}
14 \\
\times\ 19 \\
\hline
126 \\
14 \\
\hline
266
\end{array}
$$

Carol's thinking could be represented as follows:

$$14 \times 19$$
$$(10 + 4) \times 19$$

$$
\begin{array}{rl}
190 & (10 \times 19) \\
38 & (2 \times 19) \\
+\ 38 & (2 \times 19) \\
\hline
266 &
\end{array}
$$

While I reminded the students that Matilda did her problem solving in her head, I asked students to show me in writing what Matilda might have done to model for them how paper and pencil can be used as a tool for keeping track of computation when they are thinking in their own ways, not necessarily following a standard procedure. Representing mathematical thinking is an important aspect of children's mathematical learning.

▲ Why do you record children's thinking on the chalkboard?

I like to record student thinking on the chalkboard, the overhead, or a class chart for several reasons. It serves as a good model to help students see how their ideas about mathematics can be represented with mathematical symbolism. When ideas are written down, it allows students to process them both auditorily and visually. Writing students' ideas shows that their thinking is valued, which often encourages further, deeper thinking. Later, students can use the ideas recorded for reference as they work independently or with partners.

CHAPTER 11
BEANS AND SCOOPS

Overview

In this lesson, students think about strategies for multiplication by figuring out approximately how many beans fill a jar. After first estimating and then counting the scoops of beans that fill the jar, students find out how many beans there are in a scoop and use this information to decide on the number of beans in the jar. The lesson not only focuses on ways to multiply but also provides the students statistical experience using data to decide on how many beans fill a scoop. The lesson also models how to assess students' understanding.

Materials

▲ jar (more than one size is optional)
▲ beans (at least two different sizes, for example, kidney beans, lima beans, small black beans)
▲ scoops (one the size used for coffee, other sizes optional)

Time

▲ three class periods

Teaching Directions

Day 1

1. Show the students the jar, the scoop, and the beans.

2. Ask students to report their guesses about the number of scoops of beans it would take to fill the jar.

3. Put three scoops of beans into the jar and show the students. Tell them: "Now that you have more information, you can revise your earlier guess and make a better estimate based on what you know."

4. Ask students to share their new estimates and explain why they make sense.

5. Continue filling the jar to the top, stopping if it seems appropriate to give students the chance to revise and share their estimates again.

6. Once the jar is filled, ask students to estimate the number of beans in the jar and share their thinking.

7. Give each table group one scoop of beans to count. Record each table's count on the board. With the students, identify the mode, the median, and the mean and ask the class to decide on a number that best represents the number of beans in a scoop.

8. Lead a discussion about the following problem: *How can we use the information we have to figure out about how many beans are in the jar?* As students share their strategies for finding the number of beans in the jar, record them on the board.

9. Pose a new problem using a different-size bean: *How many scoops of beans will it take to fill the jar?*

10. Repeat the process as before.

Day 2

To assess students' understanding about solving multidigit multiplication, ask each to solve the following problems in two ways:

1. *A jar holds 16 scoops. There are about 53 beans in each scoop. About how many beans are in the jar?*

2. *Another jar holds 6 scoops. There are about 28 beans in each scoop. About how many beans are in the jar?*

Day 3

1. Introduce students to Jack, a student from another class. Tell them: "Jack was trying to solve thirty-two times fourteen. His strategy was to multiply thirty by ten and two by four and add the partial products."

2. Lead a discussion about why Jack's strategy didn't work and about what strategies would work.

3. Have students write letters to Jack about why his strategy didn't work.

Teaching Notes

In addition to providing students with a context for practicing multidigit multiplication problems, *Beans and Scoops* also gives students experience with analyzing statistics.

Students find out the number of beans in their group's scoop of beans. After this data is gathered from each of the table groups, students use this information to identify the mode (the outcome that occurs most frequently), the median (the middle number when data is arranged in order), and the mean (the average). The class decides on a number that best approximates how many beans fill a scoop and then figures out about how many beans are in the jar.

Students later predict the number of scoops it will take to fill the same jar using the same scoop with different-size beans. Students discover that even though the size of the beans is different, the number of scoops remains the same if the scoop size does not vary. This is a startling discovery for many students. Their number sense is used throughout the lesson as they investigate a variety of multidigit multiplication problems based on different-size beans, different-size scoops, and different-size jars.

A misconception I have seen before came up during the lesson. Rachel was trying to solve 20×19. Her strategy was to find the answer for 19 groups of 19 (19×19) and then add one more group of 19 (19×1) to make 20 groups of 19. This idea is correct. However, to multiply 19×19, Rachel used a strategy often used by students—splitting the factors to make smaller problems—and computed $(10 \times 10) + (9 \times 9)$. What Rachel did was to think only of 10 groups of 10 (10×10) and 9 groups of 9 (9×9) and then combine the partial products. This answer would not be equivalent to 19×19. This is a difficult idea to understand and explain, made even more difficult in this situation because both factors are the same.

As an example of using Rachel's initial strategy correctly, a student might think of 19 groups of 19 as 19 groups of 10 (19×10) and 19 groups of 9 (19×9) and then combine the partial products. Following is a mathematical representation of this idea:

$19 \times 19 = (19 \times 10) + (19 \times 9)$.

Another example of how a student might correctly use this idea is to first change 19×19 into 19×10 and 19×9, find the answer to the first part of the problem (19×10), which is 190, then break down 19×9 into $10 \times 9 = 90$ and $9 \times 9 = 81$, and finally combine the three partial products, $190 + 90 + 81$. Following is a mathematical representation of this idea:

$19 \times 19 = (19 \times 10) + (10 \times 9) + (9 \times 9)$.

The use of arrays is a helpful way to understand why Rachel's way of figuring 19×19 doesn't work. (See Figure 11–1.)

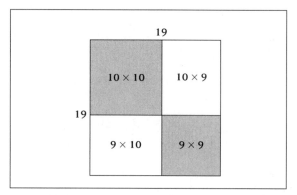

▲▲▲▲▲▲**Figure 11–1** *The student multiplied 10×10 and 9×9, as shaded on the array. The missing partial products, 10×9 and 9×10, became apparent on the array.*

Arrays were not used in this lesson because the student was able to make sense of the situation in her own way. Had she continued to struggle, an array is one tool I could have used to help her more clearly understand. Also, using arrays to explore this misconception is a good next step to help other students in the class that are still confused.

The Lesson

▲▲

DAY 1

I began by showing the students what I had brought to class—a jar, a coffee scoop, and a baggie of lima beans. "How many scoops do you think will fill the jar?" I asked the class.

After several students reported their guesses, I said, "Answering this question is difficult, I think, because you have no information to help you decide. Unless you have had a good deal of experience scooping beans into jars, you just have to make a guess. Before I ask you for more ideas, I'm going to put three scoops of beans into the jar. Then you will have some information to use." I put three scoops of beans in the jar, tapped it lightly on the table to settle the beans, and held it up for the students to examine. Hands shot up.

I said, "Now you can revise your earlier guess and make an estimate based on the information you now know." I paused for a moment to give students a chance to think. "Who thinks it will take more than thirty scoops to fill the jar?" No one raised a hand. I continued, "Who thinks it will take between twenty-five and thirty scoops?" Several students quickly raised their hands. "What about fifteen to twenty-five scoops?" A few more raised their hands. "Less than fifteen scoops?" About half the students raised their hands.

The students were eager to share their individual estimates. I said, "When I call on you to share your guess, you will also need to explain your thinking." Several students volunteered.

Sue, for example, said, "I think it's ten because it looks like you could take what's in there now and put that same amount in two more times and maybe a little more."

I then put three more scoops of beans into the jar, tapped it to settle the beans, and again asked for estimates and explanations. Then I filled the jar with scoops as the class counted, tapping it on the table to settle the beans, which Tomas had requested. The jar held twenty scoops.

"Let's do another estimation problem," I said. "It took about twenty scoops to fill the jar, but about how many beans do you think filled it?" Hands shot up, but I waited a moment to give all of the students a chance to think.

I called on Claire first. "I think one hundred thirty-two," she said.

"Why do you think that?" I asked.

"Because I think there are maybe seven beans in a scoop," she said.

Jesse blurted out, "I think that, too, but I think there are one hundred forty."

I reminded Jesse and the rest of the class about waiting to be called on. Claire now looked confused. I asked Jesse to explain.

"I counted by sevens," he said.

"Can you do that out loud so everyone can hear?" I asked.

Jesse nodded. I was impressed that he said a good deal of the sequence easily: "Seven, fourteen, twenty-one, twenty-eight, thirty-five, forty-two, forty-nine, fifty-six, sixty-three, seventy, seventy-seven . . . " Then he slowed down and thought some, then said, "Eighty-four, . . . ninety-one, . . .

ninety-eight, . . . one hundred five, . . . one hundred twelve, . . . one hundred nineteen, . . . one hundred twenty-six, . . . one hundred thirty-three, . . . one hundred forty. That's how I got one hundred forty."

I looked at Claire. She nodded that she agreed. Other hands went up.

"I think more like two hundred twenty-five," Lela said. "I think more beans fit into the scoop."

"How many do you think fill the scoop?" I probed.

"I don't know," Lela said. "Maybe eight or nine." I didn't comment on Lela's response even though I knew that that there would have to be more than ten beans in a scoop for there to be 225 total from the twenty scoops. I made a mental note to check on Lela's thinking in other situations and, if needed, offer guidance. Right now, I chose to keep the conversation moving.

Saul offered his idea next. "I think two hundred because I think that ten beans can go into a scoop." I glanced at Lela and noted that she didn't seem at all interested in revising her thinking after hearing what Saul said.

Other students wanted to make estimates, but I decided to move ahead. I told the students that I would put a scoop of beans at each of their tables and each group could count how many there were. "When you've made your count, let me know and I'll record it on the board," I said. I began placing a scoop of beans on each table. As I walked around the room, several students made comments.

"We'll get different amounts," Michelle said.

"Yeah, we have to," Andrew added.

"We can take the average," Cindy said.

As students reported their counts, I recorded them in a list on the board. Also, I asked Tomas to go around the room and collect the beans as groups finished counting. I've learned from experience that the beans can be a distraction if they're left on the tables. I recorded on the board:

19

22

19

17

20

20

19

The students were interested in this data and began talking among themselves.

"There are a lot of nineteens."

"Twenty-two is the biggest."

"They're pretty close."

"I think that nineteen is the average."

"I think that twenty is."

While they were examining the data and commenting, I wrote on the board next to the list:

mode

median

mean

The students had studied these ideas the year before and also again this year. I called them back to attention, pointed to what I had written on the board, and asked, "Who can tell us something about what the mode is?" Almost half the students raised their hands.

Claire answered, "It's what happened most. I remember because they both start with the same letters."

"It's nineteen on our list," Jamie added.

The median was more difficult. A few made guesses, but no one remembered. "It's the number that's in the middle when the data are arranged in order," I told them. I had them help me reorder the data from smallest to largest so we could see that nineteen was also the median:

17

19

19

19

20

20

22

We then calculated the mean. We added the seven numbers and divided by 7, which provided an opportunity for the students to practice their computation skills. We agreed that the mean was just about $19\frac{1}{2}$. The class agreed that 19 was the best number to represent the number of beans in a scoop.

"OK," I said. "So now here's the problem to solve. How can we use the information we have to figure out about how many beans are in the jar?" It was obvious to the students that we needed to multiply 19×20. A few students began to reach for pencils and paper, but I asked them not to.

"I'm interested in how you think about doing this multiplication," I said. "This will give me a way to learn about your arithmetic understanding and skill. I'll record your thinking on the board."

Representing on the board how students reason is a way for me to model for them how to use paper and pencil to record their thinking. Too often we think about paper and pencil in the context of performing algorithms we've taught. However, I want the students to see paper and pencil as tools for keeping track of thinking and for representing their ideas, not necessarily for replicating methods they've learned.

I called on Tim. "I'd do twenty times nine. I got the nine from the ones column in nineteen. Then I would do twenty times ten. I'd add them up."

I wrote:

(20 × 9) + (20 × 10)

"What would you add?" I asked.

"The one hundred eighty and the two hundred," Tim explained.

"Where did you get one hundred eighty and two hundred?" I asked Tim.

"Twenty times nine is one hundred eighty and twenty times ten is two hundred," Tim said. I recorded:

(20 × 9) + (20 × 10)

180 + 200

380

I called on Ellie next. "I'd do nineteen times ten and add it twice. I'd do it that way because half of twenty is ten and multiplying by ten is easy. But that is only half of the problem, so I have to add it twice." I recorded:

19 × 10 = 190

190 + 190 = 380

"I'd do it by rounding," Ben shared. "Twenty is one more than nineteen, so I would round nineteen up to twenty. The problem is really easy then. Instead of twenty times nineteen, it's twenty times twenty. That is four hundred. It is also one twenty extra, so I would subtract out twenty." I recorded:

20 × 20 = 400

400 – 20 = 380

Rachel had been listening to the other students carefully. I had noticed that she seemed to look more perplexed as the discussion went on. Rachel is a strong math student and I was interested in what was bothering her. She raised her hand and I quickly called on her.

"I'm confused. I have an idea about this problem, but I didn't get the same answer when I solved the problem in my head. I did it several times and none of the times was the answer three hundred eighty. My way makes sense and so do the others. I don't get it and I want to know why."

"Tell me your way," I said to Rachel.

Rachel explained, "I thought I'd do nineteen times nineteen. Then I'd multiply ten times ten, which would be one hundred. Next I'd do nine times nine. That's eighty-one. Then I'd add one hundred and eighty-one, which is one hundred eighty-one and one more nineteen, for the twentieth group of nineteen, and altogether that's two hundred. My way makes sense to me, but so do the others. Why doesn't it work?" I recorded:

$(10 \times 10) + (9 \times 9)$

$100 + 81 = 181$

$181 + 19 = 200$

Rachel's error in thinking is one I've seen before, but I was surprised that she had made it. Her math reasoning is usually insightful and correct.

After a few moments Rachel repeated, "I don't see why my answer came out differently than the others. I have been thinking about it. I need one hundred eighty more if the others are right. But I don't see why. How come? I don't get it! I'd like to, but I don't!"

A flurry of comments bombarded Rachel as students tried to help her see why her way didn't work. Rachel couldn't really attend to what was being said. Because Rachel is a confident student, I decided to let her grapple with the problem and not try to solve her dilemma. I told her, "You can keep thinking about this now or let it go for now while I give you some other things to think about. I'll be sure to help you clear up the confusion later." I'm never completely sure about when to intervene and when to give students time, but I think my decision at this time made sense for Rachel.

"Does anyone have other ideas to share about how to solve this question?" I continued.

Trevor suggested, "You could write nineteen twenty times and add 'em up!"

"Or you could write twenty nineteen times and add," Michelle added with a giggle. "That's too much for me!"

Ben was waving his hand, desperate for a chance to share what he was thinking. "I have an idea about what happened with Rachel's idea. Can I share it?"

I looked over at Rachel, who nodded her head, indicating she wanted to hear what Ben had to say.

Ben began, "I think she left stuff out. I think you can think of it as four smaller problems. Ten times ten equals one hundred and nine times nine equals eighty-one are two of the smaller problems. You have to multiply the ten from the bottom nineteen times the nine from the top nineteen. So that's ten time nine. Then you have to multiply the nine from the bottom nineteen by the ten from the top nineteen and that's nine times ten, which equals ten times nine. It's like you have to cross multiply. You multiply the tens by the tens, the ones by the ones, and then the tens by the ones and the ones by the tens. When you do the ten times nine and the nine times ten, that is ninety and ninety, which is one hundred eighty, which is the same as the amount that was missing with Rachel's way."

I recorded:

$10 \times 10 = 100$

$9 \times 9 = 81$

$10 \times 9 = 90$

$9 \times 10 = 90$

"What should I do next?" I asked Ben.

Ben said, "Add one hundred plus eighty-one, which is one hundred eighty-one. Then add ninety plus ninety, which is one hundred eighty. Then add one hundred eighty-one plus one hundred eighty plus nineteen. You have to add the nineteen because we only figured out nineteen groups of nineteen and we have to figure out twenty groups of nineteen." I recorded:

(10 × 10) + (9 × 9)

100 + 81 = 181

(10 × 9) + (9 × 10)

90 + 90 = 180

181 + 180 + 19 = 380

Rachel was busy drawing a picture as Ben was explaining his thinking. She had drawn twenty circles with the number 19 written in each circle. "I get why my way didn't work and where the extra problems are in Ben's way. I drew a picture of twenty circles with the number nineteen in each one."

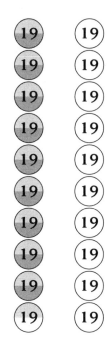

"Why did you do that?" I asked.

Rachel replied, "There were twenty scoops in the jar. Each circle is a scoop. Then there were nineteen beans in each scoop. I didn't want to draw nineteen beans so I just put the number nineteen in each one. When I multiplied ten times ten, I colored in one-half of ten circles. I did that because one of the tens stands for ten groups, so that's ten circles. The other ten stands for ten things in a group. Ten is about half of nineteen, so I colored in half of each of the circles because each one has

nineteen and ten is about half of nineteen. Then I still had nine times nine. That means nine groups of nine. So nine is about half of the beans in the circle. I went back and colored the other half of nine of the circles. I only colored nine circles instead of ten like before, because this time it was nine groups of nine. When I finished, I still had a lot of circles and beans I hadn't colored, so I knew I hadn't done the whole problem and what Ben said explains why." Rachel had a long-winded explanation that made sense to her, but I was not so certain about the rest of the students.

James had one more way to share. "I'd do it by multiplying twenty by ten, which is two hundred. That leaves nine more groups of twenty. So I'd multiply nine by ten, which is ninety and nine by ten again, which is ninety more. I did ten times nine two times because ten is half of twenty. Then I would add two hundred and one hundred eighty." I recorded:

20 × 10 = 200

20 × 9 = (10 × 9) + (10 × 9)

20 × 9 = 90 + 90 = 180

200 + 180 = 380

I then posed a new question. "How many scoops of *black* beans do you think will fill the jar?" The range of students' responses was similar to what I hear whenever I ask this sort of question to children or to adults. Some felt that a scoop was a scoop, so twenty scoops of black beans would fill the jar. Some thought it would take more because the smaller black beans would settle better. Of these students, some thought just one or two scoops more, while some thought five or six more. A few thought maybe it would take fewer scoops. For students who felt sure that there would still be twenty scoops, I asked if they felt that twenty scoops of anything would fill the jar, like rice or water. This revealed that some weren't as sure about the "a scoop is a scoop" theory in those instances, but others were.

Finally I resolved the situation by doing the scoops. There were cheers and oohs when the students saw that twenty scoops filled the jar.

After a few moments, David got a look of surprise on his face and blurted, "Of course it's the same number of scoops, the scoop doesn't change size, so it always takes away the same-size piece of the pile of beans or whatever you're scooping! I get it!"

"Oh yeah," mumbled several students.

"Here's a number sense kind of question," I said, changing the direction of the lesson. "How many black beans do you think are in the jar?"

"Why is that a number sense question?" Brendon wanted to know.

"Because you have to use information that you have to make a numerical decision in a new situation. You have to make sense of this new question," I answered. Students made estimates, and then I repeated what I had done with the lima beans, putting a scoop of beans on each table for groups to count. I recorded their counts, then rewrote them in order from smallest to largest:

63

64

67

69

71

73

74

As with the other data, we talked about the mode (there was none) and median (69), and then figured the mean (a little more than $68\frac{1}{2}$). They decided that 69 was the best number to use for how many black beans filled a scoop.

"So now we need to multiply sixty-nine times twenty," Andrew said. I did what I had

done before, recording suggestions from the students. I was interested in Mariah's suggestion that we do 70×20 and then subtract 20. If she hadn't offered this idea, I would have made the suggestion and asked students to explain why it made sense.

The entire lesson took an hour and didn't leave any time for individual work. While the lesson gave me some information about the class in general, it didn't help me assess each student's understanding.

DAY 2

I decided on the next day to devote some time to find out about individual students. I explained this to the students. "It's important for me to learn about how each of you is thinking so that I'm sure to help you each learn the multiplication skills you need," I began. "Yesterday we talked about how to solve two different problems with beans and scoops. Today, instead of actually using other size jars, scoops, and beans, I'm just going to give you two problems to solve."

I then presented the problems. "For one problem, imagine that a jar holds sixteen scoops and there were about fifty-three beans in each." I wrote on the board:

16 scoops

about 53 beans in a scoop

How many beans are there in the jar?

"Wow, that has to be a large scoop," Lela said.

"Or really small beans," Andrew added.

"You'd have to do fifty-three times sixteen," Cindy said.

I continued, "The other problem is to figure how many beans in a jar that held only six scoops with about twenty-eight beans in each." I wrote on the board:

6 scoops

about 28 beans in a scoop

How many beans are there in the jar?

"Oh, a really small jar," Claire said.

"You do twenty-eight times six," Ellie said.

"Can we work together?" Samantha asked.

"No," I replied. "My goal is to find out how each of you thinks. I'd like you to work on these problems by yourselves without help from anyone else, not even from me, unless you're really stuck. Also, I'd like you to try to find two ways to solve each problem." The students were used to my doing this from time to time. They reached for paper and began to work.

The students worked hard on these papers, and the room took on an unusual hush as they worked quietly. As some students finished quickly, I asked them to add an explanation of what they had done.

Andrew explained, for example, how he thought about money to solve 28 × 6. He wrote: *Since 25 is easy because of quarters, I changed 28 to 25. (25 × 6) which equals 150 + (6 × 3) = 168. The reason I did that was because 28 − 3 = 25.*

Mariah explained why she solved 53 × 16 by solving 53 × 8. She wrote: . . . *I did half of 16 which is 8. Then I did 8 × 53 or 53 × 8 2 times because there are 2 parts in a half and got 424. then I did 424 and 424 and got 848.*

DAY 3

The exchange between Rachel and Ben on the first day was unique to this class. Both students were in their second year with me as their teacher. They had learned to question and explore ideas they were wondering about. While their exchange and thinking had been very powerful, I was not so certain what the other students understood. With this in mind, my goal for this lesson was to return to Rachel's incorrect reasoning on the first day about finding the answer to 19 × 20 by thinking of the problem as 19 × 19 and calculating (10 × 10) + (9 × 9) and finally adding the one more group of 19 to make 20 groups of 19. To do this, I decided to

introduce how Jack, a student from another class, solved 32 × 14 by calculating (30 × 10) + (2 × 4), the same misconception that Rachel had confronted. By using Jack as a student from another class, this situation can be presented to any class, even when this particular misconception does not come from the class.

To begin class, I explained that Jack, a student in another class, had been solving beans and scoops problems as we had. In one problem, the jar held fourteen scoops of thirty-two beans.

I asked, "What would Jack need to do to find the number of beans in the jar?"

Tom explained, "He would need to multiply thirty-two times fourteen."

"Who can explain why Jack would need to multiply thirty-two times fourteen? Raise your hand if you think you can explain." I waited to see whose hands were raised and then called on Ellie.

"We know that there are fourteen scoops of beans in the jar," she said. "And we know that there are thirty-two beans in a scoop." Nods from the other students assured me that most understood the context for the problem.

Andrew offered a comment. "If it's like the problems we have solved, then there aren't thirty-two beans in every scoop," he said. "That's the average." There were more nods and I agreed.

I wrote on the board:

32 × 14

"Who remembers a way to figure out the answer?" I asked. I was interested to see who would volunteer and hear what their approaches would be. I called on Thea first.

"You do four problems," she said. I recorded what she described:

4 × 2 = 8

4 × 30 = 120

10 × 2 = 20

10 × 30 = 300

"The answer is four hundred forty-eight," she said after adding the partial products.

"That's how I do it," Samantha commented. A few others nodded.

"Can anyone describe a different way?" I asked. I called on James.

"You do two times fourteen and that's twenty-eight," he said. "And then ten times fourteen times three and that's . . . four hundred twenty. Then you add four hundred twenty and twenty-eight." I recorded on the board:

$2 \times 14 = 28$

$10 \times 14 \times 3 = 420$

$420 + 28 = 448$

James continued, "I did ten times fourteen because it's easier than thirty times fourteen and then I was able to multiply it by three. I got the same answer as Thea."

Claire reported next, describing the same approach she had used to solve previous problems to arrive at 448. I recorded what she described:

$32 \times 10 = 320$

$32 \times 4 = 128$

$320 + 128 = 448$

"Any other ways?" I asked. There weren't any volunteers, so I offered one.

"I can do it by adding," I said.

"Oh yeah," Trevor said. "You can add fourteen thirty-twos." I wrote on the board:

32	32	32
32	32	32
32	32	32
32	32	32
32	32	

I added aloud, inviting them to join in with me. Again, we got 448.

"That takes way too long," Andrew said.

"Yes, it does," I said. "It was a useful approach when you were first learning mul-tiplication and using smaller numbers, but it's not very efficient for larger numbers."

Samantha raised her hand. "You could write down fourteen thirty-two times," she said.

Jeremy groaned. "That would take even longer," he said.

I explained to the class about Jack's method. "Jack, a student from another class, solved this problem by thinking thirty times ten and two times four." As I explained I wrote on the board:

$(30 \times 10) + (2 \times 4)$

$300 + 8 = 308$

"Hey, that's what happened to me! Jack tried to solve his problem like I tried to solve mine," Rachel recognized.

I continued, "After our last class, I thought a good deal about your ideas and the different ways you were thinking. I've learned from thinking about mathematics for a long time that sometimes mistakes can be wonderful opportunities for thinking about something in a new way. And even though I thought about all the correct ways you suggested to find the answers to multi-plication problems, I heard about Jack's way and thought most about it. Rachel said her way of solving nineteen times twenty was the same way Jack had tried to solve thirty-two times fourteen. Jack had an idea that made sense to him, as did Rachel, and both were willing to share their thinking with us. We know the correct answer to Jack's prob-lem, but that doesn't tell us where his method went wrong. I think that's interest-ing to think about." I wondered what the students would say about it.

"Can anyone explain to Jack why his idea doesn't make sense?" I asked.

Several students tried. Most of their expla-nations were unclear or seemed incomplete, but I didn't interrupt or probe any of them. I just let all the students who had an idea express it to see what I could learn.

"Jack didn't use all of the numbers," Andrew said. "He can't just leave out some of them."

"Jack's answer isn't big enough," Lela said. "He only did thirty times ten and he has to do thirty-two times ten."

"He left out thirty times four and ten times two," Cindy said.

"He didn't finish it," Jeremy said.

Ben said, "He only did two parts. If it's two digits times two digits, he had to do four parts."

Each student who spoke seemed to have a glimmer of an idea. I noticed that some students expressed ideas that were similar to something already said, but they used different words and didn't seem to notice similarities among their explanations. I wasn't sure if students weren't listening to or weren't understanding what others were saying. It seemed to me that each student was invested in his or her own way of thinking and explaining. This didn't surprise me, as I've found that we all invest in particular ways to think about numbers that make sense and are comfortable to us.

After all who wanted to had offered their ideas, I gave the students a writing assignment. "First I'd like you to multiply thirty-two times fourteen in two different ways," I said. "Then write a letter to Jack explaining to him what you think is wrong with the method he first used."

Some of the students did the multiplication in only one way. Even though all the ways students had offered were still on the board, these children didn't copy another way from the board. They had learned to explain only what they understood. Jeremy wrote on his paper: *I only know one way.*

The students' comments to Jack revealed a range of ideas. Here are some of them:

From Jeremy: *I think Jack way diden't work because he diden't finish the probelm.*

From Lela: *I think Jack's way didn't work because he didn't take care of all of the prob-*

lem but he thought he did, all he did was made 32 into 30 and made 14 into 10. Then he thought he took care of the 2 and the 4 by doing 2 × 4, but really it was wrong.

From Ben: *Jack forgot to do 4 × 30 and 10 × 2 and those are importin because it is not a two and a one diget number.* He gave an example (see also Figure 11–2):

$24 \times 8 =$

$8 \times 4 =$

$8 \times 20 =$

From Brian: *Your answer is wrong because you didn't do 2 × 10 and 30 × 4 which are 2 of the 4 problems you have to do in a multiplicaton cluster which I think that's what you are trying to do.* (See Figure 11–3.)

▲▲▲▲▲▲Figure 11–2   *Ben included an example in his letter to Jack.*

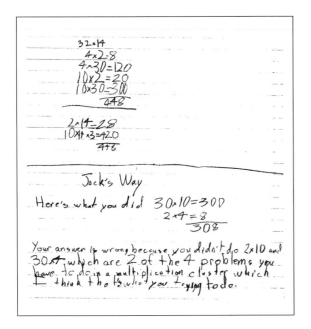

▲▲▲▲▲▲Figure 11–3 *Brian showed Jack his mistake.*

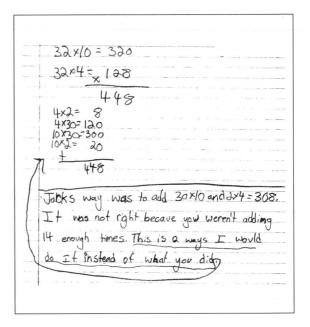

▲▲▲▲▲▲Figure 11–4 *Mariah showed how she solved Jack's problem.*

From Samantha: *But your way didn't work because you only did half of the problem. You needed to do 14 × 32 instead of doing only the didgets. You left out 30 × 4 and 10 × 2.*

From Saul: *Dear Jack, your way is wrong because you are looking at it as two problems.*

From Mariah: *Jack's way was to add 30 × 10 and 2 × 4 = 308. It was not right because you weren't adding 14 enough times. This is 2 ways I would do it instead of what you did.* Mariah then drew an arrow up to the two ways she solved the problem. (See Figure 11–4.)

From Claire: *Dear Jack, your way didn't work because [you] left out the rest of the number. With a double didjet one you have to use the numbers twice.*

From Tomas: *I think Jack's way didn't work because 30 × 14 makes a lot more than 30 × 10.*

From Andrew: *This is what went wrong. when you operate a multiplication problem the entire number has to be used. You have to use the digits with another numbers entire digits.* (See Figure 11–5.)

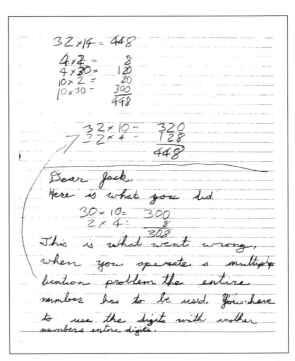

▲▲▲▲▲▲Figure 11–5 *Andrew tried to tell Jack where he went wrong.*

And Rachel wrote: *My way (Jack's way) is wrong because each number has to be used twice in a computation.*

These lessons, and the students' papers, were good reminders that partial understanding and confusion are natural to the process of learning. From these experiences, and all of the others provided with multiplication, students' understanding and skills grow stronger.

Questions and Discussion

▲▲

▲ *In the vignette, Rachel was able to make sense out of her misconception. What could you have done to help her if she had not been able to do this?*

Because Rachel had a strong conceptual understanding of multiplication as equal groups, she was able to create a drawing of twenty circles with a 19 written in each. Her drawing represented twenty scoops of nineteen beans. She was able to see the representation of 10×10 and 9×9 in her drawing and discovered that there were many circles and beans that hadn't been accounted for with her strategy.

Had Rachel not been able to make sense of the situation herself and if it were clear she needed intervention from me, I would have begun by talking with her. My goal in talking with her would have been to establish for myself what she did and did not understand. Among the tools I would have used to help Rachel is the idea of arrays. By using an array, Rachel would have seen how her idea was the beginning of an idea of what would work. She would also have seen what she still needed to do and why Ben's explanation made sense.

Also, using arrays to explore partial products would be a good follow-up for other students involved in this lesson to strengthen and clarify their understanding.

▲ *At the beginning of Day 2, you chose not to use jars, beans, and scoops and instead just gave the students problems. Why?*

One of my jobs as a teacher is to know when concrete materials make sense and enhance the lesson and when they are unnecessary. The students in the vignette had had enough experience and no longer needed the actual materials. For this reason, I chose not to use the materials and instead simply presented them with problems based on their experience with the materials. Had the students still needed additional experience with beans, scoops, and jars, I would have used them.

▲ *Why not just give students problems and skip the beans and scoops altogether? They could spend more time practicing rather than counting beans.*

Giving students problems without context takes away the opportunity to think about the problem in a way that makes sense and connects to the real world. While it does take time to go through the process, the process supports the students' development of number sense, problem solving, and computation.

Had I just given students the same series of problems to practice, there would have been no way for them to make sense of them. The practice would have been tedious and devoid of any meaning or context. The addition of the beans and scoops made the practice interesting and meaningful because it connected to real objects. The activity allowed students to practice, to make sense of the mathematics, and to use their number sense and problem-solving skills, and it allowed me to find out more about how they thought and what they understood.

▲ What is important to consider about the numbers of scoops and beans for these problems?

I learned from teaching this lesson that numbers close together such as 19 and 20 can lead to problems with communicating ideas clearly. In this lesson, students had a difficult time explaining strategies as a result. For example, it was difficult to clearly explain strategies involving taking away or adding one group, as this resulted in two of the same factors. Some students thought of the problem as 20×20. Another student thought of the problem as 19×19. The difficulty with clear communication was even more apparent when Ben and Rachel were exploring the error in Rachel's strategy for solving 19×19.

By experimenting with different-size jars and scoops before teaching the lesson you can find a jar and a scoop that generate numbers that facilitate clearer communication during classroom discussions about strategies. Examples of pairs of numbers that are easier to talk about might be 14 and 28 or 23 and 41, or even 19 and 30 or 20 and 43. Because no two digits are the same and the numbers are not close together, potential confusion and unclear communication can more easily be avoided.

CHAPTER 12
FRENCH FRIES

Overview

The book *How Much, How Many, How Far, How Heavy, How Long, How Tall Is 1000?*, by Helen Nolan (Kids Can Press, 1995), provides children with an opportunity to develop and practice their computational skills by using multiplication or division to solve a problem using two-digit numbers. Number sense, problem solving, and place value are also incorporated into the investigation.

Materials

▲ *How Much, How Many, How Far, How Heavy, How Long, How Tall Is 1000?*, by Helen Nolan (Kids Can Press, 1995)

Time

▲ one class period

Teaching Directions

1. Begin reading aloud the book *How Much, How Many, How Far, How Heavy, How Long, How Tall Is 1000?* As you read, discuss any points that you or the children find interesting.

2. Stop after reading the page about one thousand french fries and ask the students how they might answer the question of how many friends a thousand french fries would feed.

3. After having a class discussion about how to solve the question posed, ask a second related question: "Sam's Burgers sells fries with fifty-two fries per bag. How many fries would be needed if everyone in our class ordered one bag of fries?"

Teaching Notes

The vignette that follows tells the story of what happened in two classes in which I taught this lesson. The students in both classes had been taught the algorithm for multiplying multidigit numbers, but I have also taught this lesson to other classes in which students did not know the algorithm. Proficiency with two-digit paper-and-pencil multiplication is not necessary for success with this lesson. You can find additional information on this point in the "Questions and Discussion" section following the vignette.

I was eager to give the students an opportunity to think about one problem in several ways and to consider the connection between division and multiplication. The central problem, *If a single serving of french fries has 40 fries, how many friends would 1,000 french fries feed?*, is an ideal way for students to explore the connection between multiplication and division. This problem lends itself to being solved by multiplying, for example, _____ groups of 40 fries = 1,000 (_____ × 40 = 1,000), or dividing, for example, 1,000 fries divided into groups of 40 = _____ groups of 40 (1,000 ÷ 40 = _____). I also wanted to continue to develop the students' number sense about one thousand and their understanding of place value. This lesson provided me with the opportunity to examine the methods and the efficiency of those methods used by students to solve a two-digit by two-digit multiplication problem that involved a multiple of 10 ($4 \times 10 = 40$) and a power of 10 ($10^3 = 1,000$).

As mentioned, this vignette describes the lesson taught to two classes. The story of the first class is typical of what I've experienced with this lesson. I included the story of the second class because the discussion took some unusual mathematical directions. With the first class, the lesson stayed focused on solving the problem posed with multiplication, although there was a bit of discussion involving division and place value. With the second class, there was a brief discussion involving multiplication and division similar to the conversations in other classes, but the students became involved in a complex discussion involving place value, ratio and proportion, and division by zero. Ultimately, several students designed and pursued their own investigations to test a question posed by a classmate.

The Lesson

▲▲▲

THE FIRST CLASS

"Would one thousand kids fit in this room?" I asked. The students pondered this for a moment, then some nodded their heads indicating yes and most of the students shook their heads to indicate they didn't think one thousand students would fit into the classroom.

"Do you mean one thousand just standing or sitting on the floor or stacked up to the ceiling?" Mark asked.

"I don't think there is any way you could do it," Dana said. "There are twenty-five of us and look how much space we take up. There are four twenty-fives in a hundred and about ten hundreds in a thousand so that would be like . . . forty? Forty groups of us?"

"I would like to share a book with you today. The book has a lot of ideas about one thousand. The problems we'll solve come from the book," I explained. On the page about french fries, I read the following, "What about one thousand french fries? Could you eat all of them? Even if you loved french fries, one thousand would be too much for one person. You could share them. A single serving has about forty fries. How many friends would one thousand french fries feed?" After reading this, I paused to give the students time to think. Then I asked, "How could you figure this out?"

I chose this question because it offered the children the chance to look at the relationship between multiplication and division. That is, the problem could be solved by division, dividing 1,000 by 40, or a student could think of it as 40 × "how many" would equal 1,000 (40 × _____ = 1,000). They could have used other approaches to solve this problem, but I was hoping to focus on multiplication and division.

"You could divide forty into one thousand," Tina answered.

"Some people might not be able to divide by double digits. So you could take a zero away from the forty to make four and a zero away from the one thousand and make it one hundred and then figure out how many fours in one hundred," Mia said.

"How many fours are there in one hundred?" I asked. I doubted that others, or even Mia, knew why her idea made sense, but I decided to focus on the calculation she had suggested.

"It's twenty-five," Carol said.

"Is that the answer to dividing forty into one thousand?" I asked Tina.

She shrugged. "I'm not sure. I didn't figure it out."

I knew that by removing a zero from both the 40 and the 1,000, Mia made a more manageable problem that was proportional

to the original problem and, therefore, would produce the same answer. But this is a difficult concept for students to grasp. Nevertheless, I recorded on the board:

$1,000 \div 40 = 100 \div 4$

$100 \div 4 = 25$

"Who has another idea?" I asked. "Maybe we can check if twenty-five is right."

Abdul raised his hand. "I thought that there were five forties in two hundred. You can count forty, eighty, one hundred twenty, one hundred sixty, two hundred, so that's five," he shared, putting up one finger each time he counted another 40 until he held up five fingers. "There are five two hundreds in one thousand. Two hundred, four hundred, six hundred, eight hundred, one thousand, that's five two hundreds. So I think you could multiply five by five and that would make twenty-five servings." I noticed a look of relief on Tina's face as Abdul arrived at 25. I recorded Abdul's thinking on the board.

5 40s in 200

40, 80, 120, 160, 200

5 200s in 1,000

200, 400, 600, 800, 1,000

$5 \times 5 = 25$ (The first 5 is the number of 40s in 200 and the second 5 is the number of 200s in 1,000.)

"Are there any questions about how Abdul solved this problem?" I asked the students.

"I don't get it at all!" Mark said.

"Do you understand where the first five comes from?" I asked as I pointed to $5 \times 5 = 25$.

"I'm not sure," Mark said.

"Count by forties to two hundred," I suggested. Mark did. "How many forties did you get?" I asked.

"Oh, I see, there were five forties and there are five groups of two hundred in one thousand. I had to do it myself to get it. I get it now!" Mark said.

"Does someone have another way?" I continued.

"You can use division," Jim said, as he came to the board to show us his idea. Jim wrote $40\overline{)1000}$ and used the standard algorithm to figure out the answer.

"Why did you use division?" I asked.

"Well you are trying to figure out equal groups of forty, I think, and how many groups of forty there would be in one thousand. I used one thousand because that is the number of french fries and I used forty because that is how many are in each group," Jim explained.

"What do you notice about Jim and Abdul's work?" I asked.

"One used multiplication and the other did division and they got the same answer," Carol replied.

"I can use multiplication to prove my answer is correct," Jim added. "If I multiply forty by twenty-five I'll get one thousand. This proves my answer is right."

"I think they're both right. They just thought about it a little differently. They got the same answer," Becky said.

The problem I decided to present next would focus on multiplication. I wrote on the board *Sam's Burgers sells fries with 52 fries per bag. How many fries would be needed if everyone in our class ordered one bag of fries?* The students studied the board for a moment. "Are there any questions?" I asked. No one raised a hand, so I continued: "I would like each of you to work independently to solve this problem. You may use any of the ideas on the board or that you have heard before that you think would help you solve this problem. You may also use your own ideas. Please be sure to show me your thinking clearly using words, pictures, and numbers." The students got to work.

"Nate wants to know if he can use the calculator," Cally said.

"That's OK. Tell him to explain how he used the calculator, what did he do and why, and then show me a second way he could find the answer without the calculator," I replied. I had no problem with the use of a calculator. In fact, for this problem, it gave students a way to check their thinking. By using the calculator, they knew what the answer should be. When asked to do the problem a second way without a calculator, students examined their work closely when their computations didn't match the answer from the calculator. This seemed to offer them a way of checking on what they were doing.

Dean was a wonderful example of this. He had used his calculator and knew that $52 \times 24 = 1,248$. He wrote on his paper:

1.
$$\begin{array}{r} 50 \\ \times 20 \\ \hline 1000 \end{array}$$

2.
$$\begin{array}{r} 52 \\ \times 4 \\ \hline 208 \end{array}$$

3.
$$\begin{array}{r} 24 \\ \times 2 \\ \hline 48 \end{array}$$

4.
$$\begin{array}{r} 1000 \\ 208 \\ 48 \\ \hline 1256 \end{array}$$

Dean called me over to his desk. "I really need help!" he said. "Look, I know the answer should end in eight. I know because the two times four equals eight and also when I did it on the calculator, the answer ended in eight. This answer I am getting ends with six." He paused and studied his work for a moment. Then Dean proceeded to explain to me what he had done. When he got to 52×4, he stopped and started to giggle. "I know what I did wrong!" he exclaimed. "When I started, I rounded fifty-two to fifty and twenty-four to twenty. But, when I did fifty-two times four I should have done fifty times four; I did too much! I did two groups of four too much, which is eight, which is why I got eight too many!" He quickly revised his work and looked up with a proud smile.

Kate, Dean's neighbor, asked Dean about what he had done. As I walked away, Dean was helping Kate understand his thinking.

I noticed that most children had some way of thinking about this problem. A few used the standard algorithm and I asked them to show me a second way they could solve the problem. Many made use of finding partial products and solving the problem that way. (See Figures 12–1 and 12–2.) Brian made a mistake initially, then used a somewhat unusual approach he said he remembered from a previous lesson we had done. (See *Silent Multiplication,* page 37.) "I figured out fifty-two plus fifty-two equals one hundred four, then doubled and doubled until I added fifty-two twenty-four times," he explained.

Having children work on an assignment like this during class gives me the opportunity to check on children's understanding and evaluate if I need to redirect their thinking. I noticed Alfredo's paper and asked him to explain what he had done, as I had difficulty making sense of his work. (See Figure 12–3.) He explained, "First I multiplied four by two to get eight. Then I multiplied four by five, which equals twenty. I put down the zero and carried the two. I multiplied two by twenty and got forty. I multiplied two times five equals ten. I put down the zero and carried one and added it to the two I already carried and got three. Then I put down the three because that is what I carried. Then I added it up." Alfredo was clearly confused in his attempt to use the algorithm.

"Let's back up. What is fifty-two times four?" I asked Alfredo. He was able to figure out on paper that the product was two hundred eight. "Where did the four come from?" I asked.

"It comes from the four in twenty-four," Alfredo replied.

▲▲▲▲▲▲Figure 12–1 *Josh made use of finding partial products to solve 52 × 24.*

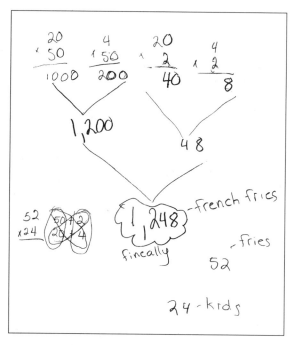

▲▲▲▲▲▲Figure 12–2 *Carol also used partial products.*

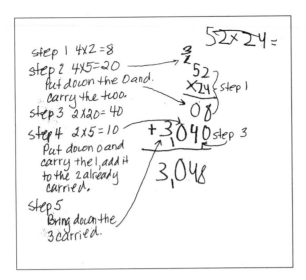

step 1 4×2=8
step 2 4×5=20
put down the 0 and.
carry the two.
step 3 2×20=40
step 4 2×5=10
Put down 0 and
carry the 1, add it
to the 2 already
carried.
step 5
Bring down the
3 carried.

52×24 =
52
×24 step 1
08
+3040 step 3

3,048

▲▲▲▲▲Figure 12–3 *Alfredo's thinking was unclear to me. As he explained what he had done, I recorded it. To help him, I had him think of 24 as 20 + 4 then multiply to find the partial products. Finally, Alfredo added the two partial products to find the answer.*

"What do you think we should do next?" I asked.

"Multiply fifty-two times twenty?" he replied tentatively.

"I agree. Do you know how to do that?" I asked. He nodded his head and proceeded to solve the problem. "Would I put the answers together now?" he wondered, referring to the 208 he had gotten when he multiplied 52 × 4 and the 1,040 when he multiplied 52 × 20. I nodded my head yes and he quickly added the partial products together to find the product of 52 × 24.

As I reflected on this lesson, I regretted that I had not taken the opportunity to more fully examine Mia's idea early in the lesson about removing a zero from both the 40 and the 1,000. When I taught this lesson again to a different class, I decided beforehand to go in this direction if the opportunity arose. It did!

THE SECOND CLASS

I began once again by reading the book and posing the same question about how many friends a thousand french fries would serve. The children came up with the same ways to solve the problem as the first class had.

Paul said, "You could do it as a division problem by dividing one thousand by forty."

"If you agree with Paul's idea, show me by putting your thumb up; if you disagree, put your thumb down," I said. The students indicated that they agreed.

After stumbling initially, Jeannie explained her idea. "Another way you could do it is there are five forties in two hundred and five two hundreds in one thousand. So you could multiply five times five and there would be twenty-five bags of french fries."

"I don't get it. Where did she get the fives?" Tony wondered. Several hands went up. I called on Felicia, who had difficulty explaining Jeannie's idea. Felicia asked if she could call on someone else to help her. After two more student attempts, it was resolved.

Brett shared next. "You could do division like Paul said, but you could take a zero off the forty and a zero off one thousand and you could then divide one hundred by four and you would get the answer," he said.

"Why did you take off the zeros?" Al asked.

"Because if there are zeros in both you can cross them out," Brett explained.

"Will this always work for numbers ending with zero?" I asked. Brett nodded his head yes. "How do you know?" I continued.

"I learned it in Korea, that's all," Brett said.

I wrote Brett's idea of crossing out zeros on the board. The class looked a bit uncertain. "Does anyone have any idea why Brett's idea seems to work and if it will work in all cases?" I pushed. I gave the students a few moments to think about this, then had them quickly share their thinking with their neighbors.

Jasmine came to the board and wrote:

4.0 = 4

100.0 = 100

"Then if you don't have the decimal point, it would still be the same way, without the decimal point you can still take away the zeros," Jasmine explained.

I was not convinced that Jasmine understood what she was saying and the look on the faces of the other students indicated that they were lost. I decided to try to clear up the confusion by asking a more basic question. I wrote *40* on the board and while pointing to the zero, asked, "In this number, forty, what does the digit zero tell us?"

"That the four is four tens, not just four," Greg offered. "The zero shows there are four tens," he continued.

Near the number 40 that I had written a few minutes earlier, I wrote the number *41*. I pointed to the four in both numbers and said, "I agree that the four in both of these numbers means four tens, but what does the one tell us in forty-one and the zero tell us in forty?" I was trying to help the students be clear about place value with tens and ones. Greg's answer told me he had some idea about tens and perhaps he even understood the meaning of the zero, but I wasn't sure.

"It tells us we have no ones," Greg responded.

"Zero divided by zero equals zero so I think you don't need to divide by the zeros, that's why you can take the zeros off," Jasmine said. Jasmine's reference to dividing by zero is a complicated idea. To think about why, it helps to remember that division is the inverse of multiplication. Because of this relationship, we can check a division answer by multiplying; for example, we know that $6 \div 2 = 3$ is correct because $3 \times 2 = 6$. Now think about dividing by zero; for example, $6 \div 0 = ?$ There isn't any number that can be substituted for the question

mark that, when multiplied by zero, would equal six. Mathematicians say that division by zero is undefined because no answer that makes sense, so we can't do it. It seems, however, that $0 \div 0 = ?$ is possible because if we substitute zero for the question mark, $0 \div 0 = 0$, it checks out because $0 \times 0 = 0$. But *any* number multiplied by zero equals zero. So the answer to $0 \div 0$ could be 6, 18, 147, or any number. It doesn't make sense to have a numerical calculation for which any answer would work! Because of the complexity of thinking about dividing by zero, I decided not to address Jasmine's comment further.

Brett came to the board and wrote:

4 tens = 40

100 tens = 1,000

"Another way to look at it is four tens equals forty and one hundred tens equals one thousand and if you just cross out the tens then you would have four and one hundred like this," he said as he crossed out the word *tens*. While the resulting math equations weren't correct, Brett's idea was based in his thinking proportionally.

"Ohhh!" responded several students as they saw the reasoning behind Brett's idea. What I appreciated so much about Brett is that even though he knew the rule and had learned it in school in Korea, he was willing to investigate the underlying reasons that rule worked.

"I have another way," Jin said. He came to the board and wrote:

$20\overline{)40}$ $40\overline{)1000}$

"You see, if you divide forty by twenty, you will get two. And if you cross out the zero in forty and the zero in twenty you will be left with four divided by two. This will also give you two. You see, it works! Well, the same is true with one thousand divided by forty. There are twenty-five forties in one thousand and if you cross off the zero in forty and the last zero in one thousand, you will have one hundred divided by four, which is twenty-five," Jin explained.

The students nodded their heads in agreement after Jin's explanation. After a moment of quiet think time, Al quickly raised his hand. Jin, who was still standing at the board, called on Al.

"OK, I see how it works with problems with no remainders, but what about remainders? What happens then?" Al wanted to know. He came up to the board and wrote the following problem:

$$20\overline{)130}$$

"What about a problem like this? There's a remainder," he said.

Jin looked puzzled. Other students started talking among themselves about this question. As a teacher, this was an exciting moment for me. The students had become totally involved with this problem. A child was actually leading a class discussion. Not only was he leading a class discussion, but the students were involved in an interesting challenge and were making conjectures and discussing ideas with passion.

"It seems many of you have ideas about this," I interrupted after a few moments. "Please record your ideas on your paper and we'll discuss them together in a few moments." Jin, still looking a bit puzzled, went back to his seat, as did Al. Both boys began to write furiously. Before too long, I looked around and noticed a group of three or four students at the board having an animated discussion about their ideas. Jin called me over.

"I've figured out about the remainders part," he said. "I believe that the remainder will always end with zero. Because of this fact, when you remove a zero from the other two numbers, you will also have to remove a zero from the remainder. Then it will work. With the problem of Al, one hundred thirty divided by twenty, that answer is six remainder ten. When I remove the zero from twenty I get two; I remove a zero from one hundred thirty and I get thirteen. Thirteen divided by two is six remainder one. You see, it works."

After a few more minutes, I asked for the class' attention once again. The students were very involved and reluctant to settle down for a discussion. Jin explained his thinking to the class as he had with me. Again Al raised his hand.

"OK, this zero thing works with these numbers. But would it work for any numbers that end with zero?" Al wanted to know.

"What numbers could you use to find out?" I asked.

Al shrugged. I paused and a few students raised their hands to offer Al ideas. I called on Lisa.

"Could he use one thousand divided by four hundred?" she asked tentatively.

I nodded my head yes and wrote her suggestion on the board.

"He could use five hundred divided by fifty," Nate said.

"One thousand divided by five hundred would work, I think," Kara said.

"One million divided by six hundred thousand," Alisa suggested as her classmates giggled about the size of the numbers.

"I think he should try his idea by using a number that begins with one and has thirty-three zeros and is divided by a number that has a five with twenty-nine zeros!" Tony suggested smugly.

"I think they'll all work," Greg said.

As I left, Jin, Al, and several other students had begun their investigations.

Questions and Discussion

▲▲▲

▲ *With the first lesson you used the numbers 52 and 24. Is there a particular reason you chose these numbers or does the choice of numbers make any difference?*

I consider both 52 and 24 to be "friendly" numbers because they are close to 50 and 25 respectively, both numbers that students can deal with easily. I consider numbers like 5, 10, 20, 25, 50, and 100 to be landmark, or friendly, numbers. Keeping in mind this idea of friendly numbers, the level of difficulty can be increased or decreased depending on the numbers used. Numbers that are close to a multiple of 10, for example 32, are easier to work with than a number like 36. Twenty-four is an easy number because it is one away from 25 and many students can think about groups of 25 easily because of their experience with money. With these ideas in mind, a problem such as 43×36 is more difficult than 52×24. I chose simpler numbers for this problem because I wanted to encourage the students to make use of the basic structure of our base ten number system in solving the problem. I believe this encourages deeper mathematical understanding, develops number sense, and improves computational accuracy and efficiency.

Other pairs of numbers that are easy for students to work with are 26×11, 24×19, and 13×49. These pairs of numbers are close to the familiar, friendly numbers of 10, 20, 25, and 50.

Problems that offer a bit more of a challenge might be 62×51 or 18×38. I consider these problems slightly more difficult than the previous ones. Each problem has one factor that is close to a familiar numbers such as 50 or 20, but the other factors are close to less familiar numbers such as 40 and 60.

Problems such as 44×36 or 27×84 offer more of a challenge. Both factors are farther away from multiples of 10 and the multiples of 10 that they are closest to are not particularly familiar.

By using this information, you can change the numbers in the problem to give students additional practice at an appropriate level.

▲ *What strategies were you expecting the students to use?*

I expected students to do essentially what they did, that is, I expected some to think of the problem as a division problem ($1,000 \div 40$), some to think of it as a multiplication problem ($40 \times$ _____ = 1,000), and some to think of it using what they knew about the number system (there are five forties in two hundred and five two hundreds in one thousand, so $5 \times 5 = 25$).

I also expected students to decompose the numbers into simpler, more manageable numbers. For example, students could have thought about 52 as $50 + 2$ and 24 as $20 + 4$. Then they could have figured out the partial products, that is, $4 \times 2 = 8$, $4 \times 50 = 200$, $20 \times 2 = 40$, and $20 \times 50 = 1,000$, and then added the partial products to find the answer of 1,248. This is the underlying idea of the standard algorithm, but looking at it like this helps children make sense of the magnitude of the answer as well as why the process works.

I did not expect the students in the second class to become so involved with the exploration of zeros and remainders. To me as a teacher, it was thrilling to have them so motivated about a complex idea. Their thinking, ideas, and justifications were wonderful. Getting so excited about an idea that they designed their own investigation to find out about one student's question is what I wanted to see happening. As they investigated crossing off zeros, not only were they gaining greater understanding of the base ten number system and ratio and proportion, but they were also doing numerous multiplication and division problems in a meaningful context.

▲ How do students who have not yet been introduced to the standard algorithm approach this problem?

I adapted the lesson slightly for the less experienced classes. I didn't give students the second problem, 52×24, although it was within their reach to solve it. These students needed time to develop their solutions in writing to the problem, *How many servings of 40 in 1,000?*

Students who don't know or haven't mastered the algorithm use similar approaches to those used by students who have learned the algorithm. The approaches that less experienced students described in their written work tended to be more varied and gave insights into their mathematical thinking. These approaches included using the distributive property, relying on the base ten number system, guessing and checking based on number sense and prior knowledge of multiplying with multiples of 10, repeated addition, skip-counting by 40 to 1,000, using number sense and knowledge of the number system to solve a larger problem, and using division to figure the number of forties in one thousand. (See Figures 12–4, 12–5, 12–6, and 12–7.)

When students are given numerous opportunities to solve problems such as this with lots of time to share ideas and strategies, they begin to learn more efficient and accurate means for solving problems that often resemble the standard algorithm we use here in the United States. Kirk's second solution is evidence of this. (See Figure 12–4.)

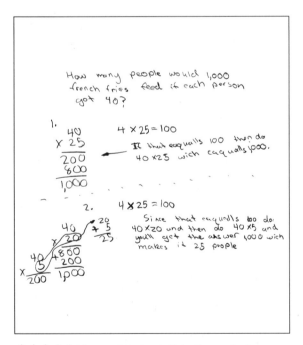

▲▲▲▲▲▲Figure 12–4 *In his first solution, Kirk used his knowledge of our base 10 number system. In his second solution, Kirk used partial products in a way that resembles the standard algorithm.*

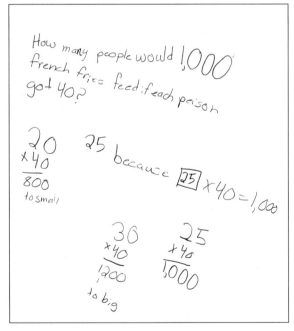

▲▲▲▲▲▲Figure 12–5 *Conner used guess-and-check and multiplication by 10 to find the missing factor.*

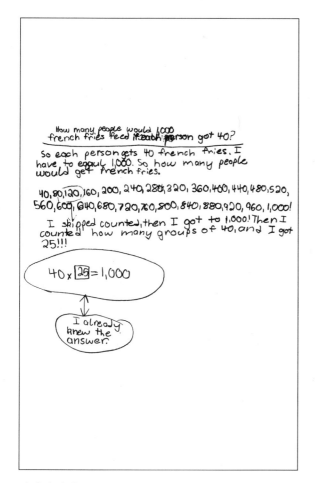

How many people would 1,000 french fries feed if each person got 40?

So each person gets 40 french fries. I have to equal 1,000. So how many people would get french fries.

40, 80, 120, 160, 200, 240, 280, 320, 360, 400, 440, 480, 520, 560, 600, 640, 680, 720, 760, 800, 840, 880, 920, 960, 1,000!

I skipped counted, then I got to 1,000! Then I counted how many groups of 40, and I got 25!!!

40 × 25 = 1,000

I already knew the answer.

▲▲▲▲▲▲Figure 12–6 *Miguel used skip-counting to find the missing factor.*

I first
How many people would
1,000 fries feed if each
person got 40?

40	40	40	40	40
40	40	40	40	40
40	40	40	40	40
40	40	40	40	40
40	40	40	40	40

200, 200, 200, 200, 200

anser 25 people

2 How many people would 1,000 french fries feed if each person got 40?

 5
× 5   it came from the 200
25 people

▲▲▲▲▲▲Figure 12–7 *Andrew used his knowledge of our base 10 number system and his number sense to solve a larger problem.*

CHAPTER 13
COLLECTING PENNIES

Overview

In this lesson, students use their skills in problem solving, number sense, and computation to figure out the number of pennies they would have if they collected one penny per hour for one year. Students also explore the relationships between units of time. For example, if they collect one penny per hour and there are twenty-four hours in one day and seven days in one week, how many hours are in a week and, therefore, how many pennies would they collect? Ultimately, students calculate the number of pennies they would collect in one year.

Materials

▲ dot paper, approximately 20 sheets per pair of students (see Blackline Masters)
▲ 12-by-18-inch construction paper, 1 sheet per pair of students
▲ scissors
▲ tape
▲ chart paper

Time

▲ three class periods

Teaching Directions

DAY 1

1. Lead a discussion about allowances to ensure that all students are familiar with this idea.

2. Explain to students they are to pretend that they are collecting an allowance of one penny per hour. Ask students to figure out the number of pennies they would have at the end of one day (twenty-four hours).

3. Brainstorm with students different time periods (second, hour, day, week, etc). List these on the board as students share. Ask the students to sequence the following periods of time from shortest to longest: day, hour, month, week, year.

4. Find and record on the board or chart paper equivalents for hour, day, week, month, and year.

5. Cut out a 7-by-24 array from a sheet of dot paper. Ask students to each talk with a partner about why the array represents the number of pennies collected in one week. Tape the array to a sheet of 12-by-18-inch construction paper.

6. Ask students to share strategies that could be used to calculate the number of pennies represented by the 24-by-7 array. Record strategies on the board or chart paper.

DAY 2

1. Ask students to make arrays from the dot paper to represent the number of pennies collected in one day, one week, four weeks, and one year.

2. Have students calculate the number of pennies collected for each time period.

3. Lead a class discussion about the students' answers for the number of pennies collected in one year.

DAY 3

Have each child write a letter to a friend, a parent, or a teacher. The letter should address the following three points:

- ▲ how much money the student earned for each time period;
- ▲ an explanation of the solution the student used to figure the amounts for each time period; and
- ▲ how the student will spend the money earned in one year.

Teaching Notes

Rick Kharas, a colleague and teacher from Syracuse, New York, created this activity and shared it with me. When I tried it with my students, I found the lesson engaged them and generated excellent discussions.

Prior to this lesson, the students in the vignette had had experience with thinking of multiplication geometrically as arrays. The students also were comfortable multiplying by 10. Some of the students were able to solve multidigit multiplication problems using the distributive property. For example, they could solve 19×12 by breaking 12 into $10 + 2$

and multiplying $(19 \times 10) + (19 \times 2)$ to get partial products of $190 + 38$ for a final product of 228.

During this exploration, students must grapple with the messiness of the measurement of time. There are at least six ways one year could be defined within the context of this problem: 365 days, $365\frac{1}{4}$ days, 52 weeks, 12 4-week months, 12 31-day months, or 12 30-day months. Depending on how they define one year, students get different answers.

Students also work with decimals as they convert the number of pennies collected into dollars.

The Lesson

▲▲▲

DAY 1

"How many of you get an allowance?" I began. Most of the students raised their hands.

Ray shared, "My mom gives me three dollars a week, but I have to take out the trash, do the dishes, and keep my room straight."

"I have to do all that and take care of my sister!" Jessi added. "Boy, it's a lot of work and not so much money!"

Melina commented, "Once I cleaned out the whole garage and my uncle gave me ten dollars. It took all day!"

The students talked among themselves about their chores and the allowances they received. After a few moments, I asked for their attention. "Let's pretend for a moment that you collect for an allowance one penny each hour." A chorus of laughs and hoots erupted.

"That's not much!" Juan said.

"You'll never get any money at that rate," Amy blurted out.

When the students quieted down I continued, "Talk with your group about how many pennies you would collect in one day with a penny-per-hour allowance."

After four or five minutes I asked for the students' attention. "What did your group decide about the number of pennies you

would have with the penny-per-hour allowance?"

I called on Shamus. "There are twenty-four hours in a day, so that would be twenty-four cents, or pennies."

"Tell how your group knew that," I pushed.

Shamus explained, "Well, there are twenty-four hours, like I said, and you get one penny each hour. So that would be like one times twenty-four, one penny twenty-four times. That's twenty-four pennies in twenty-four hours!"

Ray interjected, "Yeah, but you don't get paid for sleeping."

I explained to Ray and the others, "In the penny-per-hour allowance system you collect one penny for each hour whether you are sleeping or awake."

Ray smiled. "Oh, then Shamus is right."

I wanted to change the direction of the conversation for a few moments. "Besides days and hours, what other periods of time can you think of?" I asked as I wrote these on the board.

"Minutes!" responded Chip.

"Century," Hal added.

"What about seconds and minutes?" Krista suggested.

"There is a year," Mike said.

"And a month, too," Sue added.

"Week," Shawna said.

"I think week is tricky," Jason said. "Do you mean a school week, which is five days, or do you mean the kind of week that is seven days?"

"I meant seven days," Shawna replied.

"Jason makes a good point. Sometimes when we think of a week, we mean five days, and sometimes we mean seven days. Let's think of it as seven days for this activity today," I said as I added Shawna's suggestion of a week to the other ideas I had written on the board. If Jason had not made this observation about weeks, I would have brought it to the attention of the students.

"Are there other time periods on our list that could be different amounts of time, like a week?" I asked. The students studied the list and hands began to go up.

"What about month?" Chase wondered. "Sometimes there are thirty days and sometimes thirty-one."

"February sometimes has twenty-eight days and sometimes has twenty-nine," Jason reminded us. "I know because my sister just missed being born on leap day."

The students were quiet for a moment as they considered the list once again. There were no further comments so I decided to move on.

"I am going to put a check mark by several of the periods of time on our list," I explained. "I would like you to work with your table group to put the periods of time I indicate with a check mark in order from the shortest to the longest." I quickly marked hour, day, week, month, and year. The students were able to accomplish this quickly and accurately. After a few moments I called the class back to attention. I went around the room, asking table groups to tell the time period that should come next. I listed these in order.

Next I asked, "Can anyone think of another way to state the amount of time in a day?"

Wally answered, "Twenty-four hours."

On the list next to day I wrote = 24 hours. "One day equals twenty-four hours," I repeated to draw students' attention to what I had just done with Wally's suggestion. "Your task for the next few minutes is to work together with your group members to write down equivalents for one week, one month, and one year like I just did for one day."

Alyssa's hand went up. "I don't get it!"

"I can show her," Melina said.

"Go ahead, " I replied.

Melina walked to the front of the room, pointed to the list and said, "It's like we did for one day, we made it equal to twenty-four hours because they are the same. Now we have to find out what these other ones equal." She pointed to one week, one month, and one year. "For example, one week is the same as seven days."

"That's just what I was thinking," I responded.

It is surprising how often students can offer explanations to their peers that are as clear and concise as what the teacher was planning to say. After Melina's explanation, Alyssa quickly reached for her pencil and began working with her table group. The students had no further questions.

As I observed the students working, I noticed that most had found only one equivalent for each time period. I interrupted the class and asked, "Is it possible to find more than one equivalent for some of the time periods?"

Kerry's hand went up. She explained, "Our group found that one month has thirty days or four weeks."

Ray commented, "But thirty days is not the same as four weeks. There are seven days in a week and seven times four is twenty-eight, not thirty."

"And some months have thirty-one days," Jason said.

"And then there is February, like Jason said," Becca added. "Sometimes it has twenty-eight days and sometimes it has twenty-nine!"

"I think all of your comments are useful," I responded. "Sometimes things are not as precise as they seem and you have to think about the situation to decide what is appropriate. We'll talk some more about this in a few minutes when we share what we have found out about the other time periods. For now, let's get back to the job of working with your group members to find as many equivalents as you can for each." After a few more minutes of work time, I asked for the students' attention.

"What did you find out?" I asked to begin the discussion.

I called on Jan. "We knew from what was said earlier that twenty-four hours is the same as one day." I recorded Jan's information on the board.

"We were sort of confused about month," Derek shared with some hesitation. "So we put down that one month was ABOUT four weeks or twenty-eight, twenty-nine, thirty, or thirty-one days! We put *about* in capital letters because we couldn't figure out what to put for sure."

"Mathematicians have a symbol to show what Derek is talking about. It's kind of a wavy equal sign," I explained as I wrote the following on the board:

1 month ≈ 4 weeks ≈ 30 days

"Even though a month can be twenty-eight, twenty-nine, or thirty-one days, I chose to put that one month is about thirty days because that is how people often think about a month," I explained. When the discussion had concluded, I had the following information listed on the board:

1 day = 24 hours

1 week = 7 days

1 month ≈ 4 weeks ≈ 30 days

1 year ≈ 12 months ≈ 52 weeks ≈ 365 days

After a few moments a hand went up. I called on Jason. "My sister, who just missed being born on leap day, says a year is really three hundred sixty-five and a quarter days and it's the fourth of a day that makes leap years happen. Is that true or is she just making it up?"

"That is true, Jason," I responded. "Every year there is an extra fourth of a day, so at the end of four years, there are four-fourths or one whole day. Leap years happen every four years and that is why leap years have three hundred sixty-six days instead of three hundred sixty-five days."

To get students refocused I asked, "How many of you remember the amount of money you'd receive in one day?" There was a chorus of "twenty-four cents." I explained to the class, "I am interested in finding out how many pennies you would collect in a week."

I held up a sheet of dot paper (see Blackline Masters). I explained and demonstrated, "Each dot represents one penny. I am going to count over twenty-four dots and down seven dots to make an array." To make sure everyone understood what had just been demonstrated I said, "Talk to the person next to you about the two numbers I used. Explain to your partner why you think I used seven and twenty-four." After each student had had the chance to share with a partner, I called the students back to order. "Why did I use the number twenty-four for the length of my array?"

Tara answered, "We get twenty-four pennies each day."

I continued, "How about the seven?"

Shamus answered, "That's the number of days in one week."

I cut out the array and taped it to a sheet of construction paper, then asked, "What strategies can you think of to find the number of dots in the array?" I paused for about twenty seconds to give students time to think about the question. As often happens, just by waiting, a greater number of students became comfortable with their thinking and consequently were more willing to share their ideas and solutions.

About half the students had their hands raised. I called on Juan, who suggested, "We could count by twenties."

"Would you come show us what you mean using the array I have taped to my construction paper?" I asked Juan.

Using the cutout array, Juan counted across the top of the array to twenty then went down the rows counting, "twenty, forty, sixty, eighty, one hundred, one hundred twenty, one hundred forty. Then I would count the rest of the fours: four, eight, twelve, sixteen, twenty, twenty-four, twenty-eight. Then I would put together the one hundred forty and the twenty-eight."

I recorded Juan's strategy as follows:

Count by 20s: 20, 40, 60, 80, 100, 120, 140

Count by 4s: 4, 8, 12, 16, 20, 24, 28

Add 140 + 28

B.J. said, "I would make two groups of seven times ten, then count the rest of the pennies, or dots, by twos."

I recorded B.J.'s idea as follows:

7 × 10 = 70

7 × 10 = 70

Count the rest by 2s

Alyssa proposed, "We could just count all the dots."

"That would take too long!" responded several students.

I listed Alyssa's idea as follows:

Count all the dots.

James was the next to share. "We could plus twenty-four, seven times."

I wrote:

24 + 24 + 24 + 24 + 24 + 24 + 24

Kerry suggested the alternative, "We could add seven twenty-four times."

I recorded Kerry's idea as follows:

Add seven 24 times.

Tara offered, "It would be quicker to just multiply twenty-four times seven."

I recorded her thought along with the others:

24 × 7

DAY 2

I began by reminding the students of what we had done the previous day. "Yesterday, at the end of class, I cut an array from dot paper to represent the number of pennies we would collect in one week if we got one penny per hour. We also shared strategies to figure out the number of pennies by figuring the number of dots in the array. Today I would like you and your partner to use dot paper to cut arrays that represent the number of pennies collected in one day, one week, one month, and one year. When you have cut your arrays, tape them to a sheet of construction paper. Later you will also need to figure the number of dots in each array. Leave space between the arrays so you will be able to show the strategy you used to figure the number of dots for each array." As I gave these instructions, I referred to the construction paper with the array I had made the previous day. "Are there any questions?" I asked. There were none.

To be sure the students had made the connection that the dots stood for pennies, I asked, "What does each dot stand for?"

"A dot stands for one penny," Anthony replied. "Each array stands for the number of pennies we get for that amount of time." The other students nodded their agreement. I paused for just a moment to see if there were any last-minute questions. Ray raised his hand.

"Can we use the chart with the stuff about time?" Ray asked, pointing to the sequenced time periods and their equivalents.

"Yes," I replied. "If you find the information about time and the strategies to figure out the number of dots in the arrays useful, please use it. That is why it is posted, so you can refer to it."

Melina smiled and said, "This is going to be easy."

The class was busy gathering materials and getting started. It was interesting to observe the different approaches the students took. I noticed that Shamus and Wally had made good progress. "What did you do to figure out how to make the one-month array?" I asked them.

Wally answered, "We traced the one-week rectangle four times and cut them out. Then we taped the four weeks together and it made one month."

Kerry and Alyssa, who were working nearby, volunteered, "We did it a different way. We counted down thirty-one dots and across twenty-four dots to make our array."

"Why did you use the number thirty-one?" I asked.

"Well, we think that four weeks really isn't enough for one month," Kerry explained. "Only February has twenty-eight days, which is four weeks, and sometimes it has twenty-nine days. Most months have thirty-one days," she continued, looking over at the information from the day before. "So we decided that since most months have about thirty-one days, we would use thirty-one."

"But not all months have thirty-one days," retorted Wally.

"More months have thirty-one days than twenty-eight," Alyssa replied.

"I guess that's why it says *about;* the months aren't all the same amount of time," Kerry said, sighing.

"If Wally and Shamus think of a month as twenty-eight days and Kerry and Alyssa think of a month as thirty-one days, will each pair have the same number of pennies at the end of a year?" I asked.

The students thought about this for a moment, then Alyssa smiled and said, "We would have more pennies because we are saying there are three days more in a month than Wally and Shamus."

This problem, like many in real life, is messy. There is not a single answer regarding the length of a month or the length of one year.

As I looked up, I noticed that Jesus and Tomas were excitedly waving their hands in the air to get my attention. "We're done!" they announced.

"Tell me how you made the array to represent one year's pennies," I said as I examined their work. Jesus started to explain, but I quickly stopped him. Jesus is a strong student and I wanted to be sure Tomas understood what they had done. "Jesus, I would like you to let Tomas explain what the two of you did. Listen carefully because when Tomas is finished I will ask if you agree and if you would like to add anything further."

After a few moments of silence it became evident that Tomas was uncertain of how the one-year array had been made. "Jesus," I began, "Tomas is your partner and it is important that he understands what the two of you did together to construct this array. I will be back in a few minutes. In the meantime, I want the two of you to talk over the process of how the array was made. When I come back I want Tomas to explain to me what you did." They both nodded, so I left them alone to talk.

I returned a few minutes later. Tomas quickly held up the one-month array. "We put twelve of these together," he said, smiling.

"Why did you do that?" I asked, trying to probe deeper.

Tomas was quiet a moment. Jesus whispered to him, "Look at the chart!"

Tomas looked up at the chart and smiled, saying, "We did twelve of these because there are twelve months in a year and this is one month."

"I like the way you two are working together to make sense of this problem," I said, wanting to encourage their cooperation.

About halfway through the period, I stopped the class and said, "After you have cut your arrays from the dot paper, you will need to use the arrays to help you figure out the number of pennies collected in each time period. Remember to use the strategies we discussed yesterday to help you with this." I pointed to the list of strategies from the day before.

As the students continued to work, I stopped and talked with various pairs of students. "How did you figure out the number of dots in the one-week array?" I asked Norris and Jake.

Norris explained, "We broke the one-week array into three small arrays. We counted the first one by tens and got seventy. We also counted the second one by tens and got seventy again, then we counted the rest by twos and got twenty-eight. We added seventy plus seventy plus twenty-eight, which equals one hundred sixty-eight."

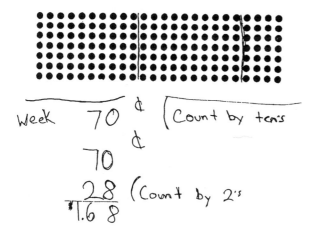

In another group, Juan was telling James, "We have to add four weeks together to get one month, so that's one hundred sixty-eight plus one hundred sixty-eight plus one hundred sixty-eight plus one hundred sixty-eight." James wrote down the numbers and added them.

"That's six hundred seventy-two pennies," James reported.

Kerry and Alyssa calculated the number of pennies in a month a different way. They used a 24-by-31 array and explained, "We counted by tens up to two hundred forty and did that two more times. Then there was only one row left and we knew it had to be twenty-four. So we added two hundred forty plus two hundred forty plus two hundred forty plus twenty-four and it equaled seven hundred forty-four."

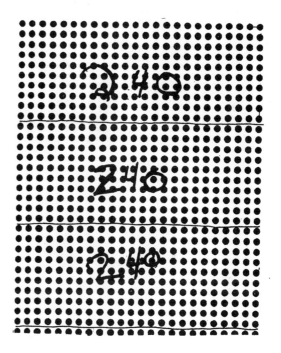

Rondi and Tawny were raising their hands excitedly as I walked over to find out what they were doing. They proudly explained, "This is how we figured out one month!" Pointing to their paper, Rondi continued, "We drew six ten-by-ten arrays because we both knew that ten times ten equals one hundred. Then we drew three more four-by-ten arrays. After that there was only one row of twenty-four left. We added six hundred plus one hundred twenty plus twenty-four and it came out to seven hundred forty-four."

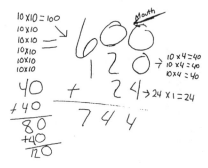

"How did you figure out the number of pennies you would receive in one year?" I asked Roy and Darren.

Roy explained, "We knew there were seven hundred twenty pennies in one month. We added seven hundred twenty together twelve times because there are twelve months in one year. For one year, the total pennies would be eight thousand six hundred sixty."

"How did you figure there were seven hundred twenty pennies in one month?" I asked.

"Well, each dot was a penny. There were twenty-four dots, or pennies, in one day.

There are about thirty days in a month, so we figured out there were seven hundred twenty pennies for thirty days," Darren explained.

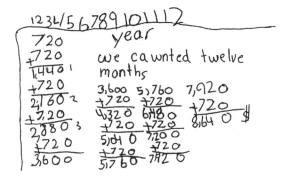

I thought it was interesting that the students were using a variety of numbers to represent the length of a month. I knew that this would make for a rich class discussion.

B.J. and Jerry were having difficulty figuring the total for one year. They had used the same approach to figure the total for one month as Rondi and Tawny had, that is, breaking each month into six 10-by-10 arrays, three 10-by-4 arrays, and one 1-by-24 array. When they tried to expand this idea to twelve months, they came up with seventy-two 10-by-10 arrays. B.J. explained, "seventy-two ten-by-ten arrays are too many to do even with a calculator!"

I paused for a moment to think about their problem. "Let's see if we can approach the problem in a different way. You've told me you have seventy-two ten-by-ten arrays. Can you think of a way to make this problem simpler?"

Neither student responded, so I decided to give a bit more information. "Do you know what ten times ten equals?"

They both answered at the same time, "one hundred!"

"How many hundreds are in the problem?" I asked.

Jerry answered, "Seventy-two all together."

"So you need to figure out what seventy-two hundreds equal," I continued.

They both nodded but looked confused. I thought about how to help the boys. I decided to have them work through a few simpler problems that involved multiplying by 100 in hopes that they might discover a pattern that would help them with the larger problem of 72×100.

I jotted down on a sheet of paper $2 \times 100 =$ _____. B.J. took his pencil and wrote 200 in the blank. Next I wrote $5 \times 100 =$ _____, to which B.J. answered 500. Finally I wrote $14 \times 100 =$ _____, to which B.J. responded $1,400$.

"Do you see any pattern to these problems?" I asked.

B.J. said, "They all are multiplying by one hundred and there are two zeros in the answer."

"Where do you think the zeros came from?" I asked.

Jerry blurted out, "Oh, I get it! It's sort of like when you multiply by ten, you just add a zero. So when you multiply by one hundred, you add two zeros. It's like we have to count by one hundred seventy-two times."

B.J. grinned as he wrote down $72 \times 100 = 7,200$. "You gave me an idea about how to solve the rest of this problem. There are thirty-six ten-by-four arrays left. I could think of it as thirty-six ten times, which is three hundred sixty, then I would have to add three hundred sixty four times, three hundred sixty plus three hundred sixty plus three hundred sixty plus three hundred sixty." Jerry looked very confused. I asked B.J. to explain his idea to Jerry again using the arrays to help Jerry see his thinking. Asking a student to explain her or his thinking helps clarify and solidify learning.

I called the class back to order to lead a quick discussion about the number of pennies that would be collected in one year.

Johnny shared, "I got eight thousand six hundred forty pennies!" I wrote Johnny's total on the board.

Shamus said, "We got eight thousand sixty-four pennies." I added his total to the list with Johnny's.

"We got eight thousand nine hundred twenty-eight," Kerry said. "Alyssa and I know why our answer is different than Shamus's. It's because we did a month with thirty-one days and Shamus did a month with twenty-eight days." I added 8,928 to the list.

"We got what Shamus got," Juan said.

"Did anyone get a different answer than the ones listed here?" I asked. I knew most of the students had one of these answers, as I had watched closely as they worked, keeping an eye out for any errors they might make. When they made an error, I questioned them immediately to help them understand and make needed corrections.

"What do you think is going on here?" I asked.

"Well," Juan said, "Kerry said she and Shamus used different numbers of days to equal a month. If they did that, the number of pennies collected in a month would be different, so they would get different answers for a year."

"Johnny, how many days did you use for a month?" I asked.

"Thirty days," Johnny replied. I wrote this next to Johnny's total.

"What about you, Shamus?" I continued.

"We thought of a month as four weeks, or twenty-eight days," Shamus explained. I wrote this information beside his total as I had done with Johnny's information.

"We did a month as thirty-one days," Kerry said.

"We did like Shamus, which is why we got the same answer," Juan added.

"I like Kerry's way the best because you get the most pennies!" Melina said.

DAY 3

"How many pennies would you collect in one week according to the penny-per-hour allowance idea?" I began. Most students remembered it was 168 pennies.

"If you wanted to tell someone how much money you had, would you say, 'I have one hundred sixty-eight cents'?" I asked. About half the students shook their heads no.

Annie explained, "You would say you have one dollar and sixty-eight cents."

The students nodded their agreement. I wrote *168 cents =* _____ on the board and asked Annie to come to the board and fill in the blank. She wrote *$1.68*.

To make sure that students could use the correct notation to write dollars and cents, I wrote the following on the board:

439 cents = _____

1,284 cents = _____

62 cents = _____

"I'd like you to discuss and solve these three problems with your partner," I said. I observed as the students worked. No one had trouble with the use of the dollar sign or the placement of the decimal.

"You are going to be writing a letter today," I explained to the class. "You may write your letter to a friend, a parent, or a teacher. Your letter should include three main points: first, how much money you collected for each time period; second, an explanation of how you figured out the amount you collected for one day, one

week, one month, and one year; and third, what you will do with the money you collected in one year."

I quickly listed these points on the board as I explained them to the students.

Tara raised her hand and asked, "Can we work with our partner?"

I responded, "You've done some excellent work with your partner, but for the letter writing I would like you to work independently. This way I will have a better idea of what each of you knows and understands. Also, when you have to write and explain your thinking in this way, it helps you clarify for yourself what you understand."

Ray asked with a giggle, "Are you going to give us that much money?"

"How much money do you think that would be?" I asked Ray.

Ray quickly checked his calculations and responded, "Eighty-six dollars and forty cents for the whole year."

"Calculating how much money it would take for me to give everyone eighty-six dollars and forty cents would be an interesting math problem for another day. Right now we have letters to write."

The students settled down and got to work writing their letters.

Questions and Discussion

▲▲

▲ *What is the value of choosing a problem that is messy?*

Often, real-life applications of mathematics are messy. Information is not always clear and numbers can vary. The person solving the problem must make sense of it in the best way possible given the context.

In this problem, students could have found at least six different answers to the number of pennies collected once an hour for an entire year. If the student defines the year as 365 days, the number of pennies will be 8,760. If the year is $365\frac{1}{4}$ days, then the number of pennies is 8,766. A 52-week year yields 8,736 pennies. For 12 4-week months, the total number of pennies is 8,064, for 12 31-day months, the total number of pennies is 8,928, and for 12 30-day months, the total number of pennies is 8,640. This kind of messiness generated wonderful mathematical discussions and comparison of results as students worked.

▲ *What do you see as the benefits to students of writing letters at the end of the lesson?*

Letter writing is a motivating and interesting format in which children describe their thinking. Writing can help students analyze and make sense of the math they have just experienced. It is important to provide students with an actual audience. Typically, I like to establish myself as the audience, giving enough feedback so that students know I have actually read and thought about what they have written. Asking students to write letters to others provides a nice change, especially if students deliver the letters and get a response. When students are writing letters to others, it is important that they be edited for spelling, grammar, and punctuation.

▲ *In a problem like this, a mistake early in the problem can ruin the final results. This would be frustrating for my students. How do you handle this?*

As the students work, I constantly observe what they are doing. I look over their shoulders and as I do this I monitor their calculations. This way, I can catch their mistakes early. When I notice errors, I ask students questions that will lead them to see and understand their mistakes, which increases the likelihood of an accurate final answer.

When monitoring student work in this way, I also gain important insights into how students are thinking. This kind of work period and monitoring also allows me to work with students individually and reduces the number of times a student may practice a procedure incorrectly.

ADDITIONAL ACTIVITIES

This section presents five additional activities that are effective for supporting students' multiplication learning. Two games, *Pathways* and *Times 10*, provide practice that is important once students have learned a concept. A whole class warm-up activity, *Don't Go Over*, also provides practice and can be varied and repeated throughout the year. The two investigations, *Consecutive Factors* and *Investigating Elevens*, engage students in looking for patterns. A brief summary and the key mathematical ideas precede the teaching directions for each activity.

Teaching Notes

Games that call for computing are effective because they generate students' interest and give purpose to computing. Playing games results in increased attention to accuracy and reduces the likelihood of students practicing a procedure incorrectly, as can happen when they are completing a worksheet of practice exercises. Also, games can develop students' number sense and problem-solving skills as they think about strategies for playing and observing the strategies of others.

It's important for teachers to investigate the mathematics in explorations before presenting them to students. Below is a way that you might organize and think about the patterns that emerge in *Consecutive Factors* (page 165). Rather than imposing this particular way of recording, however, be sure to listen first to students' ideas about the patterns they see. Then, if you wish, you can introduce this way of organizing information to help students see patterns in the differences among consecutive products.

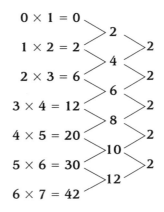

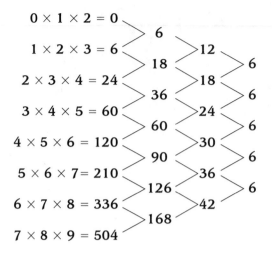

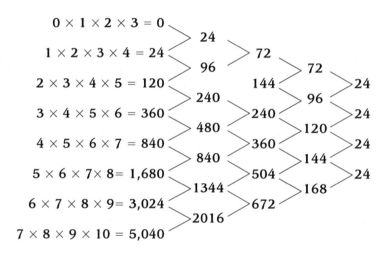

Investigating Elevens was actually suggested by one of my students who noticed that the product of single-digit numbers when multiplied by 11 were made up of two of whatever number had been multiplied. For example, 7 × 11 = 77 and 9 × 11 = 99. She wanted to know if there were any pattern to the digits of the products when 11 was multiplied by a two- or three-digit number. Structuring a class investigation based on a student's interest acknowledges her mathematical curiosity and gives the message to the class that you value their ideas.

Pathways

OVERVIEW

Pathways is a two-person game that provides practice with some of the harder multiplication facts. The object of the game is to be the first player to complete a continuous pathway from one side to the other across the game board. To allow you to choose the level of practice most appropriate for your students, several different game boards are included.

MATERIALS

▲ cubes, tiles, or other game markers in different colors, about 15 per student
▲ paper clips, 2 per pair of students
▲ *Pathways* game board, one per pair of students (see Blackline Masters)
▲ optional: rules for game, one per pair of students (see Blackline Masters)

TEACHING DIRECTIONS

1. Project an overhead transparency of the game board or post a large version that all of the children can see.

2. Explain the rules for play. Either write the directions on the board or distribute a copy to each pair of students.

Pathways

You need:
a partner
game board
2 paper clips
cubes, tiles, or other game markers in two colors,
about 15 of each color

Rules
1. Each player uses a different color of cubes, tiles, or game markers.
2. Player 1 chooses two numbers from those listed at the bottom of the game board, places a paper clip on each, and marks the product of the numbers on the game board with a marker of his or her color.
3. Player 2 moves just one of the paper clips to another number, multiplies the two factors indicated, and places a different color marker on the product.
4. Play continues. Note: It is legal to start the game with both paper clips on the same number, or to move a paper clip to the same factor as the other paper clip.
5. The winner is the first player to complete a continuous pathway in the same color across the game board. A completed pathway may include boxes that share a common side or a common corner, as seen in the figures below.

3. Play the game several times with you as one player and the whole class as the other.

4. When you feel the students understand how to play, have them play the game in pairs.

5. After the students have become familiar with the game, initiate a discussion about the strategies they use.

Times 10

OVERVIEW

This two-person game provides practice with basic facts and multiplying by 10. The game extends *Pathways* by requiring students to multiply by 10 after they multiply the two factors they select. The game can also be changed to *Times 100* to give students further practice.

MATERIALS

▲ cubes, tiles, or other game markers in different colors, about 15 per student

▲ paper clips, 2 per pair of students

▲ *Times 10* game board, one per pair of students (see Blackline Masters)

▲ optional: rules for game, one per pair of students (see Blackline Masters)

TEACHING DIRECTIONS

1. Project an overhead transparency of the game board or post a large version that all of the children can see.

2. Explain the rules for play. Either write the directions on the board or distribute a copy to each pair of students.

Times 10

You need:
a partner
game board
2 paper clips
cubes, tiles, or other game markers in two colors, about 15 of each color

Rules

1. Each player uses a different color of cubes, tiles, or game markers.
2. Player 1 chooses two numbers from those listed at the bottom of the game board, places a paper clip on each, multiplies the factors, and then multiplies the resulting product by 10. Player 1 then marks the product on the game board with a marker of his or her color.
3. Player 2 moves just one of the paper clips to another number, multiplies the two factors indicated and then multiplies by 10, and places a different color marker on the product.
4. Play continues. Note: It is legal to start the game with both paper clips on the same number, or to move a paper clip to the same factor as the other paper clip.
5. The winner is the first player to complete a continuous pathway across the game board. A completed pathway may include boxes that share only a common side or a common corner, as seen in the figures below.

3. Play the game several times with you as one player and the whole class as the other.

4. When you feel the students understand how to play, have them play the game in pairs.

5. After the students have become familiar with the game, initiate a discussion about the strategies they use.

Variation: Students play *Times 100*, using the factor of 100 instead of 10.

Don't Go Over

OVERVIEW

This whole class warm-up activity provides students practice with estimation, which improves their number sense, computation, and problem-solving skills. Students also practice basic facts and can use the relationship between multiplication and division as a strategy for solving the problem. You can repeat the warm-up many times throughout the year, varying the difficulty of the problems to meet your students' needs.

TEACHING DIRECTIONS

1. Write a problem on the board or overhead transparency, for example, $4 \times \underline{} = 25$.

2. Ask the students to figure out what factor when multiplied by 4 comes closest to 25 without going over. When students offer an answer, ask them to explain their thinking. This helps students consider one another's ideas and increases their flexibility in reasoning.

3. Continue with other problems, varying the difficulty to challenge your students, for example, $\underline{} \times 11 = 103$ or $10 \times \underline{} = 151$.

Consecutive Factors

OVERVIEW

In this activity, students investigate the patterns that result when they multiply consecutive factors. In the investigation, students apply their computation skills first by multiplying factors and then by searching for patterns in the products. The activity also gives students experience analyzing what happens when numbers grow in an orderly and predictable way. (See "Teaching Notes," pages 161–162, for additional information.)

TEACHING DIRECTIONS

1. List on the board or overhead transparency pairs of consecutive factors and ask students to identify the products. Record them.

$0 \times 1 = 0$
$1 \times 2 = 2$

$2 \times 3 = 6$
$3 \times 4 = 12$
$4 \times 5 = 20$
$5 \times 6 = 30$
$6 \times 7 = 42$

2. Ask the students to examine the list for patterns. To assist and focus students' thinking, ask the following questions:

What do you notice about the products?

Are the products even? Odd? Both?

What do you notice about the difference between consecutive products? [See "Teaching Notes," pages 161–162.]

3. Repeat the experience for three consecutive factors. Ask students to look for patterns that are both similar to and different from multiplying two consecutive factors.

$0 \times 1 \times 2 = 0$
$1 \times 2 \times 3 = 6$
$2 \times 3 \times 4 = 24$
$3 \times 4 \times 5 = 60$
$4 \times 5 \times 6 = 120$
$5 \times 6 \times 7 = 210$
$6 \times 7 \times 8 = 336$

4. For students who are interested and willing to persist, have them investigate the results of multiplying four consecutive factors. Then ask them: "Can using what you have learned so far about multiplying consecutive factors help you make predictions about multiplying five consecutive factors? Why or why not?"

Investigating Elevens

OVERVIEW

This activity engages students in looking at patterns in products when 11 is one of the factors. Students are generally pleased by the pattern that exists when multiplying 11 by a one-digit factor. The pattern of repeating digits in the products makes these facts easy to learn. However, the pattern changes when multiplying 11 by two- and three-digit factors, making it an interesting investigation for students.

TEACHING DIRECTIONS

1. List on the board or overhead transparency pairs of factors with 11 as the second factor in each. Ask students to identify the products.

$1 \times 11 = 11$
$2 \times 11 = 22$
$3 \times 11 = 33$

$4 \times 11 = 44$
$5 \times 11 = 55$
$6 \times 11 = 66$
$7 \times 11 = 77$
$8 \times 11 = 88$
$9 \times 11 = 99$

2. After discussing the pattern in the products, ask the students to investigate what happens if you continue the list to include multiplying two- and three-digit factors by 11. Discuss what the students discover.

ASSESSMENTS

This section suggests ten assessments, all intended to take students a short time to complete, generally ten to fifteen minutes. The first assessment, *Why Does 4 × 3 = 3 × 4?*, monitors students' understanding of the commutative property; this assessment can be repeated by changing the numbers involved. The second assessment, *True or False: □ × △ = △ × □*, also addresses the commutative property and asks children to consider it in a generalized form. *Twenty-Four Tiles* assesses students' understanding of the relationship between multiplication and rectangular arrays. The next three assessments, *True or False: □ × 1 = □*, *Prove or Disprove 0 × □ = 0*, and *Even Times Even*, relate to number theory. *True or False: 30 × 6 = 6 × 3 × 10* and *True or False: 400 × 8 = 8 × 4 × 100* address multiplying by 10 and multiples of 10, critical ideas for multidigit multiplication. In *Solve and Explain*, students explain how they get the answer to a multidigit multiplication problem. *Multiplication Stories* reveals if students can connect multiplication to real-world situations.

Teaching Notes

Assessing student understanding through writing gives teachers insights into what students have and have not learned. For students, writing assignments provide opportunities to reflect on their learning, solidify their thinking, raise questions, reinforce new ideas, and review older ideas. I typically give students writing assignments several times a week.

Class discussions are important to the writing process. A discussion before writing provides students ideas to consider and include in their writing. This can be especially helpful when learning is new and fragile. Leading a discussion after students write gives them the chance to share their own thinking while considering the ideas of others. These discussions help students become flexible thinkers.

When students are working on writing assignments, I circulate throughout the class, offering assistance. When students need help, I begin either by asking them to explain their ideas to me or asking them questions to spark their thinking. After I listen to students' explanations, I suggest that they begin by writing down the exact words they spoke. I sometimes tell a student to make her thoughts go from her brain, past her mouth, down her arm, and out her pencil onto the paper.

While teaching the lessons in this book, I used two kinds of writing assignments frequently to give me information about the students' progress and to inform my instructional decisions. One was to ask students to respond in writing to prompts I designed; another was to ask students to write and solve multiplication stories. Both kinds of assignments served as ongoing assessments that provided me valuable information about what the students knew and their misconceptions, thus guiding my instructional choices.

Why Does
4 × 3 = 3 × 4?

PROMPT

Explain using words, pictures, and numbers that 4 × 3 = 3 × 4. Be sure to include rectangles as part of your explanation.

This prompt monitors students' understanding of the commutative property. Understanding and applying the commutative property makes learning the multiplication table more manageable for students. When they completed *Learning the Multiplication Chart* (see page 15), the usefulness of the commutative property became more evident to the class.

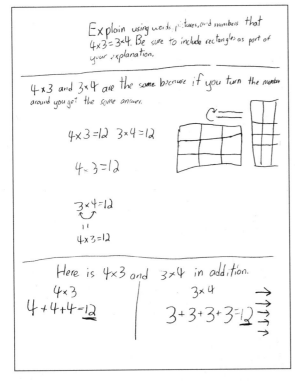

▲▲▲▲▲▲Figure 1 *James's work is typical of most students. He showed his understanding of the commutative property numerically and geometrically.*

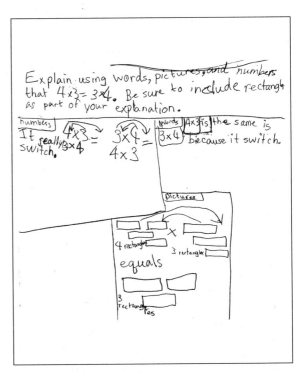

▲▲▲▲▲▲Figure 2 *Juan's work showed that he understood he could switch the order of the factors. However, his drawing showed a lack of understanding that multiplication is about equal groups. Juan needed additional work in this area.*

True or False: □ × △ = △ × □

PROMPT

True or false: □ × △ = △ × □? Show how you know.

This assessment also addresses the commutative property and asks students to think about it expressed in a generalized form. Important for students to know is the rule for substitution, that whatever number goes in the box goes in all the boxes in the same sentence. The triangle indicates a different number, but the same number must be used for all of the triangles in the same sentence.

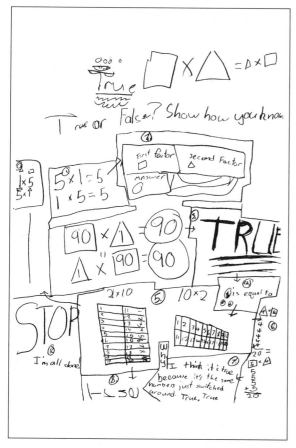

▲▲▲▲▲▲Figure 3   *James gave many examples indicating he understood the commutative property. He showed understanding numerically and with arrays.*

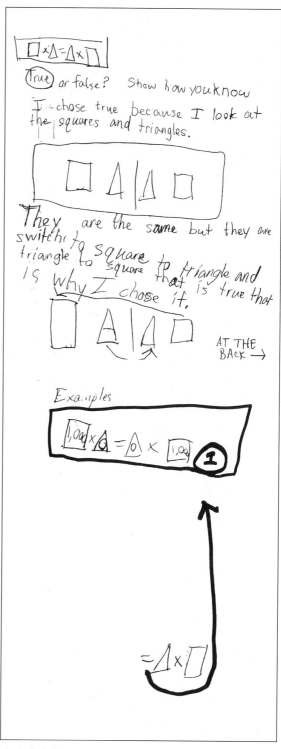

▲▲▲▲▲▲Figure 4   *Juan's written word indicated an understanding of the commutative property. When I questioned him about what 1,000 × 0 would look like, he explained, "It would look like zero groups of one thousand or one thousand groups of zero, which is nothing, so I didn't draw a picture of nothing."*

Twenty-Four Tiles

PROMPT

You have 24 tiles. Show all the ways you can arrange them in rectangular arrays. How are arrays related to multiplication? To division?

Prior to being given the third prompt, the students had experienced *Multiplication Chart* and *Related Rectangles* (see pages 15 and 56). My purpose for this prompt was to find out about students' understanding of the relationship between multiplication and rectangular arrays. I was also interested to know if students understood how multiplication, division, and rectangular arrays related to one another.

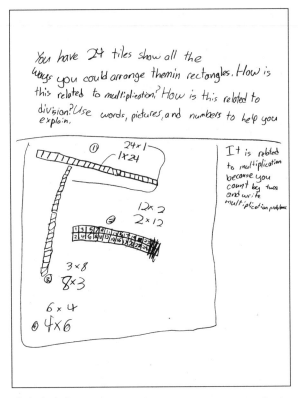

▲▲▲▲▲▲**Figure 6** *James's paper was typical. He indicated partially how to arrange the 24 tiles into arrays. His explanation about how multiplication and division are related showed little understanding. More work in the area was needed for James and most other students.*

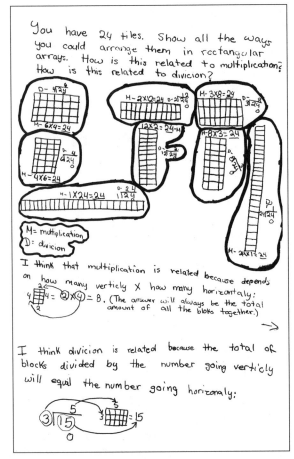

▲▲▲▲▲▲**Figure 5** *Anamaria's paper showed a strong understanding.*

True or False: $\square \times 1 = \square$

PROMPT

True or false: $\square \times 1 = \square$? *How do you know?*

The number 1 is the identity element for multiplication, also called the multiplicative identity. That's because 1 multiplied by any number is equal to that number. While this may seem obvious to adults, it's valuable to call students' attention to this aspect of our number system.

▲▲▲▲▲▲Figure 7 *David's work was representative of most students and indicated his understanding that the identity for multiplication is the number 1, because 1 multiplied by any number equals that number.*

Prove or Disprove:

$0 \times \square = 0$

PROMPT

Prove or disprove this: $0 \times \square = 0$.

This prompt assesses students' understanding of another important property of our number system—the zero property. This property states that any number multiplied by zero is zero.

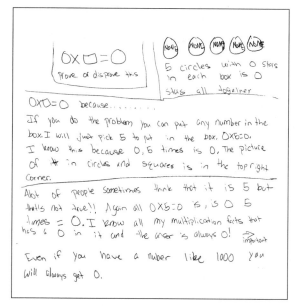

▲▲▲▲▲▲Figure 8 *Cori's work demonstrated clear understanding of the zero property of multiplication. Her understanding was typical.*

Even Times Even

PROMPT

What happens when you multiply an even number times an even number? Explain how you know.

You can extend this prompt by asking students to consider the results when two odd numbers are multiplied and when an odd and an even number are multiplied. Be sure to ask students to discuss why this happens.

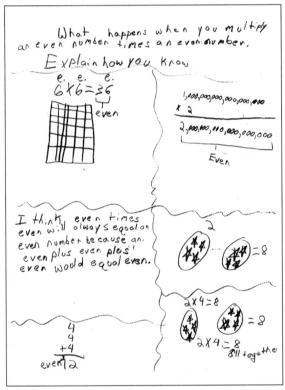

▲▲▲▲▲▲Figure 9 *Ben's paper showed he understood that the product of two even factors is even.*

True or False:
$30 \times 6 = 6 \times 3 \times 10$

PROMPT

True or False: 30 × 6 = 6 × 3 × 10? Explain.

This prompt addresses multiplying by 10, being able to factor 30 into 3 × 10, and rearranging factors when multiplying. These skills are necessary for students to become efficient with computation. To monitor students' understanding, I presented many opportunities for written responses similar to this.

> True or false:
> $30 \times 6 = 6 \times 3 \times 10$.
>
> Explain your thinking.
>
> $6 \times 3 \times 10 =$ It is true because $30 \times 6 = 180$
> $6 \times 30 = 180$ and 3×10 is multiplying by 10 so it would be 30 then you do $30 \times 6 = 180$.
>
> $30 \times 6 = 180$

▲▲▲▲▲Figure 10 *Tom's work indicated he was able to multiply by 10 effectively.*

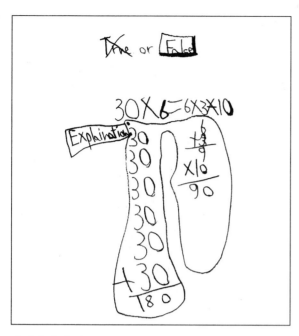

▲▲▲▲▲▲Figure 11 *Steve used repeated addition to solve 30 × 6. He made an error when attempting to solve 6 × 3 × 10, adding 6 + 3 rather than multiplying 6 × 3.*

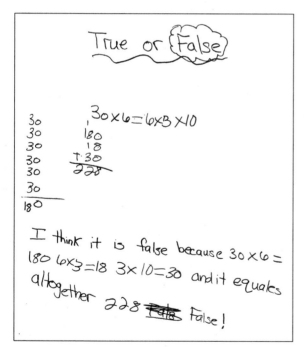

▲▲▲▲▲▲Figure 12 *Amy used repeated addition to solve 30 × 6. She showed her failure to understand the meaning of the equals sign when she added 180 + 18 + 30. She also showed a lack of understanding about three factors.*

True or False: 400 × 8 = 8 × 4 × 100

PROMPT

True or False: 400 × 8 = 8 × 4 × 100? Explain.

This prompt addresses multiplying by 100, being able to factor 400 into 4 × 100, and rearranging factors when multiplying. These skills are necessary for students to become efficient with computation. To monitor students' understanding, I presented many opportunities for written responses similar to this.

▲▲▲▲▲▲Figure 13 *While Cori's written explanation was more elaborate than most students', her basic understanding was typical.*

Solve and Explain

Explain one way to solve the following problem: 13 × 12.

Computational efficiency is an important goal for students. Lessons such as *French Fries* (see page 137) and *Matilda* (see page 113) provide a context for practicing computation similar to the computation in these prompts. To monitor students' progress toward computational efficiency, I periodically give prompts such as this one. The student samples show the growth toward efficient computation that can occur over time. For some of these assessments, such as the student work shown for 52 × 19, I also asked students to write a related story problem.

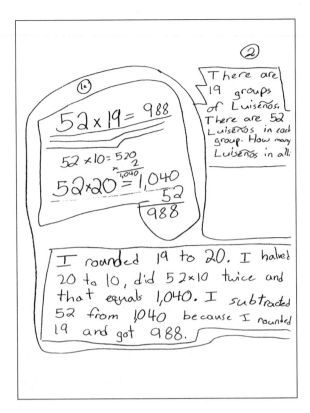

▲▲▲▲▲▲**Figure 15** *James shows his solution to 52 × 19.*

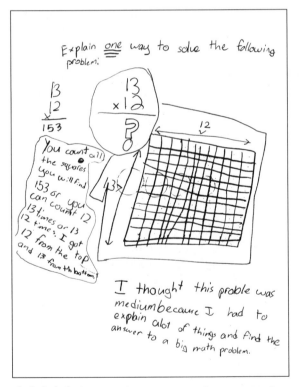

▲▲▲▲▲▲**Figure 14** *James used a rectangular array to solve this problem. When solving multi-digit problems, an array is not particularly efficient. In this case, James arrived at an incorrect solution.*

Multiplication Stories

PROMPT

Write a story problem that includes a question that can be solved using multiplication.

Having students write multiplication stories is another way to assess their understanding while also providing multiplication practice. In order to write a story including a question that can be solved using multiplication, a student must have a basic understanding of the concept. If a student does not understand the concept of multiplication, this will become apparent when he attempts to write multiplication stories. (See Figures 16 and 17.) Also, writing multiplication stories clarifies and deepens their understanding of multiplication.

I have included samples from two classes. The students in the first class were still working on learning the basic facts. In the second class, students used facts about animals to write multidigit multiplication problems. In both instances, the students solved their own problems. After editing and revising, the students took their work to the computer lab to produce final copies of their multiplication stories (see Figures 18–20). I gathered a copy of each student's multiplication story, photocopied them all, and bound them together to create a problem-solving booklet for each member of the class. Each day we solved and discussed one problem from the booklet. The author of the day was, of course, quite proud!

An African elephant eats about 300 pounds of food per day.

The elephant has been eating 300 pounds of food a day for 10 days. How many pounds of food has the elephant eaten in the 10 days?

The way to figure it out is with multiplication. This is the problem, 300 X 10, Here are some ways to solve this problem,

The easiest way is to add a 0 on to the end of 300. You can do this because anything X 10 can have a 0 added onto it. Then it would be 3000

You could count by 300's,

300, 600, 900, 1,200, 1,500, 1,800, 2,100, 2,400, 2,700, 3,000

The answer is 3000

▲▲▲▲▲▲**Figure 16** *Cori's work shows she clearly understood that multiplication is about equal groups.*

An anaconda can grow to be 27 ft. long. An Etruscan shrew can grow to be 21 ins. long. How many ft. and inches all together?

27 ft. 21 inches

7×7=49 I know that an Anaconda is longer than a Etruscan because what equals 49 is 7 and 27 is more than 21.

▲▲▲▲▲**Figure 17** *Allie's work showed her confusion. She had written an addition problem rather than a multiplication problem. Her solution was also confusing.*

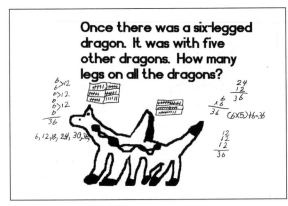

Once there was a six-legged dragon. It was with five other dragons. How many legs on all the dragons?

6)12
6)12
6)12
6
36

6, 12, 18, 24, 30, 36

24
12
36

6
x6
36   (6x5)+6=36

12
12
12
36

▲▲▲▲▲▲Figure 18 *Melissa solved her own problem correctly. Most other students solved this problem correctly, also.*

Once there was a six-legged dragon. It was with five other dragons. How many legs on all the dragons? 30

5, 10, 15, 20
25, 30

▲▲▲▲▲▲Figure 19 *Allison misunderstood the problem. There were a few other students who made the same error.*

African elephants eat about 300 pounds of food everyday. How much do five elephants eat in five days?

By Nicole

AFRICAN ELEPHANTS EAT OVER 300 POUNDS OF FOOD PER DAY. HOW MANY POUNDS OF FOOD IN 5 DAYS? HOW MANY POUNDS OF FOOD IN ALL APRIL? (1 MONTH).

AMANDA

Giraffes grow 19 feet tall.

If 17 girraffes stand on top of each other, how tall will they be altogether?

Cindy

Anacondas can grow to twentyseven feet long. How many feet long are ten of them attached to each other?   Steve

▲▲▲▲▲▲Figure 20 *Multiplication stories based on animal facts.*

PARENT COMMUNICATION

At the end of a unit of study, or whenever it seems appropriate, I ask students to create mini-portfolios of their work to take home and share with their parents. To begin the process of creating mini-portfolios, I give students time to go through their work that I have been collecting throughout the unit of study. When students have had a chance to review and reflect on their work, I explain they will be taking some of it home to share with their parents. Together we brainstorm reasons they might want to take a piece of work home to share. As the students discuss their ideas about sharing their work, I record them on the board.

The first time we do this, it is difficult for students to generate reasons to share with their parents. To help them over this hurdle, I suggest appropriate reasons such as the following:

This is my best work because ———————.

A new discovery I made was ———————.

I made a mistake but learned ———————.

This work was challenging because ———————.

This was my favorite work because ———————.

When I finished this assignment I was still wondering ———————.

I clearly explained my thinking when I ———————.

I ask the students to choose three pieces of work to take home to share. There is nothing magical about the number 3. Choose what seems right for you and your students. Once the students have chosen their work, I ask them to write a paragraph for each piece of work explaining to their parents why they chose it. At this point, the list of reasons on the board becomes very useful.

The students spend a short period of time daily over three days reflecting and writing about their work. Each day they write about one piece of work. As the students work, I circulate throughout the room, reading over their shoulders and editing their work when necessary for spelling, punctuation, capitalization, complete sentences, and mathematical accuracy.

I collect each student's three work samples along with the written paragraph about each and attach them to a letter I have written explaining the unit (see Figure 1). I usually ask students to take the packets home on Monday and return them, signed with comments, no later than Friday.

In all the years I have done this I have gotten wonderful, supportive comments about the students and their work. Parents have asked some excellent questions, giving me the opportunity to explain further what I am doing and why it makes sense.

Dear Parents,

For the past several months we have been studying multiplication of whole numbers. The students have learned that multiplication has to do with combining equal groups. This can be represented in many ways. Some of the ways include pictures, skip-counting, repeated addition, and rectangular arrays. Students used the preceding methods early to help them understand the concept of multiplication and to help them begin to memorize the facts.

As students gained confidence and understanding of multiplication, we moved from the basic facts into multiplication of two-digit numbers by one-digit numbers and then two-digit by two-digit numbers. As the numbers got larger students found that many of the early ways they used to multiply no longer were efficient. They are beginning to see the usefulness of finding partial products. As an example, a student might solve 23×9 by thinking of 23 as 20 + 3, then multiplying both the 20 and the 3 by 9 to get $20 \times 9 = 180$ and $3 \times 9 = 27$. Then by combining the products 180 and 27, she gets 207. Or a student might realize that 23×9 is only one group of 23 less than 23×10. $23 \times 10 = 230$. The student would then subtract the extra group of 23 from 230 to get 207. These are just two examples of how students might solve this problem efficiently and accurately. An advantage to thinking about multiplication in this way is that students use their number sense and make fewer computational errors.

Your student has selected three pieces of work to share with you to show his/her learning in multiplication. Please discuss with your student why he/she chose the work and what was learned. Students chose work for one of the following reasons:

- ▲ best work
- ▲ challenging
- ▲ made a discovery
- ▲ something he/she is still wondering about
- ▲ worked very hard on the assignment

Please sign below and write any comments and questions you may have. Please have your child return this sheet and his/her work by Friday.

Sincerely,

parent signature _____

Comments/questions:

▲▲▲▲▲▲Figure 1   *Letter to parents.*

BLACKLINE MASTERS

Multiplication Table

1	2	3	4	5	6	7	8	9	10	11	12
2	4	6	8	10	12	14	16	18	20	22	24
3	6	9	12	15	18	21	24	27	30	33	36
4	8	12	16	20	24	28	32	36	40	44	48
5	10	15	20	25	30	35	40	45	50	55	60
6	12	18	24	30	36	42	48	54	60	66	72
7	14	21	28	35	42	49	56	63	70	77	84
8	16	24	32	40	48	56	64	72	80	88	96
9	18	27	36	45	54	63	72	81	90	99	108
10	20	30	40	50	60	70	80	90	100	110	120
11	22	33	44	55	66	77	88	99	110	121	132
12	24	36	48	60	72	84	96	108	120	132	144

 From *Lessons for Extending Multiplication, Grades 4–5* by Maryann Wickett & Marilyn Burns. © 2001 Math Solutions Publications

1–100 Chart

1	2	3	4	5	6	7	8	9	10
11	12	13	14	15	16	17	18	19	20
21	22	23	24	25	26	27	28	29	30
31	32	33	34	35	36	37	38	39	40
41	42	43	44	45	46	47	48	49	50
51	52	53	54	55	56	57	58	59	60
61	62	63	64	65	66	67	68	69	70
71	72	73	74	75	76	77	78	79	80
81	82	83	84	85	86	87	88	89	90
91	92	93	94	95	96	97	98	99	100

Centimeter Squares Grid Paper

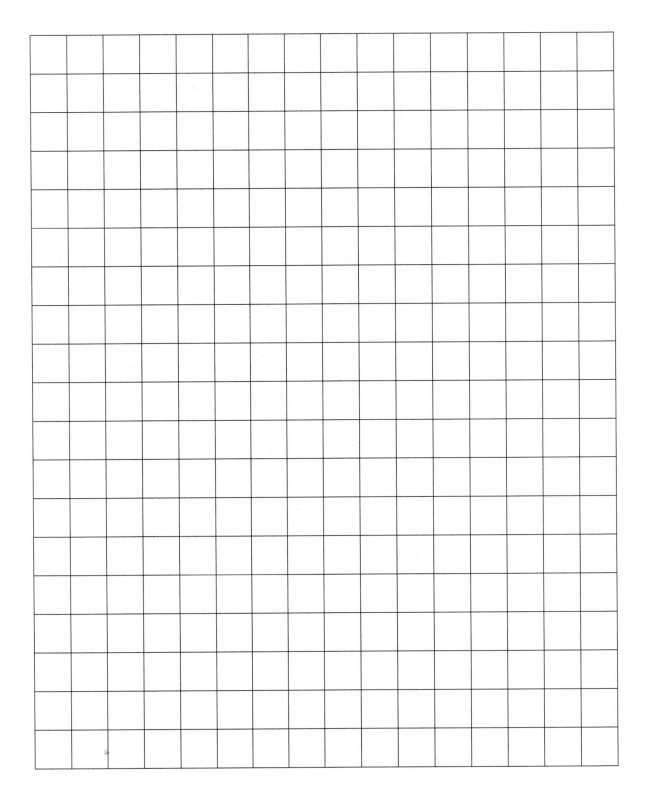

Related Rectangles
Assessment Grids

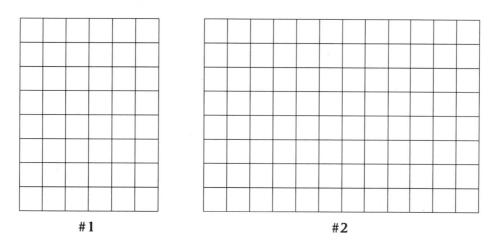

#1   #2

Explain how rectangle 1 is related to rectangle 2.

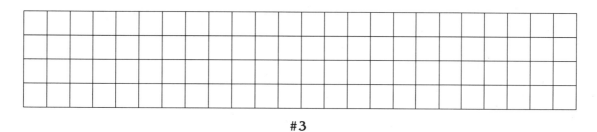

#3

Explain how rectangle 2 is related to rectangle 3.

Target 300

You need:

    a partner
    1 die

Rules

The object of the game is to be the player whose total is closest to 300 after six rolls of the die. This means that the total can be exactly 300, less than 300, or greater than 300. Each player must use all six turns.

1. Each player draws a two-column chart on a recording sheet as shown, one column for each player.

2. Player 1 rolls the die and decides whether to multiply the number rolled by 10, 20, 30, 40, or 50, keeping in mind that each player will have six turns and the target amount is 300.

3. Both players write the multiplication sentence representing the first player's choice and product. For example, Player 1 rolls a 2 and multiplies it by 20, and both players write the multiplication sentence $2 \times 20 = 40$.

4. Player 1 hands the die to Player 2 and Player 2 follows the same steps as Player 1.

5. At the end of each turn, the player adds his new amount to his previous score to keep a running total.

6. At the end of six turns, players compare scores to see whose score is closest to 300 and record underneath the chart:

    _____ won.

    _____ was _____ points away from 300.

    _____ was _____ points away from 300.

Player 1	Player 2

Player 1	Player 2
$2 \times 20 = 40$	

From *Lessons for Extending Multiplication, Grades 4–5* by Maryann Wickett & Marilyn Burns. © 2001 Math Solutions Publications

Dot Paper

Game Boards
Pathways and Times 10

Pathways

81	54	63	36	72
28	18	32	81	24
48	64	21	16	56
12	9	42	49	27

3　　4　　6　　7　　8　　9

Pathways

81	64	48	36	63
30	42	32	35	28
72	25	49	24	45
16	54	20	40	56

4　　5　　6　　7　　8　　9

 From *Lessons for Extending Multiplication, Grades 4–5* by Maryann Wickett & Marilyn Burns. © 2001 Math Solutions Publications

Pathways

54	28	42	72	63
77	36	16	99	64
49	32	44	81	121
56	48	66	88	24

4   6   7   8   9   11

Pathways

72	36	49	88	54
84	77	96	132	56
63	81	48	108	121
66	99	144	64	42

6   7   8   9   11   12

From *Lessons for Extending Multiplication, Grades 4–5* by Maryann Wickett & Marilyn Burns. © 2001 Math Solutions Publications

Times 10

90	450	300	810	200
180	630	540	350	250
240	150	210	270	360
420	280	160	490	120

    3   4   5   6   7   9

Times 10

810	480	540	640	630
210	360	160	720	560
280	120	180	90	320
420	810	490	240	270

    3   4   6   7   8   9

Times 10

560	400	200	540	160
720	250	490	240	450
300	420	320	350	280
810	640	480	360	630

4   5   6   7   8   9

Times 10

540	630	990	440	480
280	770	640	810	660
420	360	490	1210	880
720	160	320	560	240

4   6   7   8   9   11

Pathways

You need:
 a partner
 game board
 2 paper clips
 cubes, tiles, or other game markers in two colors,
 about 15 of each color

Rules

1. Each player uses a different color of cubes, tiles, or game markers.

2. Player 1 chooses two numbers from those listed at the bottom of the game board, places a paper clip on each, and marks the product of the numbers on the game board with a marker of his or her color.

3. Player 2 moves just one of the paper clips to another number, multiplies the two factors indicated, and places a different color marker on the product.

4. Play continues. Note: It is legal to start the game with both paper clips on the same number, or to move a paper clip to the same factor as the other paper clip.

5. The winner is the first player to complete a continuous pathway in the same color across the game board. A completed pathway may include boxes that share a common side or a common corner, as seen in the figures below.

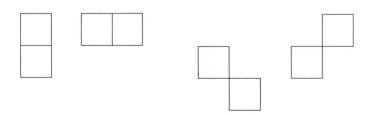

 From *Lessons for Extending Multiplication, Grades 4–5* by Maryann Wickett & Marilyn Burns. © 2001 Math Solutions Publications

Times 10

Rules
1. Each player uses a different color of cubes, tiles, or game markers.
2. Player 1 chooses two numbers from those listed at the bottom of the game board, places a paper clip on each, multiplies the factors, and then multiplies the resulting product by 10. Player 1 then marks the product on the game board with a marker of his or her color.
3. Player 2 moves just one of the paper clips to another number, multiplies the two factors indicated and then multiplies by 10, and places a different color marker on the product.
4. Play continues. Note: It is legal to start the game with both paper clips on the same number, or to move a paper clip to the same factor as the other paper clip.
5. The winner is the first player to complete a continuous pathway across the game board. A completed pathway may include boxes that share only a common side or a common corner, as seen in the figures below.

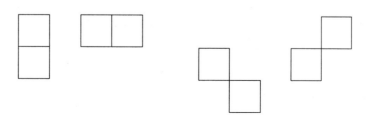

INDEX